BLACK AND GOLD

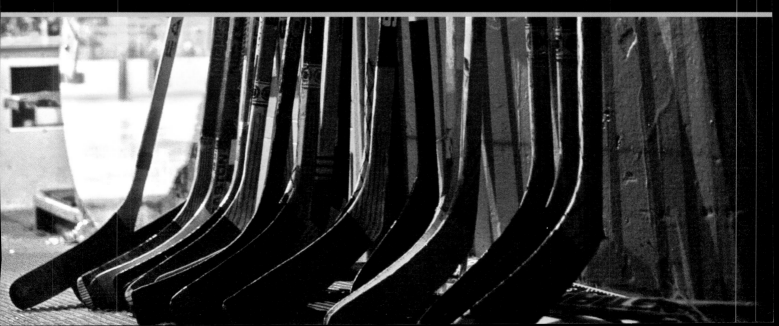

BLACK AND GOLD
FOUR DECADES OF THE BOSTON BRUINS IN PHOTOGRAPHS

Rob Simpson

**Photography by
Steve Babineau**

WILEY

John Wiley & Sons Canada, Ltd.

Library and Archives Canada Cataloguing in Publication Data

Simpson, Rob, 1964–

Black and gold : four decades of the Boston Bruins in photographs / Rob Simpson ; photography by Steve Babineau. — Rev. and updated.

Includes index.

ISBN 978-1-118-17278-0

  1. Boston Bruins (Hockey team)—History. 2. Boston Bruins (Hockey team)—History—Pictorial works. I. Babineau, Steve II. Title.

GV848.B68S54 2011   796.962'640974461   C2011-906113-9

Production Credits
Cover and Interior text design: Adrian So
Cover concept: Brian Babineau
Front jacket photo: Steve Babineau/Boston Bruins
Back jacket photo, top left and right: Steve Babineau
Back jacket photo, bottom: Steve Babineau/Boston Bruins
Jacket photo, spine: Steve Babineau
Typesetting: Adrian So, Indianapolis Composition Services
Printer: Quad Graphics

John Wiley & Sons Canada, Ltd.
6045 Freemont Blvd.
Mississauga, Ontario
L5R 4J3

Printed in the United States

1 2 3 4 5 QG 16 15 14 13 12

CONTENTS

Foreword		ix
Preface		xi
Acknowledgments		xiii
Chapter 1:	Basic Babs	1
Chapter 2:	The Garden	17
Chapter 3:	Bruins Legend: John Bucyk	39
Chapter 4:	Bruins Legend: Bobby Orr	51
Chapter 5:	Bruins Legend: Phil Esposito	65
Chapter 6:	Bruins Legend: Terry O'Reilly	77
Chapter 7:	Bruins Legend: Ray Bourque	95
Chapter 8:	Bruins Legend: Cam Neely	111
Chapter 9:	The Lunch Pail Gang	129
Chapter 10:	Coaches	145
Chapter 11:	Masked Men	159
Chapter 12:	Blueliners	177
Chapter 13:	Scorers	195
Chapter 14:	Enforcers	211
Chapter 15:	Grinders	229
Chapter 16:	A Winter Classic	241
Chapter 17:	Lord Stanley	251
Scrapbook		270
Index		283

above:

Don relaxing at home in his basement with his dog, Blue, the original.

left:

Don Cherry in his prime as coach of the Bruins.

Fran Rosa, a writer for the *Boston Globe*, described our Boston Bruins team of the '70s as the "Lunch Pail Gang," meaning that we punched in the time clock at 7:30 and never stopped working. Fran was right. Sometimes teams would outscore us (not often) but never, never would they outwork us, and that is why the Lunch Pail Gang was so popular with the Boston Bruins fans (especially the Gallery Gods).

Fortunately for us, Steve Babineau was there to catch the excitement. I remember the first time I met Steve. I was the Boston Bruins coach and I noticed this young kid always taking pictures at our practices, almost every day. One day he introduced himself and showed me some of his pictures. I was blown away, how he had captured the image and flow of hockey and our club. I knew he would go far.

Steve has taken wonderful pictures and I know you will agree with me when you see them. Steve has the touch, and I must admit that I get a little misty and sweet memories flow back when I see Steve's pictures of the "Lunch Pail Gang." They were a great bunch.

Don

Brian Babineau

Brian Babineau

above:

Babs with Nikon film camera.

left:

Babs taking the 2006–2007 Boston Bruins team photo.

The illustrious Bruins' names jump off the pages: Orr, Esposito, Cherry, Bourque, Neely, Babineau…Babineau!?

Photographer Steve Babineau, covering the NHL in Boston since 1973, probably wouldn't describe his career as illustrious, although he should. In almost four decades shooting hockey in Boston, he's taken *the* photos, and had them appear in countless magazines, newspapers, hockey collections, and websites the world over.

Black and Gold recounts the careers of the aforementioned players and other Bruins legends through vintage photographs, many of them never before seen. The coaches, the players, the famous and infamous moments, and the original Boston Garden—are all preserved in written and illustrated detail for real hockey fans and historians to enjoy.

Aside from recollections from the players, *Black and Gold* also takes fans behind the scenes, when the shutter wasn't clicking, when the flash wasn't going off, for Steve Babineau's perspective behind the camera. "Babs" has scanned through hundreds of thousands of photographs to select the few hundred found inside these pages. Six chapters are dedicated to specific Bruins legends, whom Babineau captured in action on Garden ice. All others who donned the Spoked-B, are categorized by position, or by their ability to fight, grind or score. Who belongs where? Let the arguments begin.

Originally, the "Basic Babs" opening chapter was entitled "Babs's Best," until we realized it was next to impossible to really qualify a select two dozen or so as the "best." Basic Babs sums it up better. The photos tell Babineau's story, while high-lighting a cross-section of his most compelling photographs for various reasons: lighting, action, angles, history, timing, and subject matter. From there, it gets pretty clear-cut. The ensuing chapters reveal the last 35 years of Bruins hockey, through the eyes of one of the greatest photographers in all of professional sports. The volume concludes with the "Scrapbook." This is Babineau's personal collection—moments when the photographer and his family became the subject. True, behind-the-scenes images of a hockey club and the man documenting its existence.

right:

Anson Carter with a leaping goal celebration in front of Ray Bourque and Jason Allison.

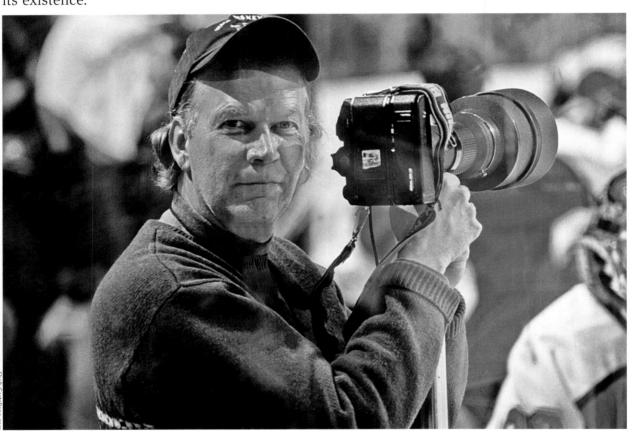

above:

Babs on the visitors' bench during the pre-game skate.

As much as anything, this book honors the life lesson of perseverance. Steve Babineau was a late blooming, shaky-legged high school hockey player who enjoyed a simple love for the game. He combined that with his overwhelming interest in sports photography. Through dedication, luck, timing, and creativity, Babineau literally turned a career dream into reality. The tangible realization of living that dream is laid out across these pages for all hockey fans, especially those who bleed black and gold, to enjoy.

Rob Simpson

Acknowledgments

Thank you to Nora for making it possible for me to write. Thank you to our friends and cohorts at Wiley for their guidance and professionalism, the illustrious Karen Milner, Liz McCurdy and Michelle Bullard for making me appear smarter than I am, and Adrian So for the lay-out of lay-outs. To Mick Colageo and Kevin Vautour for their input on our player categories and backgrounds; you've started many an argument. To Kate Stanley for her assistance compiling backgrounds and statistics. To Amy Latimer, Dan Zimmer, and Kerry Collins with the Bruins, and to the multiple others associated with the organization who contributed reflections. Special thanks to the many Bruins alumni for making themselves available, lending a helping hand, and with rare exception, always being supportive of my many multi-media efforts. You're good friends and a great bunch. All the best.

Rob

Thank you to my rock and soul mate Anita, for giving me the freedom to live out a dream the past 35 years. To the Bruins: the Jacobs family, Harry Sinden, Nate Greenberg, Paul Mooney, Heidi Holland, Peter Chiarelli, and Sue Byrne. To Joyce Papaamoroso, the electricians, the security team, and all the guys in the bull gang. To the many photographers/assistants: Armen James, Brian Babineau, Robert Rooks, Lee Calkins, Shelly Castellano, Glen James, Andre Ringuette, Graig and Dave Abel, Jim Turner, Dave Lyons, Chris Relke, Paul Whalen, Keith Babineau, Richard Lewis, Rick Marshall, Leo Echavarria, Steve Malloy, Jamie Babineau, Renata Greene, and Chris Babineau. Thank you to the players and coaches for making my job special by treating me as more than just a photographer.

Babs

CHAPTER

1

BASIC BABS

Brian Babineau

above:

Steve Babineau, in his new "studio," the Fleet Center [now the TD Banknorth Garden].

left:

Arguably the two greatest defensemen of all time, and they both spent the great bulk of their careers in Boston. Ray Bourque and Bobby Orr.

Steve Babineau is a rink rat: a rink rat with a camera, who happens to be the team photographer for one of the most storied franchises in hockey history. What the Bruins lack in Stanley Cup victories over the course of their proud history, they make up for in grit, toughness, and personality. The number of characters and legendary moments captured by Babineau in just the past 38 years are more than most organizations could hope for if they stayed in business for a century. Maybe it's the attitude. Maybe it's hardy New Englanders and their love for a game played on ice, by generation after generation: by grandpa on a pond, by grandson in the Sunday morning squirt house league. Whatever draws the locals to love the finesse, the skill, the sound, the banter, and, most importantly, the physicality of the game, is what attracted Cambridge, Massachusetts, native Steve Babineau.

"My Uncle Lenny always took me to Celtics games," Babineau remembers. "I was wiry and tall, and he wanted me to be a basketball player. His buddy was a writer for the old *Record American* and we got great seats."

To Babineau, naturally ordained "Babs" via the hockey world, the hoops just didn't seem to fit. Fortunately for him, an intervention occurred.

"My next-door neighbor Paul Harrigan in 1964 took me to a B's game. I'll never forget it. It was Original Six hockey. The B's were the doormats but it just didn't matter," Babs recalls. "Jerry Toppazzini, Murray Oliver, John Bucyk, Orland

Kurtenbach, and Eddie Johnston in net. I loved watching these guys and the uniforms were classic."

The game stirred quite a bit of passion in a kid who didn't even skate.

"I was born in 1952. When I was eight, I remember watching the 1960 U.S. Olympic team win the gold medal in Squaw Valley. It was on *Wide World of Sports* or something," Babineau ponders. "From that point forward I was out in the street playing hockey, or banging it around somewhere playing floor hockey. I was the best street hockey player on the planet; even the kids who played ice hockey wanted me on their street team."

Living in North Cambridge, Babs used to walk to a ballpark in West Cambridge to play baseball, with the same kids who were already skating. Lack of family funds for equipment and transportation to the rink, and living in a different part of the city, hindered his opportunity to play the frozen variety of hockey early on. Finally, in eighth grade, with encouragement from the other kids and families, he took up the game on ice.

"I picked up the skills of passing and shooting pretty quickly. I just couldn't put it together with my feet," he says.

Ah, but of course, therein lies the basic challenge to the greatest game on the planet.

above:

Early ticket stubs and photos from Babineau attending the Boston Braves and Bruins games in the early 70s.

bottom:

The lanky photographer can skate, sort of. Since his high school team lost 44 straight, he's improved dramatically.

Armen James

Nevertheless, despite lacking skill, a demographic shift of sorts opened up an opportunity for the poor skater. With an influx of African-American kids into the neighborhood, the more popular sports at the time became basketball and track. Very few of the new kids, if any, played hockey at the time. The hockey and baseball teams at Rindge Technical High School suffered for a lack of talent and numbers. Babineau tried out and made the freshman hockey team.

I would cut physics class and lunch to hustle down and watch about 30 minutes of practice.

(By the way, the athletic swing continued. Where hockey and baseball were popular and very successful at Rindge in the 1950s, by the mid-1960s the emphasis was on football, track, and basketball. Georgetown and NBA great Patrick Ewing came out of Rindge, as did many exemplary track athletes.)

"Playing our games at the old Boston Arena, where the Bruins started," Babineau recalls, "I'd go in and skate and practice and sit on the bench and say, 'Gee, I wonder if Eddie Shore sat here, or Dit Clapper.'"

Meanwhile, with Babineau's father being a union laborer, a carpenter, and a painter, it seemed safe to assume that young Steve might follow in his footsteps in some way or another. The idea at Rindge Technical was to load up the grades for college, or in most cases, line oneself up with a vocational opportunity.

below:

Phil Esposito of Boston just misses against his younger brother, Chicago netminder Tony, after leaving Black-hawks defenseman Keith Magnuson in his wake.

left:

"Turk" and "Pie," Derek Sanderson and John McKenzie, walking to practice at Harvard's Watson Rink.

In Babineau's mind, his vocational opportunity, official or not, within the scholastic curriculum or not, was photography.

"I had an attraction to the Bruins," Babs recalls. "They used to practice at Harvard's Watson Rink, about two miles from my high school. I would cut physics class and lunch to hustle down and watch about 30 minutes of practice and then return to school. I'd go on my own with a little Instamatic camera. I have a picture of Johnny McKenzie and Derek Sanderson walking across Harvard Yard carrying their skates. Then my friend Rick Marshall and I would jump on the bus and the trolley to go on Saturday mornings to watch the Bruins practice at the Garden."

It remained to be seen whether Steve Babineau's photo-graphy career showed early promise. His hockey career, despite plenty of opportunity, did not.

"Coach Dick Kelly, a former Boston University star, used to call me 'Alice,' because when I was in high school I was 6-foot-2, and dripping wet I was lucky to weigh 115 or 120 pounds. 'Hey Alice, get out there.'

"I remember one game he benched me after my first shift. I made a bad pass, so he benched me. We only had 12 skaters. We're losing the game 10-nothing to Waltham, and with 35 seconds left in the game, he put me back in to take a face-off. I won the draw. Ned Yetton was in goal for Waltham. Our point guy took a slap shot, the rebound came right out to me, and I put it top shelf. The game ended two seconds later."

Not bad for 35 seconds, eh coach?

below:

Ray Bourque as a rookie. Babineau documented Bourque's entire career in Boston.

"We had so few players, anybody who made freshman was eligible to play junior varsity. I was playing both," Babs says with astonishment. "I played about 30 games that year. We went at it six days a week; practice Monday, JV game on Tuesday, practice on Wednesday, and so on. As a sophomore I made varsity, and if you weren't captain of varsity, you could also play JV. I was getting a ton of ice time."

But the team was awful. In fact, Babineau played for one of the most infamous teams in the Commonwealth's hockey history. They weren't cheap or dirty or delinquent; they were just bad.

"We set the high school league record for most consecutive losses," Babineau points out. "The streak started when I was a freshman, and it went until my first game as a senior. We lost every single game, 44 straight. We beat Brockton the first game of my senior year 1-0, and you'd think we'd won the Stanley Cup. It was in all the papers."

Babineau scored three goals his entire senior year.

below:

Don Cherry coaches the Rochester Americans at the Garden against the Braves. That's Brave's defenseman, part-time Bruin, Nick Beverley along the boards.

"A typical game: we'd play Arlington," Babineau says. "There would be three hundred fans for Arlington, three fans for us. I remember we were tied nothing-nothing after one period, and the Arlington fans gave us a standing ovation. Between periods we said to each other, 'Let's just try to keep it under five goals this period; let's hold 'em to five.' We were gassed. We went down 9-nothing after two."

Despite his less-than-stellar experience on the ice, Babineau's love affair with hockey was raging. About the time Babs was playing high school hockey, some guy named Orr was on the top of his game.

below:

Shots of the great Bobby Orr when Babineau was still an amateur photographer, taken from his seat in the Garden. Left, Orr's lone game as a Boston Brave [against the Bruins] played as a charity exhibition, and right, Orr as a Bruin.

"I remember when I was a bit younger...the talk of the 'second coming.' I saw Bobby play an exhibition game at the Garden when he was still a defenseman with Oshawa. It was the Oshawa Generals with Orr against Niagara Falls featuring star forward Derek Sanderson. Orr had the shaved head. Sanderson was gritty. I remember Orr and Sanderson fought at center ice," Babs says with a smile. "It was unreal."

By 1969, Orr established himself as the best overall player in the League, while Babineau's interest in photography had taken off. Hockey and photography dominated his young life.

above:

Self-portrait of teenager Steve Babineau at home in Cambridge in front of his framed hockey collection. At the time Babs worked as a rink attendant at Harvard.

"I lived in Porter Square, North Cambridge, and I worked at the rink at Harvard making ice. I have a picture of me when I was 17, 18 years old, sitting in a chair in my house, with all of these framed pictures I had taken behind me.

"I also remember trying to get Bobby Orr's autograph," Babs continues. "At the old Garden, North Station, there were double doors that were used as the main entrance, and one of the doors was open. Rick and I used to get there early and sneak up to the level where the players came in through security. I remember Orr and Gilles Marotte walked in."

When Babineau asked for an autograph and Orr obliged, Babineau froze. Orr tried to hand Babineau his coffee to hold while he signed and Steve's hand didn't open. Orr spilled coffee on both their hands.

"I was young, not much younger than him," Babs states the obvious, "but I was nervous then."

Within the same decade, those nerves would turn to pure adrenaline and emotion for Babineau. After being a fan and seeing Orr lead the organization to two Cup wins, Babineau would have the opportunity to shoot a brief stint of Orr's career before it ended, and then be on hand for the ultimate night: Bobby's jersey retirement on January 9, 1979.

"Needless to say he was an unbelievable player and to have a chance to overlap with his time here just a little bit is special to me," points out Babineau. "He was one of a kind and I still get emotional when I watch clips of the night they hoisted number 4. A great night for probably the greatest player."

Because of Orr and others, Babineau gradually learned to keep his composure around superstar players. He also recalls another valuable job-related lesson from watching those blessed with the ultimate in talent: always have your camera ready.

"We got in to see a Red Wings practice: Howe, Delvecchio, Gadsby. After practice Gordie Howe was standing in front of the crease like a baseball batter, Roger Crozier [the goalie] was crouched behind him in front of the net like a catcher, and Andy Bathgate was sending slappers in from near center ice. Pow. Pow. Pow. Gordie is swinging his stick like a baseball bat and hitting pucks upstairs. He got a piece of everything. I don't know how he did it. I kept yelling at him to give me his stick. He kept hitting the pucks into the balcony, and finally the stick shattered into a million pieces. I remember him looking at me with the end of the broken stick and wondering if I still wanted it. I passed, but he gave me an autograph instead."

From that point forward Babs always carried his camera along, his nerves settled, the comfort level from the experience of being around the NHLers started to kick in, and Babineau started to get a feel for the building.

I went out and bought season tickets to the Boston Braves.

As is often the case, getting something one wants badly enough also means making small sacrifices. He gave up a crack at the best hockey tickets to the best games, just to improve his opportunity to work on his craft.

above left:

Normand Leveille, whose career ended suddenly during a game in Vancouver in October 1982 when he suffered a cerebral hemorrhage, returns to the Garden for the first time. Bruin Barry Pederson (#10) is clapping to the left, immediately next to retired Bruin Jean Ratelle in a plaid jacket. Media man Nate Greenberg is next to security guard clapping.

above right:

Leveille with "Mr. Hockey" Gordie Howe at the Fleet Center, during festivities for the 1996 NHL All-Star game.

"I just needed to get into the building to take pictures at hockey games, which I could do before the game by walking down to the glass," Babineau recalls. "The glass was short, I was 6-foot-2, and I could walk down and shoot right over it. Plus, I could shoot from my seat. It may have been the year the WHA [World Hockey Association] started [1972]. I went down to buy Bruins tickets on a wicked cold night. The mayor didn't want the fans waiting outside, so they funneled us inside and into two lines: Original Six or expansion tickets. I thought, well, everyone's going to want to see the Canadiens and Red Wings, so I'll get in the expansion line. I really wanted to see the better teams but I knew it would be next to impossible. Rick and I were third in line for expansion games. We get to the front, looking to buy seats for the Blues and Flyers and such, and they hand us obstructed view. The season ticket holders had already bought all of the rest of the seats before they opened it up to us.

"How can this be? This sucks. I went out and bought season tickets to the Boston Braves."

The Bruins American League affiliate, the Braves, also played at the Garden. Even with six extra teams at the NHL level in those days, the talent wasn't that watered down, and the hockey at both levels was outstanding.

Babs bought season tickets to the Boston Braves, plus a ticket package for the first seven games of the season of the New England Whalers of the World Hockey Association (WHA).

below:

What Babineau calls a "onetimer" shot, a posed effort outside the norm. Here, goalie Andy Moog, Ray Bourque and Cam Neely don three different Bruins sweaters; black, white and NHL 75th-anniversary "throw back," worn by the Original Six teams.

9

Basic Babs

"I saw guys when they were young play against and for the Braves like [Larry] Robinson and [Terry] O'Reilly. I have pictures of Terry O'Reilly playing for the Braves. We used to keep track of how many times O'Reilly would fall down during a game. He made himself into an unbelievable player. Not a great skater then, but he turned himself into a solid skater and a great player. First on, last off. By the end of his career, in his heyday, you couldn't knock him off his skates. He might fall after running through you, but you're not knocking him down. He was best ever at controlling the puck in the corner with his skates. Pass it or keep it, he'd protect the puck with his body."

O'Reilly is one of only two non-Hall-of-Fame players [Lionel Hitchman is the other] with his name and number in the Garden rafters. He's the mold of a true Bruin.

"I was dating my soon-to-be-wife, Anita, at that time. I used to take her to games," Babs recalls. "I remember us watching O'Reilly chasing Dave Schultz down the runway. Schultz butt-ended me once when I leaned over and called him a p——. O'Reilly chased him down the rink. O'Reilly probably doesn't remember that and obviously he'd have no idea that was me. Pretty cool actually when you think about it."

Babineau's season tickets were in the third row. His simple plan: he'd take photos leaning over the glass before the game, and from his seat during.

The next big step in the young photographer's development: ironic luck.

A burglar broke into the Babineaus' house one spring afternoon while Steve was down the street playing baseball. When he and his father came home, the crook was still in the house. The front chain was still hooked; the man had come in and was about to go out a back window.

"He heard us, jumped back out, and ran across a field and crossed the railroad tracks," Babs recalls.

The burglar had swiped a strongbox out of Steve's uncle's room, and he had also taken Steve's camera.

"I had a simple SLR [single lens reflex]. One fixed lens. I was able to go out with the insurance money and get a camera with lenses. I started shooting my second year of the Braves with a good camera," Babs says thoughtfully.

Babineau got married in 1973, two days before he turned 21.

"Getting married set my life in motion," Babineau says. "I had to get a job."

He sold his first photo to *The Hockey News* that same year.

"I was an avid reader of *The Hockey News*. My neighbor Paul Harrigan got it, and then I started getting it when I could afford it," Babs recalls. "After three or four issues, I worked up the nerve to call them."

"The middle of *The Hockey News* had three pages dedicated to the new league [WHA] but no photos, so I called Charlie Halpin, the editor in Montreal," remembers Babs.

Babineau explained that he was an avid reader of the weekly, and wondered why photos of the WHA never showed up inside. He added a little passion behind his argument, by pointing out the fact that he had turned his bathroom into a darkroom, and had a number of great photos of the WHA's burgeoning stars. He then sent in some black-and-white photos of Tim Sheehy playing for the Whalers and Bobby Sheehan playing for the New York Golden Blades.

above:

The first Steve Babineau efforts to make The Hockey News. *He was paid three dollars a piece for these WHA images of Tim Sheehy and Bobby Sheehan. Printed in Montreal at the time, this was the November 2nd, 1973, issue of the weekly.*

below:

New England Whalers of the WHA, Boston Bruins of the NHL, and Boston Braves of the AHL. As an amateur, Babineau was shooting all three during the same season.

Halpin not only bought some shots, he offered to get Babineau a season pass to cover the Whalers games.

"I got six bucks, three dollars each, for my first two published photos," Babs says with a smile. "And I got a season credential. The Whalers went on to win the championship that year. I came across the great Gordie Howe again that year. He was playing for Houston."

The second year, the team split its games between the Garden and the Boston Arena.

"I'd come full circle," Babs adds. "I was back in the same rink where I played high school hockey, photographing professional hockey."

Events were working out well for the young, up-and-coming photographer. The next logical step was the "big show."

When the WHA moved to Springfield and then Hartford, Babineau convinced *The Hockey News* to get him a press credential to shoot the Bruins. The timing was fortuitous. The Boston Braves of the American Hockey League (AHL) disbanded, and their PR guy, named Nate Green-

above:

An image from the first Bruins game Babineau attended on a press credential. Left to right: Phil Esposito, former Bruin turned Atlanta Flames defenseman Doug Mohns, goalie Phil Myre, Flames d-man Noel Price, with Bruins Wayne Cashman and Bobby Orr swarming.

berg, moved over and replaced Bruins PR guy Herb Ralby. Greenberg gave Babineau his first NHL credential in 1975. On top of *The Hockey News*, Babs started taking photos for four or five other different hockey publications. What came next seemed inevitable.

"The Bruins had two photographers during the Cup years," Babineau explains. "Al Ruelle took the black-and-white shots, while Jerry Buckley did color. Jerry left and went to work for the Red Sox, and the guy who took over was Dick Raphael. After a couple years, he and the Bruins apparently had a falling out at one point. He left, but I don't think it was a big deal for Dick because he was also shooting for the Celtics, the Sox, and the Patriots, as more of a freelance guy. Meanwhile, I had taken a few NHL photos along the way for *The Hockey News* and for *Hockey Illustrated*, beginning in 1974, which would open the door when Raphael left. The media guy Nate Greenberg came up and said, 'We need your photos for the

Boards and Blades Club. I thought he was proposing photos for the press room, but it turned out to be for the 'B and B' season ticket holders' room, which was literally underneath the ice."

Babineau received a call about a meeting. He met and showed photos to former coach and assistant general manager Tom Johnson, general manager Harry Sinden, Greenberg, and Garden president Paul Mooney, who ran the building. They ordered about forty 16-by-20 framed prints and also wanted to use some photos in the Bruins yearbook. Soon after, they offered Babineau the job as full-time Bruins color photographer. It was 1977.

"You're the team color photographer until I tell you otherwise," Greenberg told Babineau.

"When Babineau came along, he gradually brought along a bit more technology," Greenberg remembers. "It worked out well for all of us because at that time we were adding more promotions and more color publications. The press guide went to color. I started doing the yearbook with a lot more color photos, so we needed a lot more than we had before."

> "You're the team color photographer until I tell you otherwise."

below:

Babineau captures the action: Bruins defenseman Kyle McLaren hammers Detroit's Anders Eriksson as Boston center Mike Sullivan looks on.

Over the course of the next three-and-a-half decades, Babineau snapped hundreds of thousands of photos, including almost every one of those found in this collection. His son Brian took the remaining few. The Babineau business became a family affair in the early '90s. They called it Sports Action Photography, and it became one of the biggest suppliers of NHL images to licensees of the League. Clients in the hockey card industry included Topps, Upper Deck, Score, and Pro Set. One of Babs's claims to fame was taking the photos for the Wayne Gretzky and Mario Lemieux rookie cards for Topps. Poster and calendar companies, video game companies like EA SPORTS, and equipment manufacturers like Bauer, Easton, Mission, ITECH, and Louisville Slugger soon came calling. Steve and Brian stayed very busy.

"Never in a million years when he was 15 years old and I let him shoot at ice level at a game against the New Jersey Devils did I think he'd be so into it and be so good at it," Babineau says proudly of Brian. "He had played the game and had a real understanding of how to capture it. I knew he had it figured out soon after he started. We were still using primitive equipment then, so to speak, but he could really capture the angles and the images. When I was young I used to go up to [highway] 128 to shoot cars zipping by to work on my timing. Brian just seemed to inherit it. He had the timing and the movement of the skaters figured out right off the bat."

Greenberg's "until I tell you otherwise" expired when, after 34 years with the team, Greenberg departed in 2007. But

above:

Prominent Bruins through the years pose together for a "onetimer." Joe Thornton, Gerry Cheevers, John Bucyk, Phil Esposito, Cam Neely, Ray Bourque and Bobby Orr.

above:

Steve and Brian (standing) Babineau with a Bruins Zamboni on the Zakim Bridge outside the big rink, fooling around during a commercial/print ad shoot.

below:

The past, present, and future of Sports Action Photography, dad Steve Babineau and son Brian.

Babineau didn't outlast him by much. With the NHL wrapping its arms around the licensing of hockey photographs, including Babineau's massive collection, 2008 became time for Babs to wind it down. The league purchased his entire collection in December of 2007.

"I felt that my work would be protected for all time by being part of the NHL image collection and would always remain intact," Babineau explains. "I'm grateful to the League for seeing the value of my work. Many other photographers I have known, their work has disappeared or been sold off into public hands, and I didn't want that to happen. My dad always told me to leave something behind.

"At the same time, moving and selling the archive is like losing a child," Babs points out, "but it makes sense, since I wouldn't really be in touch with the clients like I always was before, with the licensing, and sales, and distribution in the hands of the NHL. So I wouldn't really have direct contact with the clients anymore anyway."

Babs's son Brian will take over day-to-day photography responsibilities with the Bruins and with the Celtics as well.

"This is my last hurrah," Babineau says, "a few hundred thousand hockey photos down the road. The path is now set for Brian to keep our name imbedded in Bruins history."

Bruins history, at least for the past three-and-a-half-decades, is unceremoniously synonymous with the name Steve Babineau. This collection culminates his efforts. A for-the-most-part anonymous existence producing images for the masses now becomes more tangible: priceless moments and memories released by the man who captured them.

CHAPTER

THE GARDEN

above:

The Boston Garden, 1928-1995.

left:

The interior of the old Boston Garden from the northeast corner above the Zamboni entrance.

The original Garden was built in 1928 with boxing in mind, but during its 70-year existence it saw a whole lot of everything—legendary fights, basketball games, political rallies, speeches, concerts, circuses, and shows. For hockey, the building was unlike any other, with its own peculiarities not found in any of the other Original Six buildings. The attendance often ballooned beyond the often uttered original hockey capacity of 13,909. Standard NHL rinks are 200 feet long by 85 feet wide, while the old Garden was nine feet shorter and two feet narrower. The small rink with its tight corners gave the Bruins a distinct home-ice advantage: intimidation on and above the ice gave the home team a feeling of dominance and comfort that literally could transfer to the scoreboard.

"The building itself when coming in to play [gave] maybe a goal-and-a-half, two-goal advantage or lead right off the bat, which was nice; the fans were right on top of the players with the balconies. It was close and just a fun place to play," sums up Don Marcotte, a Bruin for 13-plus seasons.

The Garden could best be described as a bandbox. The fans seemed to hang from the balconies right out over the playing surface. The crowd noise was deafening, inspiring, and sometimes simply hard to believe.

In 70 years it saw Stanley Cups lifted in celebration, it saw Bobby Orr revolutionize the game, and it saw legendary names hoisted to its rafters.

Kevin Paul Dupont, 30 years a Bruins observer for the *Boston Globe*, describes the feeling.

"You were just perched right over. You felt like you could reach right out and touch it, and almost like you were overlooking a slot-hockey game. You felt like you could control it," reflects Dupont. "Beyond that, you not only watched it, you were just immersed in it. The game was so much more emotional then anyway because of the fighting and hitting. You were just absorbed by it, so that was wonderful."

Hall of Fame left winger John Bucyk, 21 years a Bruin, says the atmosphere was unforgettable.

"It was fun because the fans were right above you in the overhang," "the Chief" recalls. "You could hear the fans cheering for you or yelling at you one way or the other and they enjoyed it too because they could hear what we were saying on the ice. It was just so much fun because the building was a little bit smaller, so you really enjoyed it."

For some fans, sitting in the stadium seats beneath the balconies meant watching just half a game. Wide pillars, support beams for the balcony, each easily a foot wide and spaced out almost evenly around the building, blocked the view of some of the fans in the last four rows of the lower section. Meanwhile, spectators in the last three rows of the upper balcony on the side couldn't see the near boards unless they

above:

Shot from the catwalk above center ice, Jacques Lemaire of the Canadiens just won back an opening face-off against Jean Ratelle of Boston.

stood up, and those on the end couldn't see the goalie's net closest to them. At times, simply for the purpose of being able to see, fans got to know each other a little bit, through all of the leaning, standing, and coercing.

"Certainly it was cozy," states Nate Greenberg, who spent the last 23 years of the old Garden's existence handling media for the Bruins, and then as assistant to the team president.

"The rink was unlike any other; today the rinks are all uniform. Boston Garden was the best. The people were right on top of the game. The entertainment value every night was off the charts, and I enjoyed every single night like you wouldn't believe. The team had a lot to do with it, but so did the building. The atmosphere was unbelievable."

below:

Just what it was like to sit "obstructed view" in the lower balcony (behind a support beam which held up the 2nd balcony) at the Garden. Babineau's partial view of the Blackhawks and Bruins in January 1971.

The Bruins played their first playoff game at the Garden on March 19, 1929, beating the Montreal Canadiens 1-0. Cooney Weiland scored the lone goal at 7:20 of the first period and Cecil "Tiny" Thompson made 29 saves for the shutout. The Bruins swept the three-game semi-final and beat the New York Rangers in a best-of-three sweep of the final for Boston's first-ever Stanley Cup. Bill Carson scored the Cup-clinching goal on March 29.

Ten years later, the Garden saw the Bruins win their second Cup. The semi-final series format had expanded to seven games, and the Bruins/ Rangers series went the distance. The Bruins won Game 7 in overtime, with a goal by Mel "Sudden Death" Hill. He earned the nickname by establishing a record that still stands today. Hill tallied three overtime winners in the series. The Bruins whipped the Maple Leafs four games to one to win the final and the organization's second Cup.

That 1939 Bruins roster featured notable names: Frank "Mr. Zero" Brimsek in goal, Eddie Shore on the blue line, and Milt Schmidt, Bobby Bauer, and Woody Dumart on the young Kraut Line up front. Shore, Dit Clapper, and Weiland had won in 1929 as well, with Weiland retiring after the '39 Cup win.

Two years later, in March of 1941, the Garden added its first four-sided clock over the playing surface, at a cost of $25,000. A month later the Bruins won their third Cup, with a seven-game semi-final win over Toronto, and a four-game sweep of the Red Wings. Bobby Bauer scored the Cup winner at 8:43 of the second period on April 12, in a 3-1 win.

For the next three decades little changed at the Garden. The improvements to the building were minimal, the team gradually fell into a playoff drought, and the curse of the Canadiens began. The last time the Bruins beat the Habs in a playoff series prior to 1988 was in 1943, when Boston won a semi-final series four games to one. The win in Game 1 of the series featured a 5-4 sudden death victory for Boston, after the team had fallen behind 3-0 in the second period. The Bruins then lost the Stanley Cup final to Detroit in a sweep.

The 1941 Cup win two seasons earlier would be the club's last until 1970.

above:

One of the Garden's great charms and advantages for the home team: the intimate proximity of the fans to the action. Here, the Boston faithful celebrate a playoff victory against Montreal.

The small rink with its tight corners gave the Bruins a distinct home-ice advantage.

By the time the core of the future Cup champions began appearing on the scene, little had changed in terms of player accoutrements. John Bucyk and Marcotte and the 20-man rosters of the 1960s, were using the same dressing room that Bill Cowley and 16 teammates had used in the 1930s and '40s.

"The first time I was in the old Garden was 1964," remembers Marcotte. "I was playing for a junior team and we walked in and couldn't believe what bad shape the dressing room was in; wood floor with cracks all over the place, filthy, dirty, one little tiny shower in the corner. I came from a junior team which was minor but our room was good there and the junior building was nice. I came back in 1968–'69 and the room was redone. It was very nice, more like a professional team. They had done a real nice job."

below:

The bandbox packed to capacity.

"First of all, when I first came in the League, the dressing room was a dump," confirms Ken Hodge. "Both locker rooms at the old Garden were dumps, but after I got traded here in '67, they made a concerted effort to make sure everyone was going to feel a lot more comfortable in the new locker room. Dan Canney [head trainer] and the Bruins staff went through a major renovation of the new locker room and made it very comfortable to live in and play in."

"The first time I went in that building, all I can remember is seeing the clock and the Original Six banners hanging

above:

Cam Neely walks to the ice surface one last time. This shot is from May 14, 1995, the last official Bruins game in the old building, a 3-to-2 playoff loss in the first round to New Jersey. The Devils wrapped up the series that night four games to one.

left:

The Bruins, including Ray Bourque, Randy Burridge (#12), and Bob Sweeney (#20), celebrate a goal. The crowd noise in the old Garden could get "beyond deafening."

from the catwalk," remembers Steve Babineau. "The ceiling seemed so far away when I was a kid.

"I had been in there for the circus and by the basketball court, but it was different for hockey," adds Babineau. "The hanging clock, the ice surface, it was amazing to me. Over time of course, I got to know the building with all of its nuances."

"All of the little nooks and crannies," remembers veteran PR woman and Bruins publicist Heidi Holland. "One thing comes to mind...there was a circular staircase that if you weighed over 120 pounds— I don't know how some of the players got down it—that went from the dressing room down to the players' lounge downstairs. That was just very bizarre."

"The hallways were small and all of the floors around the concourse were sloped," adds Babineau. "At the Zamboni end, it seemed like the floor dropped away; I wonder if they did it for drainage in case the ice melted and they had a flood. And speaking of the Zamboni, it would literally leave the ice, cross the concourse where people were walking to their seats, up through an overhead door that they'd open, out through a weird little alley between the Garden and 150 Causeway, and dump the snow."

Outside in the arena area, aside from the chicken wire above the boards changing to glass, little changed. Intimate meant intimidation: the bigger, taller, faster bodies of the expansion era on the same small ice surface equaled less time and space.

"To play in that building with the people right on top of you, things happened so quick in that building and you either hit, or got hit," reminisces Andy Brickley, a former Boston forward turned TV commentator. "It's what hockey's supposed to be. It's supposed to be about scoring chances, it's supposed to be about being physical, it's supposed to be about fights, and in that building it happened every game."

The key factor in the noise adding to the aura, and to the influence the fans had on driving the home team, came from the vertical nature of the spectator area. While the Garden and the other Original Six buildings were built "up," almost all modern arenas erected since are built "out," tapering away from the rink. The bandboxes placed fans on top of the action.

"That was the best," Brickley continues. "When you think of the Garden you think of places like Chicago, Buffalo, where the people were right on top of you. The building had a pulse, and that's the thing you appreciated most about the Garden. Obviously, the great players that played there, the sweater, putting that on, and playing in front of fans that had an unconditional love for the team…"

"The proximity of our crowd to the action, that was probably an advantage. They were right on top of the play," affirms longtime Bruins coach, GM, and executive Harry Sinden. "The other thing about the old Garden was that the players, as they entered the building and left the building, they did it right through the middle of the crowd, and that kind of touchy-feely atmosphere between the players and fans was great."

Onetime Bruins captain and current off-ice official Ed Sandford remembers the adrenaline rush from "the walk" across the concourse— the home players as heroes, the road team as villains.

"Ted Lindsay of Detroit, I remember he used to jab his stick at the fans as he went by," Sandford says. "They'd get into it. It was a unique time. The players would walk right along and the crowd

below:

Another perspective on the fans' proximity to the ice and the action, especially in the tight corners. Left to right during a playoff game on May 7, 1995: Bruin Dave Shaw (#34), Devil Neal Broten against Adam Oates on the draw, Blaine Lacher in net, and Ray Bourque.

above:

In 1988-89, Bruin Andy Brickley crashes the net against Sabres goalie Jacques Cloutier and backchecker Pierre Turgeon.

would be yelling for us on one side and against them. It was different."

That same area of the concourse took on a different feel on non-game days and during morning skates.

"One thing I really liked was on weekend game days, guys would come in for the skate, and a lot of times they'd bring their kids and they'd bring their dogs," remembers Holland. "And the kids would be out on the concourses playing hockey with balls of tape, what have you, and because there were—no rats in the Garden—very large mice, the way the stands were set up, the dogs would just be having a field day, running all over the place chasing the mice. It was a neat atmosphere. Nobody was around, and it was unique to that building. In traveling around I never saw that at morning skates anywhere else except for the Garden."

Mice?! Rats?!

"There were a few animals running around, four legged, with long tails," adds Ken Hodge. "They'd come across—you'd listen to them at night—they'd come running across the [locker room] ceiling and you'd hear them. A couple times, animals fell out of people's pockets or fell into their hockey pants and stuff like that, but that's what it was all about, the old Garden."

As for the canine camaraderie, that tradition came to a screeching halt.

"I remember one guy had a cute Labrador puppy...it may have been Jay Miller, I can't remember for sure...but one day the dog hopped the boards and started running around the ice during practice," reflects Holland. "The coach, I think Taz, absolutely lost it. The guys were skating around trying to get ahold of it, while the coach was yelling, 'Get that bleeping dog out of here.' That was the end of dogs in the building."

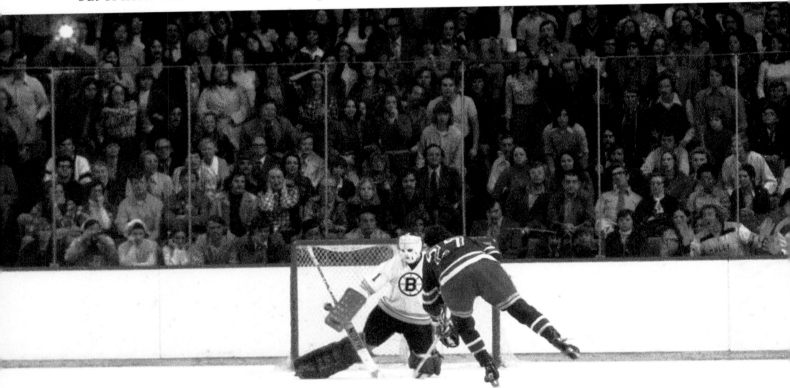

Photographer Steve Babineau remembers the Garden for a special reason of a completely different sort: it's where he broke into the full-time sports photography business.

"Being a new kid on the block, there were a lot of old-timers, and any time a 'foreign' photographer came in it was like, 'What the heck are you doing here?' There was a breaking-in period," Babs remembers. "When I finally got *The Hockey News* credential, in the mid-'70s, I was accepted somewhat, but I was still low guy on the totem pole in terms of shooting positions in the building. In those days, everybody wanted the side holes, along the face-off circles. The problem was,

above:

Ted Irvine of the Rangers against Bruins goalie Gilles Gilbert. A fan back left gets a clutch photo of his own.

above:

The Bruins score on the Flyers during the 1992-93 season. From left to right, Steve Leach, Flyer and former Bruin Gord Hynes, Dave Poulin, Flyer Brent Fedyk, netminder Stephane Beauregard, Flyer Dmitri Yushkevich, and Ray Bourque.

you couldn't turn all the way and shoot down the ice in either direction. Guys wanted the Bruins' attacking zone twice, and they were happy shooting the action there. I was fortunate enough to get a hole on the curvature of the boards, so I could shoot one goal, and all the way down the ice. Those are the preferred holes still today, because you can shoot more of the ice surface. I was in a spot ahead of its time by accident."

As for handling the photographers and the rest of the media, that job belonged to Greenberg.

> I was fortunate enough to get a hole on the curvature of the boards, so I could shoot one goal, and all the way down the ice.

"When I first started, the press box was in the first balcony, and the things that happened to us there, you wouldn't believe," Greenberg professes. "We had problems with the power. We used to put out these little black-and-white televisions because we televised all of our games in the '70s, and we'd have these little TVs we'd put out across the press box, and sometimes those wouldn't work. If it wasn't the TVs it was the phones. The stuff was put in place in the '20s, and very little had been done, of course. Nothing ever seemed to work right. It probably took about 10 years off my life, that building. But I enjoyed it immensely. It was unique and it was wonderful."

above:

Long time Bruins PR man and executive Nate Greenberg overlooks the proceedings from his perch in the Garden balcony.

From his start in 1973 until 1984, when he hired Holland as an assistant, Greenberg worked alone. Most of the NHL teams worked with just one PR person.

"At one point we moved the press box to the second level, probably in the mid-80s, and that was like moving to a new building for us," Greenberg remembers. "To go up to the second balcony, there was a lot more room, but you were still hanging off a balcony. I wouldn't go as far as to say it was plush, but it certainly was better than the first balcony. The one issue was to get up, there was this little fire escape. You had to duck down and kind of sneak your way through. If you tended to be on the portly side, it could be a challenge."

"When [the press box] moved up, it wasn't all that bad; in fact, by today's standards it was excellent," chips in Dupont. "Your angle was vastly different then, especially that first balcony. You were almost even with the boards, that near board; that's how pitched the angles were in the old buildings."

"It was very steep. You had to watch yourself coming down and often times things would fall over into the seats," Greenberg adds. "In the original balcony we had people sitting right behind us where the balcony went up, and occasionally we'd have someone from the road team come in and we'd have some issues. We knew everyone. We'd have NHL officials come in, or supervisors, visiting GMs or visiting scouts, former players, and there was some interesting give and take there over the years. The visiting GMs, because there were no boxes, they'd be sitting right out in the press box and they'd be mad at a call or something, and they were close enough where the players and officials could actually hear them from the press box. They'd be that close and they'd be givin' it to 'em. It was unique; I'll tell you that."

Longtime *Boston Globe* reporter Fran Rosa describes it another way.

"At one time, the press box at the old Garden was in section 60, part of the balcony at center ice. There was just one row on top of the other, about six or eight rows, like a desk top," Rosa describes. "Officials used to come in with other teams, general managers, and people like that—they would sit up there, too. One guy, King Clancy from Toronto, who was kind of a legend, and a very charming guy—when he used to come in the Garden, he'd always come in through the east lobby, and I think all the women who were hockey fans would stand there and wait to talk to the King, because he was a very charming guy…. Anyway, he'd go up in that press box, that old press box, and overhead, in the second balcony, is where the Gallery Gods were."

below:

The penalty box at the old Garden, a home-away-from home for many a Big Bad Bruin and for those in the Lunch Pail Gang. The near bench now resides in photographer Steve Babineau's home in Florida (if anyone's wondering what happened to it).

The Gallery Gods, led by Revere's Roger Naples, were vocal season ticket holders who occupied the first couple of rows of the second balcony. They've been attending Bruins games in both Gardens, old and new, for the last half-century.

"They had a section chief who got all the tickets," Rosa continues. "One guy up there, I think he came from Medford, I'm not sure, he was known as "Foghorn" because he was always yelling, nothing dirty, just always yelling. So Clancy would come up to the press box and Foghorn would yell down to him, 'Clancy, we named a town after you!' Clancy would look up at him, and Foghorn would yell,

'Marblehead!' So you know what Clancy did? He'd go buy a strong case of beer, get the ushers and Gallery Gods to send down a piece of rope; [then] he'd tie the case to it and send it up."

Often, more so by accident, that same beer or two might find its way back down the stairs and into the press area. Coats hanging in the back would change flavors, depending on what came trickling down the steps. Getting your clothes occasionally doused by beer wasn't supposed to be part of the allure of covering the team.

"God forbid you had to go to the bathroom," Greenberg adds. "You had to fight your way over to the corner where it was loaded with smoke, that beer smell…it was unbelievable. The press had to stand in line with the masses to get to the facilities."

Later, the Bruins let me in the penalty box and I was right in the game.

Being a photographer downstairs much of the time, Babineau didn't have to deal with similar confinement and traffic. In fact, his opportunity to discover new spaces and places around the building actually grew with time.

"Gradually, as ushers and other people always saw me around, I was recognized, and at the same time, I started adding more advanced equipment," Babineau declares. "As the Bruins became more popular, and more photographers started to show up, they added spots. I started to have access to everything. I wasn't under a deadline like a newspaper guy, so I would hang out in cool spots and patiently wait for the best shots. Eventually I ended up in the balcony and the catwalks.

"By the time everybody knew me," Babs continues, "I added strobes in the ceiling. [A building-wide system of high-powered flash units, which are wired together in a sequence, and tied to a line that ran down to where the strobe could be triggered remotely by Babineau's camera. Early on, a single wire ran all the way down to where Babs would plug in. Today, the system is wireless, and essentially triggered electronically by remote control.] Later, the Bruins let me in the penalty box and I was right in the game. The game was two inches away; I could feel the breeze as guys went by; I could feel the game."

above:

Normand Leveille, whose Bruins career ended due to a cerebral hemorrhage in October of 1982, took the ice with the help of Ray Bourque. Bruins in the shot left to right: Bob Armstrong, Terry O'Reilly, a glimpse of Bourque, Leveille, Bobby Orr, Phil Esposito, Gary Doak (#25), Doug Mohns (#19), Fred Stanfield, and Ed Sandford. Harry Sinden is on right, on skates in the white sweater.

left:

The Boston Garden from Causeway Street in 1995.

next spread:

The Bruins Honored Numbers, honored players, family representatives of the deceased, and other former Bruins left to right: John Bucyk, Doug Mohns, Derek Sanderson, Fred Stanfield, Phil Esposito, Ed Sandford, Jerry Toppazzini, John Peirson, Bobby Orr, Ken Hodge, Bob Armstrong, Jean Ratelle, Eddie Shore's son, Don McKenney, Ed Westfall (obscured), Dit Clapper's daughter, Terry O'Reilly, and Lionel Hitchman's descendant.

On September 28, 1995, the final Garden party was held: the Last Hurrah. Following a preseason game against the Montreal Canadiens, the Bruins brought back every legend possible for one final skate in front of a packed house.

Milt Schmidt, Bobby Orr, Johnny Bucyk, Terry O'Reilly, other legends, other members of the Big Bad Bruins and the Lunch Pail Gang all took laps around the ice for one last time. To cap off the emotion, Normand Leveille, a talented young Bruins winger whose 75-game career ended when he suffered a cerebral hemorrhage during a game in Vancouver in 1982, skated out onto the ice with the help of Bruins Superstar defenseman Ray Bourque.

"It was incredibly emotional," Bourque recalls. "It was a special moment I'll never forget and an incredible evening."

Literally inches behind the old Garden, the new TD Banknorth Garden, originally ordained the Fleet Center, had been built. It offered restaurants, luxury suites, and a seating capacity of 19,600. One night after the Last Hurrah, a gala event opened the new building.

With the increase in luxury, came the inevitable decrease in personality. The original Boston Garden had a distinct feel and persona likely never to be seen or felt again. The venerable old barn, unable to be razed by dynamite due to its proximity to the new building, came down in chunks—back-hoe and power-shovel-sized mouthfuls over the ensuing months. Hockey lost a shrine, while Bostonians lost their home away from home.

JOHN P. BUCYK 9 1955-1978

PHILIP A. ESPOSITO 7 1967-1975

ROBERT G. O 4 1966-197

EDWARD W. SHORE
2
1926-1940

AUBREY V. CLAPPER
5
1927-1947

LIONEL HITCHMAN
3
1925-1934

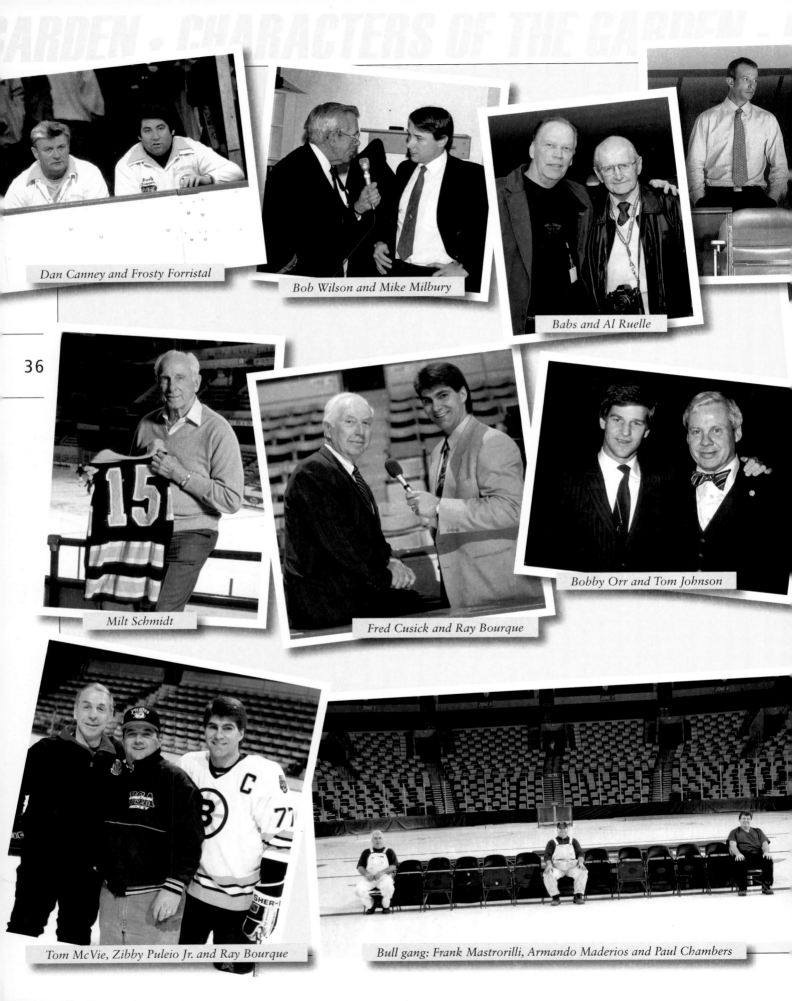

Dan Canney and Frosty Forristal

Bob Wilson and Mike Milbury

Babs and Al Ruelle

36

Milt Schmidt

Fred Cusick and Ray Bourque

Bobby Orr and Tom Johnson

Tom McVie, Zibby Puleio Jr. and Ray Bourque

Bull gang: Frank Mastrorilli, Armando Maderios and Paul Chambers

Bruins Execs

Joe Curnane, Nate Greenberg and Harry Sinden

Ed Sanford

Tony Nota and Pat Considine

Paul Mooney

Rene Rancourt

Anthony Velente – garden pizza

Locker room crew

Doc Fleger

Babs and Andy Carroll

CHAPTER

BRUINS LEGEND: JOHN BUCYK

above:

The most recent "Chief Night" on February 13th, 2007, celebrated Bucyk's 50th year in the Bruins organization.

left:

John "Chief" Bucyk was inducted into the Hockey Hall of Fame as a player in 1981.

Hundreds of Bruins players and employees have come and gone during John Bucyk's tenure with the organization. He's presently past the 50-year mark and counting with the hockey club. He's known by everyone as "Chief," a moniker first applied to him in the 1950s by teammate Bronco Horvath.

"Bronco said I took care of business. I'd do all of the running around, arranging things," Bucyk remembers. "I also scored goals, so he called me the Chief. 'Hey, you get everything done; you're the Chief,' he said."

Many associate the name with an assumed Native North American background. However, one shouldn't let Chief's appearance fool them; his complexion and native look and his nickname are purely coincidental. John Bucyk is of Ukrainian descent.

Chief is *still* getting everything done as he continues in his sixth decade with the Bruins. After retiring as a player in 1978, Bucyk jumped on the radio broadcasts as color commentator at the invitation of play-by-play man Bob Wilson.

"It was great fun, and I appreciate Bob asking me to do it," Chief says. "It was a great second career. Heck, I was on there for years."

During his two-plus decades on the air, Chief gradually added other job responsibilities. He handled public relations,

media relations, and travel secretary chores along the way. Today, he's still the full-time road services coordinator.

"Chief could do it all, on and off the ice," says Bruins legend Milt Schmidt. "He had a great hip check. He was a solid defender. He reminded me of my teammate Woody Dumart in that area, and he's still a Bruin today—just the way it should be."

"He'd set up the postgame socializing, get everyone out to eat and whatever," recalls former Bruins goalkeeper Gerry Cheevers. "He'd get you a starting time at your local golf club. If you needed a submarine, he'd get it for you."

"When you think of the Bruins, you think of John Bucyk," says former Bruins captain Wayne Cashman. "He was a great leader, a leader on our winning clubs, and he's a great guy on and off the ice. To this day, he helps Bruins players and ex-players."

If a man wore the Spoked B, there's a good chance Bucyk helped him with something along the way, and there's equally as good a chance he'd still help that man today.

"I enjoy it," says Chief. "Nowadays, traveling with the team, I like helping the kids, teasing them a bit, and it's fun. They joke around with me and all in all we have a good time."

The best of times for Boston in terms of on-ice success came with Bucyk in his elongated prime. During the three-season span in which the Bruins won two Stanley Cups, from 1969–72, Bucyk tallied 114 goals and 154 assists in the regular season, and added an impressive 22 goals and 24 assists in 36 playoff games. He barely missed being a point-a-game man over the course of his entire playoff career.

above:

Bucyk battling in the final months of his final season 1977-78, against LA Kings defenseman Steve Short.

Of course, as was the case for all of the Bruins over the years, the Chief's main playoff nemesis was the Montreal Canadiens. Bucyk's Bruins never beat them head-to-head in a series, although he did earn their respect.

"They had very good players. It was scary every time we played them," Canadiens Hall of Famer Guy Lafleur recalls. "Bucyk was late in his career when I played against him but he was strong, a scorer, and a real gentleman on the ice. He was very good with the younger guys. He'd help out the younger players a lot, I remember."

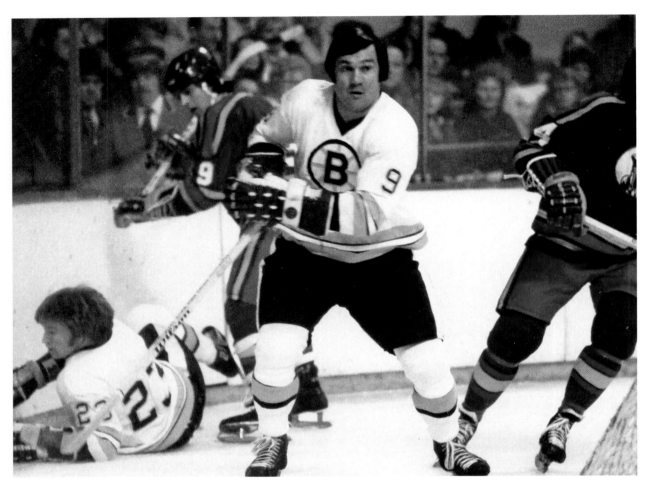

Twice Bucyk earned the NHL's Lady Byng Memorial Trophy, awarded each season to the player who exhibits the best type of sportsmanship and gentlemanly conduct combined with a high standard of playing ability.

"He was very sneaky," adds Pierre Bouchard. "You wouldn't chase him up and down the wing or anything; he'd just know where the puck was going to be."

Bucyk found the puck in the right spot enough times to pot 545 goals as a Bruin, still the club record and one unlikely to be broken for a very long time. Ray Bourque passed Bucyk in the games played, assists, and overall points categories. Bucyk took over the career points mark in 1967 and held it for thirty years, until Bourque passed him with his 1,440th point on February 1, 1997. Both men played 21 seasons, with Bourque catching Chief in actual number of games played during Ray's next-to-last season in Boston.

"I've always said that records were made to be broken," Bucyk says. "I'm happy for the guys. I remember when Ray passed me for points. I mean that's fine. It was good for him, and the team, and it's going to happen. The younger

above:

Chief's NHL career lasted 23 seasons, almost four times longer than the Colorado Rockies franchise, which lasted six (1976-82), before moving to New Jersey and becoming the Devils. Bucyk leaves behind teammate Al Sims (#23) and Colorado's Wilf Paiement (#9).

generation is going to come along and it's time to move on, and the records get broken. I still have a few."

In 1970–71, Bucyk scored 51 goals, his career high for a single season and the only time he eclipsed the 50-goal mark. He's still the oldest player ever to do it in the NHL, turning the trick at age 35.

Bucyk still holds the NHL career record for assists by a left wing, with 813, 19 of those coming in his first two seasons in Detroit.

> Bucyk found the puck in the right spot enough times to pot 545 goals as a Bruin, still the club record.

"It was those years in Detroit I learned the ropes," Chief says. "Gordie Howe was my idol, still is, and he and Ted Lindsay, the captain back then, took the young guys under their wings and showed them around. They really took care of all of the players, and that's where I learned it."

The 20-year-old from Edmonton played just 38 games his first season with the Red Wings, and scored only one goal.

"It was tough. You'd sit on the bench for 45 minutes and then he'd [the coach] tell you to go out," Bucyk explains. "You'd be stiff. It was tough to do your job properly. But they had some great players and I was a rookie and I had to wait my turn."

The following year the youngster played 66 games, and reached double-digit figures in goals with 10—maybe not enough to be a top-liner just yet, but apparently enough to catch the eye of the Boston Bruins. On June 10, 1957, the Red Wings sent Bucyk and some cash to the east coast, in exchange for goaltender Terry Sawchuk. Number 9 has been here ever since. Bucyk would have plenty of opportunities to burn his former team, given the nature of playing in a league with only six teams.

"The kids nowadays don't know the type of hockey we used to play," Chief explains. "I mean we had full-scale bench-clearing brawls. It was different. It was tough. There were only six teams at that

below:

Chief battles the Flames, another team that changed locations, from Atlanta to Calgary. Known for his hip checks and lower body strength, Bucyk holds off Atlanta's Dave Shand (#8) while Ken Houston looks on.

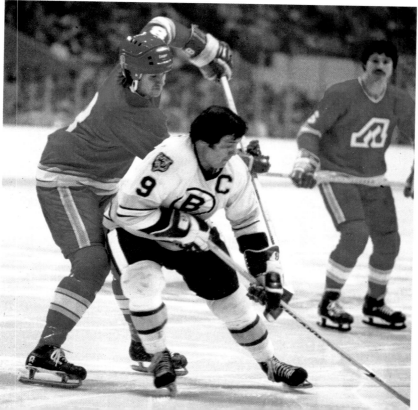

time and you'd see the same players night in and night out. We'd play in Montreal on a Saturday, jump on the train and play in Boston on the Sunday. And we'd ride down on the same train, us in one private car and the Canadiens in another."

Even with frequency and familiarity, the fights and battles would soon be forgotten.

"We'd never let it carry over much, maybe every once in a while. But we'd usually just play, forget about it, and move on. I do remember Rocket Richard separated my shoulder once. Nothing malicious, just a hit along the boards, but he separated my shoulder. I remember that, and I remember playing against him."

It was late in the Rocket's career. One legendary time span winding down, the other one practically just gearing up, and the Chief was paying attention.

"He was a competitor, I'll tell you that," Chief says of the Rocket. "He was fierce; he'd play every game hard. It was neat to play against a guy like that and of course knowing who he was."

During an eight-year span in the '60s, the Bruins failed to make the playoffs, but the team, and the hardy fans in Boston, still managed to have a good time.

"We got beat up sometimes," Chief recalls, "on the scoreboard. But we would fight. I mean, we might lose a game 6- or 7-1, but if we had one big fight, and we won that, the fans would go home happy."

For the most part, rather than fists, Bucyk preferred to leave a physical impression with his hips. He had a devastating old-fashioned hip check.

"Great hip check," proclaims Milt Schmidt. "One of the best. Chief would give hip checks and score goals."

Bucyk continued to produce through his penultimate season, with 43 points in 49 games in 1976–77. The next season, the Chief wound down with just 18 points.

below:

Bucyk powers through the offensive zone against Pittsburgh's Dave Burrows and Colin Campbell (#6). Teammate Wayne Cashman follows. Bucyk holds the Bruins team record with 545 career goals.

right:

Chief at the old Garden. In his fifty-plus years as a member of the organization, Bucyk has been a player, a broadcaster, a media relations man, and a travel secretary among other things. He continues as the team's road services coordinator.

It was during this time period, during the latter stages of the sturdy left winger's career, that photographer Steve Babineau appeared on the scene.

"He was more old-school in my mind," Babs remembers. "I was a little more intimidated by him when I first showed up. He was part of the old regime and I'm pretty sure he was friends with the previous photographer. It took a little while for him to warm up to the new kid, I think."

It was clear to Babineau at the time: the Chief was the man.

"Whenever players were doing promos or anything, or had to be somewhere for an event, it seemed like everything filtered through Chief. As a player and then obviously since then, he was the guy you went through to get things done."

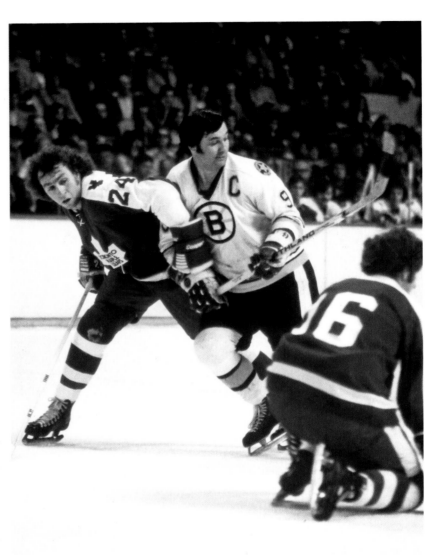

Bucyk bowls through Brian Glennie (#24) of the Maple Leafs. That's Toronto's Rod Seiling on one knee.

"His longevity makes him as important as anyone, any of the legends I've photographed retiring, and that's what makes it special for me. Growing up in Cambridge, when I was a kid, 8, 10, 12 years old, I used to listen to the games at night on the transistor radio and Chief was *the* star. Before Orr came along and Esposito, Bucyk was the star and he was on the BOW line [Bucyk, Oliver, Williams] with Murray Oliver at center and Tommy Williams streaking down the other wing. They didn't win much, but that was the line, and Chief was the main guy."

Bucyk wore the C for two separate stints as a Bruin, and even during a time when they didn't have a formal captain, Chief was the unnamed, de facto captain.

"He was the captain when I first got there," Babs remembers, "and even when he wasn't wearing the C, he was the guy the players looked up to."

After the 1977–78 season, Bucyk hung up his NHL skates for good. Two seasons later, on March 13, 1980, the Bruins retired his jersey, and hoisted number 9 to the rafters.

"That's when I really started to get to know Chief," Babineau recalls. "I took the shot of the ceremony—him watching his number go up—and we decided to make and sell a limited edition print of the occasion. It was sold in the pro shop for a couple of years. Chief was like 'sure, let's do it.'"

Twenty-eight years later, in early 2007, the Bruins had Chief Night number two, to honor Bucyk's 50 years with the organization.

below:

Boston greats honor Chief in his 50th season. Ray Bourque, Bronco Horvath, Tom Johnson, John McKenzie, Doug Mohns, Don Marcotte (face in back), Chief, Cam Neely, Terry O'Reilly, Billy O'Dwyer, Derek Sanderson, and Ed Sandford.

"That's really cool," states Babineau. "Again, as a kid, I'm listening to him play hockey; he's the star. Then I'm shooting pictures of him still as a player and I'm a young adult, don't know anything, and then here he is, all this time later, still with the club and I'm still taking his picture. I mean, with Orr, I caught him towards the end, but then he just went on his way. Chief is *still* going; he embodies my whole existence with the team."

At one point along the way, Babineau knew he had been accepted into the fold, old school, and otherwise.

"Chief was already an old-timer, and he and Gary Doak, and Pie McKenzie and Don Marcotte were playing in an alumni game against the Medford Youth Hockey coaches. I was one of the coaches. They left the other guys alone but every chance they got, they gave me an extra elbow, or a playful hook, or a whack, or would run me into the boards when they could. It was fun. They could get away with it with me, but they weren't going to do that with guys they didn't know."

Through the course of Babineau's career, Bucyk provided countless opportunities to add to the scrapbook. The awards and recognition he has received are as diverse as anyone's in hockey.

While still a player, during his final season in fact, Bucyk earned the Lester Patrick Award for service to hockey in the United States. Four years later, and in his first season of eligibility, he earned induction into the Hockey Hall of Fame.

Bucyk also holds the unofficial record for vehicles obtained from one team.

"You're gonna say that's a record," Chief laughs. "Yeah, I got one in 1965 when they thought I was going to retire because of a bad back. They gave me a '65 Mustang convertible. That was the fans' gift. They had a night for me."

For John Bucyk Night number one after his retirement, he received a hefty stipend from the team toward a motor home, and then for John Bucyk Night number two almost three decades later, he picked up a Volvo SUV.

In 2008, Bucyk and his wife, Anne, celebrated their 50th wedding anniversary, while Bucyk's been married to the Bruins for 52 years...and counting.

"I can't believe it's been that long," Chief says of his relationship with the Bruins. "It goes by quick. I enjoy it. I've had fun every year."

above:

Chief receiving congratulations from Bruins Executive Vice President Charlie Jacobs, a member of the ownership family. Bucyk has worked for three different owners: the Adams, a local TV conglomerate, and the Jacobs.

Chief is *still* going; he embodies my whole existence with the team.

right:

On the first "official" Chief night, March 13, 1980, former teammate Stan Jonathan presents Bucyk his head dress. Jonathan is native American, Bucyk is Ukrainian, but often mistaken for indigenous, especially given his nickname.

below:

Former teammate and Bruins captain Wayne Cashman presents Bucyk his # 9 Bruins sweater.

right:

Chief watches his banner go up. That's Harry Sinden to his immediate right.

JOHN BUCYK (LW) Edmonton, AB | #9 | 50-plus years in organization

BRUINS REGULAR SEASON STATISTICS	GP	G	A	Pts	PIM
1957–1978	1,436	545	794	1,339	436
Bruins Postseason Statistics	124	41	62	103	42

CHAPTER

4

BRUINS LEGEND:
BOBBY ORR

above:

Orr stood alone as a hockey player. Knee injuries shortened a career that would have been the greatest in history, for a player who may have been the greatest in history anyway.

left:

Bobby Orr, working on his stick, which normally featured a single width of tape wrapped once around the blade.

In Boston, "Bobby" is all one needs to say to instantly bring to mind the man who revolutionized the game of hockey from the blueline—the man many argue became the greatest player of all time. Robert Gordon Orr hailed from Parry Sound, Ontario, along the shores of Lake Huron's Georgian Bay, but it's Boston where his image will forever be immortalized.

To say his arrival in New England was anticipated would be an understatement, as the Bruins would have to wait until Bobby was 18 years old to play in the NHL. It became obvious well before that that Orr had extra special qualities and the potential to be a star. Signed by Bruins agent and Oshawa coach Wren Blair at age 13, Orr began playing in junior-A (then the Ontario Hockey Association, precursor to the OHL) at age 14. Despite playing with teenagers four and five years older, the Oshawa Generals' defenseman dominated.

Boston Globe sports writer Fran Rosa covered the Bruins occasionally starting in the early 1950s, and began covering them on a regular basis early in Orr's professional career.

"He was gonna be the savior. For so many years they [the Bruins] had finished last or next to last. It was between them and the Rangers as to who was going to finish last, back with only six teams," Rosa relates. "So the hockey experts and the Bruins people all said this kid was going to lead them out of the wilderness, and he did. He lived up to the expectations.

"You also have to remember that the Bruins made a big trade. I believe it was Milt Schmidt, the General Manager at the time," Rosa recalls. "They got Phil Esposito from the Blackhawks."

The deal is still referred to as "The Trade" by many from the time period. It occurred on May 15, 1967, and along with Espo, the Bruins received Ken Hodge and Fred Stanfield, in exchange for Pit Martin, Gilles Marotte, and goalie Jack Norris.

He would amaze you with the next thing you didn't know he could do.

"That deal filled out what they needed," Rosa adds, "and with Orr along, they had something special."

After averaging two points a game his final year of junior, Orr led his team to the OHA championship and was named Most Valuable Player. The next season, his first in the NHL, he won the Calder Trophy, the award given to the Rookie of the Year. Despite only playing in 46 games the following season, 1967–68, Orr earned himself the first of an astounding eight consecutive Norris trophies, awarded to the League's best defenseman.

"The greatest player who ever played, and to be on the ice with him was just great," states Bruins netminding legend Gerry Cheevers. "Every game, every shift, you just marveled at what he could do. I'm sitting here right now watching Tiger Woods on TV, and I'm watching Tiger do things that no one else can do. I'm watching him do new things all the time, and that's exactly like Orr in his time. You loved watching him do it, and he would amaze you with the next thing you didn't know he could do. He was incredible and a tremendous team player to boot."

"Obviously he stood alone," recalls former Bruins coach and executive Harry Sinden. "He was the guy around whom we focused and how we operated."

below:

Orr in a battle for the puck with Vic Hadfield of the Penguins as Terry O'Reilly follows.

One can find Orr's list of awards and accomplishments anywhere. What's most impressive and enduring to New Englanders is the impact he had on hockey and its growth in the region.

"I work for the Department of Conservation and Recreation, what used to be the MDC," explains Cup-winning Bruins defenseman Gary Doak. "They did have 20 rinks in the area, and then about 20 more went up outside of Boston basically because of us winning the Stanley Cup in 1969–70. That's the era of Bobby and when hockey exploded in New England."

Doak lived with Orr for a couple of seasons, and as a fellow Bruins D-man from 1965 to '70 (and later '72 to '81) he watched Orr's ascension firsthand.

"He's still the best player I've seen," Doak continues. "I've seen a lot of players, the players now and then. The things that he could do on the ice, he had like four or five different speeds, he played power play, he killed penalties, he did it all, and individually. I've never seen a player do all that he could do. You'd just sit on the bench and be amazed at what he could do."

Steve Babineau never worked directly with the legendary defenseman. He received his first full-time NHL press credential during Orr's last full season in Boston, and became team photographer after Orr had left. Prior to that, like all the other kids, moms, dads, staffers, and players for that matter, Babineau was simply an awestruck fan.

"When Orr hit, I was a youngster of six or seven years old, and my parents immediately gravitated to the Bruins and they used to watch all of the games on channel 38, or whatever channel they were on at that time," former Bruins' defenseman and Melrose native Frank Simonetti remembers. "You couldn't help but get sucked into the Orr era. Whatever team you played for, everybody wanted number 4, regardless of the team, growing up in the late '60s and early '70s. He changed the game of hockey, but he kind of put defensemen on the map too, where it became a position kids actually strived to play, instead of the glory positions of center or wing with scoring all the goals. Bobby made it cool to be a defenseman."

It's easy to look up to a guy who in the 1969–70 season won his first of two Art Ross trophies as the League's leading scorer with 120 points —the only defenseman ever to do it—the Hart Trophy as League MVP, the Norris, and the Conn Smythe Trophy as the playoffs' Most Valuable Player. He also scored the Stanley Cup winning goal against St. Louis, on a feed from Derek Sanderson, while being upended by Blues defenseman Noel Picard. The image of Orr flying through the air while beginning the celebration is the most famous hockey photograph of all time. Although there were almost a dozen different photos of the goal sequence from different angles, the definitive shot was taken by the late Ray Lussier, a New Hampshire resident, working for the *Boston Record American*.

above:

From a shaved head as a teenager in the sixties to long flowing locks in the mid-seventies, Orr was the most popular figure around Boston. During that span he won an unprecedented eight consecutive Norris Trophies as the NHL's best defenseman.

Before injuries shortened his final season in Boston and free agency took him to Chicago in 1976, Orr played a grand total of ten games with Brad Park, who came to the B's in a controversial multi-player deal for Phil Esposito in November of 1975. That's Bruin Hank Nowak (#18) in the background.

"That was the first image everyone saw," Steve Babineau points out. "As the story goes, he was a guy who showed up unexpectedly. He was able to get the shot and get out of the building quickly. I watched the game on TV and they kept replaying that moment over and over and over. The fact that he was able to snap that moment was incredible, especially for a guy who wasn't normally a sports shooter. He found a crevice between the fans that was a prime spot most people didn't know about. It was a position I used years later."

Rumor has it another photographer had vacated the position to get a drink, go to the restroom, or to change ends. Lussier stepped in.

"The picture has been bootlegged a thousand times. It's everywhere," Babs continues. "The guys you'd expect to get it, didn't get it. Regular beat photographers, they could go to a thousand games and never get a shot like that, where Lussier showed up and gets this unbelievable shot. That's just the way it works sometimes.

"In fact, Frank O'Brien from the *Globe*, a photographer I idolized, took a sequence from up where the TV guys were, and he had all the shots, but from Orr's back and above. It was from the TV-38 overhang, from a perch above the blueline.

Not to say it was a bad shot or sequence; it was cool. It just didn't include *the* shot. I did notice that O'Brien had a motor drive camera, which shot a sequence of two or three frames a second. I was thinking the next day, 'I'd love to get one of those.'"

Babineau would later experience an incredible and opportunistic moment involving Orr's famous goal.

"Years later, when I was the team photographer, I was sitting in my office in Medford Square, and this little, old guy walks in," Babineau recalls. "His name is Ernie Cormier, and he knows who I am, and he introduces himself as a former season ticket holder and Gallery God member. From an envelope he pulls out some slides, and being busy at that moment, I was wondering if I even wanted to go through them. Well, I literally trembled when I pulled the first image out of the envelope. It was a 35mm slide transparency, on 'available light' film, from the first row of the Gallery Gods, reverse angle

Chapter 4

below:

Orr pursued by Los Angeles King Butch Goring, who would later play the last 39 games of his NHL career for Boston, and then would coach the Bruins for just more than a season. Chasing Orr was a full time endeavor for opponents, as was watching Orr for teammates and opponents alike. From left to right on bench, Bruin Dallas Smith, while on the ice it's King Bob Nevin, Gregg Sheppard, and King Bob Murdoch

right:

Orr on the end of the bench as his injury plagued career winds down in Boston. That's head coach Don Cherry in the background, and next to Orr: Dallas Smith, Don Marcotte, and John Bucyk. Question is: who's the kid? How's that for fan proximity to players.

of the goal. He had the whole offensive zone, from about the blue line on the opposite side. You could see Lussier in the photograph. You can see every player on the ice in the picture except for [goalie Gerry] Cheevers, who's at the other end of the ice."

"Can you do anything with this?" Ernie said at the time.

"Holy moly!" reacted Babs, trembling.

At the time of the actual goal, Babineau remained just a fanatic.

"The photo standing alone needed something, so we added a shot of Orr holding the Stanley Cup, over the expanse of the white ice in the foreground," Babineau explains. "We struck a deal, made posters and prints of the two images together, and we shared a percentage of the sale when we sold the photos. It was later available on Bobby Orr's website. Might still be."

At the time of the actual goal, Babineau remained just a fanatic. He had watched the Cup win from home, and his official credential days were still a few years away. Meanwhile, Orr led the Bruins to the Cup finals in 1971, only to be upset by the Canadiens, and then back again for triumph in the 1972 final against the New York Rangers. Orr continued his Norris Trophy string, of course, and after the second Cup win, he once again earned the Conn Smythe MVP.

left:

Known for his skating skill and his offensive prowess, Orr would combine all of his talents to also guard his own net, here working with Carol Vadnais against the St. Louis Blues.

"I met him when we were both kids, with his shaved head, and then I watched him become this flying defenseman with the long hair," Babineau remembers, "and it was amazing to watch his transformation take place. He was literally toying with guys. On the penalty kill, he'd be chased around the ice. He'd skate back into his zone, pass it up, get it back, and keep going. He was so far ahead of his time, such a great skater, it seemed like the other guys were skating in sand.

"That was the pace of the game then, and then you threw this body out there; he almost seemed out of place," Babs continues. "It was like everyone was using triple-A batteries and Orr was using a car battery. No one else really did it. Coffey did it 10 years later, in terms of going end to end, but Orr did it consistently. Orr also used to set up behind the other net, something Gretzky made famous two decades later. Even when he had the knee problems, his vision of the ice surface was just unbelievable. Unfortunately for Orr, the deking and weaving left him vulnerable to being clipped in the knees and legs, and unfortunately for me, my first couple of seasons around the team were his last."

He was so far ahead of his time, such a great skater, it seemed like the other guys were skating in sand.

The aforementioned three-season period from 1969–72 may feature the most impressive sustained performance by any player in history. Orr won the League regular season MVP award all three seasons on top of the playoff accolades, and he set records for a defenseman that still stand almost four full decades later. In 1971, he finished with 102 assists and 139 points.

above:

Orr and Phil Esposito in pre-game warm-ups. In their ultimate season as a defenseman/forward scoring machine in 1970-71, the two combined for 291 points (Orr 139). Orr's 102 assists that season remains the NHL's single season record for a defenseman.

With the personal accomplishments came fame, obviously, but for Orr it may have also brought about a certain awkwardness, a shyness, an aversion for the ridiculous amount of attention and exposure, reserved in a more modern day and age for divas, rock stars, and heads of state. In the hockey world at the time, the media demands were simply overwhelming.

"I always used to say, one of my toughest jobs in the day was trying to get Orr to come out of the trainer's room to talk to the press," remembers longtime Bruins PR man Nate

Greenberg. "The reason he wouldn't or didn't all the time was that he really wanted his teammates to get proper accolades, while everybody, all the time, wanted him. Especially on the road. I remember one time we were in the Olympia in Detroit, and he was holed up in the trainer's room—in this old, old building, the room which was the size of a closet—and I used to have to go in and plead with him to come out. I knew what was going on: every night, every guy wanted to ask him the same old stuff, and he really felt like his teammates were being slighted at times. He would try to withstand it by staying in the trainer's room. He'd try to get his teammates some publicity."

To present, Orr still has never "authorized" a biography, and his desire to avoid the center of attention remains. He is active with the Bobby Orr Museum in his hometown in Ontario, an entity that inducted longtime friend, former Bruins coach, and Canadian icon Don Cherry in the summer of 2008.

Occasionally on his *Hockey Night in Canada* "Coach's Corner" segment, Cherry will still order up highlights of Orr skating around as a Bruin. "Look at him; isn't he something?" Cherry will say in awe. His on-air co-host Ron McLean oohs and aahs and reacts with "unreals" and "something elses" right along. The video and the response bring chills of sentimentality.

above:

Constantly hounded by the media game to game, Orr attempted to deflect some of the attention to his teammates. Well spoken but shy, Orr would often delay post-game interviews as long as possible.

"It seemed to me, and I don't know if anyone else felt it," adds Rosa, "that the better he played, the more difficult it was to find him in the dressing room after the game. He didn't want to take credit; he wanted the other players to get credit for the game. If you could afford to be patient, with your deadline and everything, he'd eventually come out and he'd be very gracious. You had to wait for it."

"I'm not sure what the reasons were but I do know that he was a very private, very shy guy," reflects teammate Terry O'Reilly, "who just happened to be the best hockey player in the world. And so, something had to give and he did what he had to do. I can tell you when he was asked to do something for a good cause for a charity he was there. I remember tapping him to be man of the year for the Liver Foundation one year, and you know, he didn't want to do it, but he wouldn't say no because it was a friend and a teammate asking him, and that's just the way he was. He couldn't say no."

below:

Hard to say whether he's being pursued behind his own net or behind the opponent's. Orr would use the entire rink surface to his advantage, including the area behind the net in the offensive zone, long before it was claimed by another NHL great and nicknamed Gretzky's office.

"Bobby Orr off the ice was a great person," states 15-year Bruin and two-time Cup winner Don Marcotte. "He was one guy I was amazed with. He'd maybe meet a person one time, and then the same person five years later and he'd know the guy's name. Unbelievable. A great guy who never thought himself a superstar, always thought of the team; he wasn't the only guy on the ice; it was teamwork. When someone was called up, they were part of the family and equal to what he was, and he treated them that way."

O'Reilly possessed a unique and well-rounded perspective on Orr, having grown up a fan of the young star defenseman.

"Well, I was a lucky kid to be growing up in Oshawa and watching Bobby," remembers O'Reilly. "He was the phenom and then, as I came up through the Oshawa organized hockey rinks, I got an opportunity to play for the junior-B team. And our dressing room was just down the hallway from the junior-A dressing room, which belonged to the Generals. So I was with the junior-B and Bobby was with the Generals and I would look out the dressing room door down the hallway and see Bobby; he'd be scraping the stick and adjusting the blade and the stick. Then a couple years later I got drafted by the Bruins, got assigned to their farm team, the Boston Braves, and it was in the Boston Garden, the old Boston Garden, down the hall from the Bruins dressing room.

above:

Orr retired from hockey on November 8, 1978. He was inducted into the Hockey Hall of Fame less than a year later on September 12, 1979, at age 31. He remains the youngest inductee ever. Orr invited Steve Babineau to the induction in Toronto, where Babs took this never-before-published photo.

It was like déjà vu—I came walking out of the Braves dressing room and I look down the hall and there's Bobby Orr working on a hockey stick getting ready for practice. It was kind of neat. Then, the following year, I had an opportunity to join the Bruins and be his teammate, so it was kind of neat chasing him at practice for a few years."

"I was drafted by the Rangers, and I really only have one recollection of Orr because it was late in his career and maybe Bobby was hurt when we played them," recalls then soon-to-be Boston forward Rick Middleton, "but I remember one time in Boston Garden on the power play, Boston was killing the penalty and Orr had the puck and he wouldn't give it to us. I remember chasing him around the net. You know, the scene from many highlights, where he skates around and nobody can get him, nobody could get the puck off of him. I remember doing that, chasing him."

It's often said a good goaltender is a team's best penalty killer. In Orr's case, goaltender Cheevers disagrees.

"I think in his case the goaltender just had the best seat in the house."

In 1975, in his last "full" season in the NHL, Orr played in all 80 games, and despite being in the latter stages of his

below:

The Bruins held Bobby Orr night and retired his jersey on January 9th, 1979. Orr, alongside bull gang worker Zibby Puleio Sr., who helped unveil it, watches his banner go up.

above:

Donning # 4, Orr, arguably the greatest hockey player of all-time, addresses the Bruins faithful.

right:

Orr and former teammate John Bucyk display # 4, a sweater number many hockey fans felt should have been retired League-wide.

career and being somewhat hobbled, he won the regular season scoring title for his second Art Ross Trophy. He finished with 46 goals, still the second-most ever by a defenseman in a single season, and tallied 135 points.

"I do believe he's the greatest Bruin of them all," declares Greenberg.

"Bobby is responsible for practically every American-born hockey player out here, because when he got here, all the rinks started springing up," says Middleton passionately, "and now New England is the hockey hotbed of the United States I believe, and I think every one of these American players should thank him for putting them on the map."

BOBBY ORR (D) Parry Sound, ON | #4 | Some say #4 deserved League-wide retirement

BRUINS REGULAR SEASON STATISTICS	GP	G	A	Pts	PIM
1966–1976	631	264	624	888	924
Bruins Playoff Statistics	74	26	66	92	92

CHAPTER

BRUINS LEGEND:
PHIL ESPOSITO

65

above:

Outspoken, Espo never feared expressing his feelings as a player, a coach, or as a hockey executive. His 2003 book ruffled more than a few feathers of ex-teammates.

left:

Phil Esposito scored 1,012 points in 625 regular season games with the Bruins, and added 102 playoff points in 72 games while helping Boston win two Stanley Cups along the way.

Of all the Bruins legends, Phil Esposito remains the most outspoken: about the game, about his time in and out of Boston, and about his life. In fact, he wrote a book about it.

"I didn't give away anyone that's still married to the same woman," states Espo, in regards to his book, *Thunder and Lightning: A No B.S. Hockey Memoir.* "If you're divorced you were free game, because I cut the hell out of myself because I'm divorced."

"I gave it to Alan Eagleson a little bit, absolutely," clarifies Espo. "I gave it to Harry [Sinden] a little bit too. Quite frankly, I didn't ever want to leave Boston. I wanted to end up my career in Boston, and that's what I wanted, and that's why I didn't go to the WHA. I thought I would end up my career in Boston, but things happen. I understand it though, because Harry had to make some tough decisions because he knew Bobby Orr was going to leave. Bobby didn't know he was going to leave at that time, but Eagleson [Orr's agent, and then the head of the NHL Players' Association] knew it, and they made the deal."

"Espo always had something to say," states former Bruins PR man Nate Greenberg. "He was outspoken. The one thing about Phil, he always wore his heart on his sleeve. No one could ever accuse him of being a phony; he was honest and outspoken."

Eight years after being acquired in "The Trade" from Chicago, Espo, along with Carol Vadnais, was sent packing to New York, for Brad Park, Jean Ratelle, and Joe Zanussi on November 7, 1975. It was a decent deal for both clubs, but one that still has Esposito a bit bitter today.

"He [GM Harry Sinden] said I would never leave Boston, or I would be there as long as he would be there," Espo states. "I shook hands with him, and I don't believe in no-trade contracts. I don't believe in them to this day. Then he traded me and I was bitter for a lot of years. I'm probably still a little upset about it—isn't that unbelievable. I was very, very sad. I didn't want to leave Boston. I could have gone to the WHA and made a million-dollar signing bonus, but I decided to stay in Boston, and give up that money, just because I loved it so much. Three weeks later I was traded, and that hurt. That hurt. That's what bothered me. Other guys like Derek Sanderson went, Johnny McKenzie went, Gerry Cheevers went…

above:

Espo tries to fire a backhander past defenseman Ron Greschner with New York captain Brad Park (#2) also heading back.

above:

A battle for the bouncing puck in front between Bert Marshall of the Islanders and Esposito, who was well known for scoring "garbage goals," an arguable term, from the slot and around the crease area.

They went, came back and he [Sinden] accepted them fine. Me, I stayed, as a loyal guy. No, that's not right."

Espo wasn't the only one upset by the deal. The fans had lost a prolific scorer, a favorite adopted son, and a two-time Cup winner.

"The guy had been a scoring machine," points out Greenberg, who was in the middle of the media maelstrom following the deal. "It was a really ballsy move by Harry Sinden, the ballsiest, and it worked out—a great deal. But at the time it created as much buzz as a Stanley Cup final. Harry had death threats. You talk about a buzz. I mean Brad Park was a good player but he was hated; he was the enemy. We traded a beloved player for a guy we hated. A lot of media was against it. Len Berman, who worked in Boston then, he was upset. He basically said any great player should spend his entire career with the same team. Now they'd laugh in his face, but back then, with Howe and others, they felt that way. D. Leo Monahan of the *Record American* took a level-headed approach. I'll never forget. He wrote, 'My heart said it was a bad deal; my head said let's wait and see.'"

He was just one of the players you loved to play with because he hated to lose.

One could understand the initial reaction. Before Gretzky, in terms of ridiculous offensive numbers, there was Esposito. In the 1970–71 season he tallied an unheard of 76 goals and 76 assists, a record at the time many believed would last a lifetime.

"Phil was a great centerman," states John Bucyk. "I spent a lot of time with him on the ice, particularly on the power play, and he could put the puck in the net."

"He was just one of the players you loved to play with because he hated to lose," adds linemate Ken Hodge. "You saw that in the Team Canada series [Summit 1972, when Canada beat the USSR in the eight-game series], you'd see it every day when he came to the rink. We just melded together—Cash, him, and I—Cash on the one wing and me on the other and we just blended. We were just a very unselfish line and Esposito started to click, started to score goals at a rapid pace, and it didn't hurt matters that we had number 4 on defense, either. That was a big thing right there. Took a lot of pressure off."

Esposito was the leading scorer in the Summit Series and in 1972 was named Canadian athlete of the year.

Similar to the overlap with Bobby Orr, Steve Babineau's experience with Phil Esposito came early in the young photographer's career. He covered number-7 as a free-lancer, and Espo's existence in Boston came to an end prior to Babineau joining the B's staff. Of the two "overlap" legends, Babineau seems to lean the way of the defenseman.

"Esposito was successful in Boston because he played with Bobby Orr," argues Babineau. "Sure, he was on a line with Cashman and Hodge, but bottom line, the puck was coming into the net because of Bobby Orr. How many goals did Espo have that Orr assisted on?"

Orr finished with 37 goals and 102 assists that season. Ken Hodge had 43 and 62, while Wayne Cashman finished with 21 goals and 58 helpers.

above:

At 6-foot-one, 205 pounds Espo used size and a scoring touch to remain a constant threat in the offensive zone. He was the first player in history to break the 100-point single-season scoring barrier, shattering it in 1968-69 with 126 points.

"Hodgy was the guy who could just force himself in front of the net, probably the strongest guy on our team," says Esposito. "People had no idea how strong Kenny Hodge was, and how good he was in front of the net. He was in front of the net, I was 10 or 15 feet out, and Cash was the best corner man in the game, without a doubt."

Esposito drools at the possibilities that would have existed for him and his power play mates then, had the current no-hook, no-hack, no-grab rules existed.

"Our power play, we would have torn this League apart, and they never would have been able to stop Bobby," urges Espo. "Never! Never would they have been able to stop Orr, because Bobby was the greatest give-and-go guy in the history of the game. There's no way you could stop this guy unless you hooked him or interfered with him all the time, and as far as I'm concerned, in front of the net, by the hash marks and all that, man, if they just touched me and I fell down, I'd draw a penalty on the other guy, and we'd get *another* power play. These rules were made for us guys in the '70s."

"Regardless of rules, it was just a phenomenal era to be a part of Bruins hockey at the Boston Garden," adds Hodge.

Of course, the main reason was Cups—1970 and 1972—the last that Bruins fans have celebrated.

The 1970 trip to the championship ended a 12-year streak without visiting the final and a 29-year drought without the Cup. The tightest battle in the postseason came in the quarterfinals, with the Rangers pushing the Bruins to six games. The Bruins won Games 5 and 6 to close out that series, then swept Chicago and St. Louis in the semis and final, respectively, for a postseason-concluding 10-game winning streak.

Esposito set an NHL record for postseason scoring, with 13 goals and 27 points. The numbers included two hat tricks, one coming against his younger brother, Tony, in Game 1 of the Chicago series.

In 1972, after splitting the first two games of the opening series at home versus Toronto, the Bruins reeled off a nine-game winning streak. The run finished off the Maple Leafs, swept the Blues, and included the first two games of the final at home against New York. Espo had three assists in Game 1 against the Rangers and finished the postseason with 24 points, tied with teammate Orr. After the 3-0 win in Game 6 to wrap up their second Cup in three years and their fifth overall, Orr once again received the nod over Esposito for the Conn Smythe Trophy as postseason MVP.

It was 1972 and Espo and the boys were living large.

"Those teams then, to sum it up, one thing they had was a hell of a lot of fun!" says Greenberg.

Among the list of adjectives to describe Esposito—scorer, entertainer, pot-stirrer—one could also add snowbird. He's gradually moved south, to where he still resides today, in the Sunshine State.

"I lived mostly in Sault Ste. Marie [Ontario, his hometown], but New York was second. I lived there [New York] for 17 years," Espo points out. "I've been living in Florida now for about 15 years. I think Florida will be the place, but Sault Ste. Marie is still close to the heart; I lived there the longest. But the greatest time of my life was in Boston, without a doubt. I mean, I was on top of my game, we were winning, we had a great team, and a great bunch of guys. The fans were fantastic. It was just the greatest time of my life."

His production while in New York, although not as prolific as when he was in Boston, remained consistent. Esposito averaged better than a point a game during his first five years in Manhattan.

While a player for the Rangers, Esposito kicked off a sequence of events one night in Manhattan that will remain etched in hockey fans' memories forever. Two days before Christmas

above:

Bobby Orr and Esposito celebrate yet another tally. Espo will be the first to admit, his huge point totals came with a great deal of help from defenseman number 4.

in 1979, in the waning moments of a game against his former club, Espo had a chance to beat Gerry Cheevers on a breakaway to tie a game with the Bruins. (Terry O'Reilly's perspective follows in Chapter 6.) As he skated in, a fan threw a tennis ball at him, and although it didn't hit Espo, it distracted him enough to screw up the play. After failing to score, Espo smashed his stick on the ice in disgust with a two-armed tomahawk chop, skated to the bench, and headed to the dressing room. After he (and Cheevers) had departed, a melee began in one corner between the remaining Bruins and the Rangers. Then some Rangers fans became involved. One threw a punch at Stan Jonathan and stole his stick, and the Boston players ended up in the stands wrestling with the spectators. Espo had nothing to do with it.

below:

Orr and Esposito discussing strategy or developments. John Bucyk is over Orr's shoulder. The patch on Orr and Bucyk's shoulder commemorates the 50th anniversary of the Bruins.

"It [the tennis ball] went just over Cheesie's head, and it bounced right in front of me and I took my eye off it [the puck], and I looked away, and by the time I looked back up, Gerry was charging, and I didn't have anything to do with the puck, and it ticked me off, to tell you the truth," recalls Phil. "And I remember after the game, him and I were in the

Looking for a tip or rebound against Atlanta Flames goalie Dan Bouchard.

above:

Always the conversationalist, Esposito as a New York Ranger chats with former teammate, Bruins goalie Gerry Cheevers during a game at the Garden.

hallway in Madison Square Garden, and Gerry comes out of his dressing room with a beer, and I come out of our dressing room with a beer, and we look and I said, "What's going on?" and he said, "I don't know," and somebody said there was a fight in the stands. Cheesie looked at me and I looked at him and he goes, 'Ahhh, the hell with it.'"

In his sixth season in New York, then in his late 30s, Espo hung up the skates midway through the 1980–81 season after tallying 20 points in 41 games. He would become assistant coach, have two stints as head coach, and later be named general manager for the Rangers.

> The greatest thing I've ever done in the game of hockey was getting the franchise to Tampa.

Soon enough, there'd be good reason for Espo's continued migration. After three years as GM in New York, where he earned the nickname "Trader Phil" for his proclivity to make deals, Esposito headed much further south to spearhead the effort to bring Tampa Bay an NHL expansion franchise. Despite intense competition from Peter Karmanos and Compuware (who eventually bought and moved the Hartford Whalers to Carolina), Esposito and his group prevailed.

"The greatest thing I've ever done in the game of hockey was getting the franchise to Tampa," insists Esposito. "I was completely out of my element. No one gave me one bit of a chance, and I like that, because when people underestimate me is when I'm at my best. I just did whatever I had to do to get the franchise. Sometimes in life you do that. Did I ever think that I would ever leave this place [Tampa front office]?... No. I never thought I would stay general manager. Eight years was a long time. I never wanted to do it for eight years. I just wanted to get the team set, but we had problems in the '95–'96 season when we built the building. We just didn't have enough money to pay some of the players. So, obviously we did some things we didn't want to do: trading players and getting rid of guys that were making too much money. That put us back two to three years. I'm convinced we could have won the Stanley Cup in 10 years, and that was the game plan going in. I get a big kick out of people who said Esposito had no plan when he came here. Well, I can tell you, I plan everything."

below:

Esposito attacks the net of the Bruins arch-nemesis, goalie Ken Dryden and the Montreal Canadiens. That's defenseman, ex-Bruin Don Awrey behind Espo.

above:

Among his superstitions, Espo kept lucky charms hanging from the top of his stall in the Bruins dressing room at the Garden.

Esposito lists his other greatest thrill as having his jersey retired and hung at Boston Garden. A dozen years after he was dealt, the man who earned five NHL scoring titles, two Hart Trophies as MVP, and two player-balloted Lester B. Pearson MVP awards while in Boston would get his due.

The celebration took place on December 3, 1987, three years after he was inducted into the Hockey Hall of Fame, and included an unforgettable turn of events. Ray Bourque, who wore Espo's number 7, had already played eight seasons in the NHL, had become a prolific scorer and was one of the League's best defensemen, decided to give Esposito a big surprise. Bourque had agreed to switch numbers to 77, to allow Espo to retain exclusive retirement rights to his number. Bourque skated out to Esposito wearing number 7, stopped, turned around, and peeled off the sweater to reveal "Bourque 77." He then handed Espo his number saying, "This is yours." Bourque and others joke it's the only time they've ever seen Esposito speechless.

"I watched him taking it off, and if you've ever seen replays you see me looking at him, and I said, 'What the hell are you doing?'" Phil recalls. "And he said, 'This is yours, big guy; it's not mine. It never should have been mine; this is yours.' I'm looking at him, like, is someone trying to play a joke on me here or what? We had talked about it that yeah, we'd put the number up, with my name on it, and when Raymond retired, they'd put his name on it. I had no problem with that and Bourqee had no problem with that, but when he did that, man, that really…I'll never forget that as long as I live."

On December 3rd, 1987, on Espo's jersey retirement night, Ray Bourque shocked everyone, especially Esposito, by taking sweater number 7 off his own back, presenting it to Phil for his exclusive retirement, and then switching to number 77 for the rest of his career. Espo is stunned, he addresses the crowd with great appreciation, while Bourque is praised by the Bruins alumni.

Phil Esposito (C) Sault Ste. Marie, ON | #7 | First NHLer with a 100+ point season

BRUINS REGULAR SEASON STATISTICS	GP	G	A	Pts	PIM
1967–1976	625	459	553	1,012	512
Bruins Postseason Statistics	71	46	56	102	81

CHAPTER

BRUINS LEGEND: TERRY O'REILLY

above:

O'Reilly was the emotional leader of the Bruins as a player, and later as head coach. Despite his intensity and his success on the ice, his humility was one of his greatest attributes.

left:

Terry O'Reilly with his eyes on the prize. Whoever stood between Taz and the puck, he went through him or them to get it. The name "Taz" came from his ferocious style and tenacity, after the Tasmanian Devil on the Bugs Bunny cartoons.

Every Boston Bruins name hanging in the rafters of the TD Banknorth Garden also resides in the Hockey Hall of Fame, except for two. One of those two, Terrence O'Reilly, hangs in the rafters simply because number 24 utterly and completely embodied what it meant to be a Boston Bruin. And although O'Reilly could be recognized in hockey's ultimate shrine for what should be the same criteria, he isn't; and maybe it doesn't matter.

He is the underrated talent, the fighter, the blue-collar worker, the emotional powder keg, the inspirational leader that belongs exclusively to Boston.

"There's nobody like the guy that I ever played with or against," states former Bruins roommate Mike Milbury. "Completely totally focused and relentless, to the point where we'd come back after a game on the road to the hotel room, and some of the guys would go out for a beer, for something to eat, but he'd come back to the room and do push-ups and sit-ups. I mean, it was really kind of sick when you think about it, but once the puck was dropped there was nobody you'd want more on your side than Terry: a physical player and a heady player, who was completely committed to winning the game."

"He played on a line with Peter McNab and John Wensink and they were a terror in the League for many, many years," points out former teammate Rick Middleton. "Most teams didn't want to come into Boston Garden and face that line, trust me. There was the unwritten O'Reilly rule [among opponents] that you might as well let him win the first one [fight], because he's just gonna keep coming back until he beats you. A lot of guys would just let him win the first one so they wouldn't have to fight him again."

The same intangible that helped him will his team to wins on so many nights is the same intangible that allowed the awkward forward to will his way into the League in the first place.

"I always said that I fell into the business," O'Reilly laughs. "You know my skating style was so rustic that I spent more time literally on the ice; before Phil Esposito nicknamed me Taz after the Tasmanian Devil, my nickname was Zamboni. And it was because I cleaned the ice with [my body]."

He made himself a player; he willed himself to be a player.

"He could barely skate the first couple years he was in the League," affirms Milbury, "and I'm one that's living in that glass house who shouldn't be throwing stones, but he made himself a player; he willed himself to be a player. He scored more than 90 points one season, which is a remarkable feat. He spent countless hours before practices; he'd play with anybody that was on the ice. He would go one-on-one, just work drills, and he developed himself into a world-class player, and certainly a player that is unforgettable in Bruins fans' memories."

below:

O'Reilly fights his way to the net against Buffalo Sabres Jerry Korab (left) and Andre Savard.

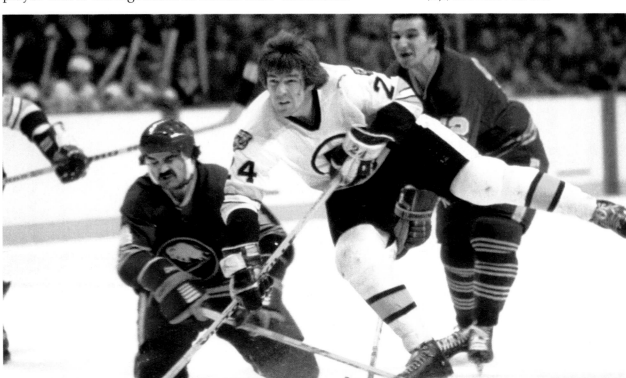

Much of a player's success can be attributed to his mental makeup, reflected in his desire, his competitiveness, his selflessness, his ability and desire to lead, and his mental toughness. In O'Reilly's case, his drive overcame his physical limitations.

"Terry was a real team player, a hard worker, did everything he had to," says Hall of Fame teammate John Bucyk. "He was a real plus to any team. I'll tell you what, a big leader for the Bruins."

"People should look at what hard work does for you," states Hall of Fame ex-Bruin and current team Vice President Cam Neely. "We've all played with guys who had more talent, but the work ethic might not have been there and they didn't last very long. And then you have a guy like Terry who didn't have the best skating ability, and came in and worked extremely hard and obviously was a very physical, tough player, and ended up being a huge asset to the Bruins organization."

O'Reilly's performance and attitude three decades ago actually remains a benchmark for the Bruins. As Neely suggests, O'Reilly can still be an example for current players, regardless of whether or not the rules or style of play have been altered. He set an example for others that transcends any era.

"No doubt, I don't think you're going to find much tougher than Terry O'Reilly," says Bruins Head Coach Claude Julien. "He's one of those guys, you knew what you would get every night, and no doubt you'd want him on your team more than you'd want him against you. He was a pretty intimidating individual, and I don't think I ever saw him back down, and I don't think you'll ever see him back down even to this day. So he brought to the Bruins what the Bruins have always wanted, and that's an identity. In Boston, they like their teams to be tough, and when you look at Terry O'Reilly, that's exactly what he brought."

above:

Bob Hoffmeyer of the Black Hawks doesn't look too excited, or ready, for an O'Reilly left.

below:

Terry O'Reilly as a Bruins rookie, after playing junior in Oshawa and 60 games with the AHL Boston Braves.

"Well, we'd like players like him, certainly," adds General Manager Peter Chiarelli. "You're not gonna get a player just like him, but you can certainly get a lot of the characteristics that he has—his fortitude, his forecheck, you know he liked to drop them, he went to the net; and he got a lot of goals in dirty areas. There are a lot of parts to how he played that I'd like to have in players, and we look to get."

Current Bruins Assistant Coach Craig Ramsay remembers the experience of playing O'Reilly firsthand, as a defenseman for the division rival Buffalo Sabres for 14 years.

"It was a long night, I can certainly say that. But one of the great things about Terry, and everyone knows how tough he was, was that he was one of those real honest tough guys. He hit you hard, but he didn't mind if you hit him back. You could play a physical game against him; you just couldn't do anything cheap, and he was always there to defend his teammates if there were cheap shots going on. In our day, there was a lot of it. Terry would jump right back in there," Ramsay states. "I always enjoyed my nights against Terry. I knew I was going to get hit, and I knew I would kind of get pounded around, but it was a fair, honest night. I always thought body contact was a great part of the game, even as a smaller player. I always thought those confrontations on the puck were what made our game very special. Against Terry, it was a long night but a very good night against a good hockey player."

"I loved hockey," O'Reilly says, explaining his basic motivation, "and at the time, that was hockey to me. I mean, that was hockey to everybody. A good, balanced, winning team, if you look at every team that won the Stanley Cup back in that era, had such a balance of skill and toughness. You know,

above:

A bear hug was one technique used to stop Taz, utilized here by Maple Leafs defenseman Bob McGill. That's Toronto goalie Allan Bester holding the post.

above:

A 1975-76 shot of Guy Lapointe (#5) and Pierre Bouchard of the Canadiens versus O'Reilly at the Montreal Forum.

the Montreal Canadiens, probably one of the best teams in the history of the game, won six Cups back in the '70s, and if you look at the tough part of their team they had, it was very well sustained. The Bruins, when they won their two Cups in '70 and '72, had a very tough contingent to their team. The Philadelphia Flyers won two Cups and they were a very physical team, and the Islanders didn't become a championship team until they added some toughness with Gord Lane and a few guys like that. Gillies, Nystrom, Howatt—that part of the game has to be addressed."

Young hockey fans now, witnessing clips of '70s-style "physical hockey," would likely be in for a big surprise. Hockey in those days featured line melees and bench-clearing brawls.

"Those were crazy," remembers O'Reilly, a man often found in the middle of the action. "You didn't know what was going to happen. We had one in Philadelphia that bled over onto the off-ice and into the runways and into the hallway behind…that connected the dressing rooms. I think [Paul] Holmgren and Wayne Cashman went at each other in the hallway, so both teams got in there and got onto the cement, more so our team than the Flyers.

"We were announced to start the next period," Taz continues. "We were trickling out because we were having our skates addressed with the sharpener. Well, the Flyers had more players on the ice, and it re-ignited on the ice, but we were vastly outnumbered. So I remember coming down the runway, after getting my skates touched up, to be met by three Philadelphia players. As soon as I came through the gate, I had a Flyer grab my left arm, my right arm, and they threw me down on my back, pinned my knees behind me, and the third guy got on my chest!" O'Reilly laughs. "I had three guys, and I couldn't even move my arms off the ice, so…I didn't do well in that one!"

Fortunately for O'Reilly, his reputation, and his on-ice way with words, defused the situation.

"Oh, it seemed like a lifetime [until our reinforcements showed up]," O'Reilly recalls. "I had to talk my way out of it. I said something like, 'OK, you got me, do what you have to do, but I've got all three of your numbers and I'll talk to you later.' That's all I said. Well, either they didn't want to hit me or someone else came to my rescue because I ended up getting out of it without getting badly hurt. I have to say, more to their credit, they just decided it wasn't the thing to do, but they did have me neutralized!"

above:

O'Reilly was a Bruin for one game in 1971-72 and then for 13 straight seasons through 1984-85.

above:

Taz with the fat lip/cut lip combo, talking with interim head coach Harry Sinden.

Not an easy task.

"Taz had both sides of the word *fear* covered. He was fearless, and you feared him," states former Boston forward and current NESN TV commentator Andy Brickley. "In the day, that was a big part of the National Hockey League, where intimidation was a big factor."

"Oh, there were a lot of guys in the League that I scrapped with that I didn't look forward to playing because I," O'Reilly thinks for a moment, "chances are, I was going to have a scrap with them. We had that one series against the Islanders [in 1980] where every time I looked up, Clark Gillies was on the ice against me. He was—I'm not sure how much younger he is than me, a few years younger [3]—but he was bigger, stronger, longer reach; other than that, I owned him." O'Reilly laughs. "But it was a tough match-up for me. All I could do was just try to get a good hold on him and hang on until the ride was over. I fully respected what he was doing for his team, and he was a great hockey player. I mean, that was...the New York Islanders having a guy like Clark Gillies, that combination of skill and toughness, was one of the reasons why they won so many championships."

It was earlier in that same regular season at Madison Square Garden, on December 23, 1979, against the other New York squad, that Taz and his teammates had their most infamous skirmish.

"What started it was the Rangers and the Rangers fans were very frustrated," explains O'Reilly. "I think the final score was 4-3; it was a one-goal game. Esposito had a breakaway for the Rangers in the last minutes of the game and I don't think he got a shot on net. I think he came down on Cheevers and the puck slid off his stick into the corner. He slammed the stick and broke it. So we're on our way home for Christmas, it's December 23rd and we've got three days off, which feels like

two weeks during hockey season. It's three days off where you don't have to go to the rink and we've got a plane waiting for us, so we want out of there. But the buzzer goes, and we get on the ice to congratulate each other. We're headed down to get off the ice and some of the Rangers players started pushing and shoving us out of frustration, so there's a little bit of a melee going on. I didn't think it was going to turn into anything, and Stan Jonathan and one of the Rangers players were over against the side wall. The side wall glass was only two feet tall at the time, and this drunk fan standing up swung one of the hardest sucker punches you've ever seen. He, he just swung down and hit Stan right in the face, and he [Stan] covered up. The guy grabbed his stick, pulled it out of his hands and started swinging it like a machete. I was maybe 15 feet away and you know this guy is gonna hit Stan, steal his stick, and then disappear into the crowd, so I just sort of snapped, and I stepped over the glass as he was swinging the stick. I don't know what I was saying or thinking, but I went in and grabbed him around the waist and got him into a sort of a half nelson and I held him until the Madison Square Garden security came along and took him from me and arrested him. But when I had him, everybody [fans] closed in on me and then my teammates came over and chased everybody out. I felt like a quarterback in a pocket. I, you know, I looked up and I was just surrounded by black and gold."

O'Reilly received an eight-game suspension for leading the way. Peter McNab and Mike Milbury, famous for ripping a shoe off a Rangers fan and trying to whack him with it, both picked up six games.

He'd charge at me, and he looked like the front end of a Mack truck.

The ensuing time off for the players led to a magical encounter for team photographer Steve Babineau. With the next five Bruins games on the road, and the three players not traveling, it led to the perfect opportunity for some pickup hockey at the Garden.

"I played with the three of them and a few other people in a pickup game," Babineau remembers. "They broke into the electrician room and turned the lights on. O'Reilly is going crazy having a good time, but scaring the hell out of me. I'd go pick up the puck behind the net and bring it out to the circle and he'd charge at me, and he looked like the front end of a Mack truck. A few times I'd hide behind the net and he'd race in and he could go either way around after me. To me, he

right:

Early in the 1979-80 season, left to right, Peter McNab, O'Reilly, and Mike Milbury at the old Garden.

looked like my motor home. It was scary. One time, he dumped the puck, came down toward me doing the theme from *Dragnet*, 'duh-duh-duh-hh, duh-da-da-da-duhhhhh.' He did a baby flip in the corner just so I'd have to pivot and chase the puck with him following. It may have been the *Jaws* theme, like 'duhh-duhh, duh-duh, duh-duh, du-du, du-du, d-d,' faster and faster. He's following me and I'm wettin' my pants laughing and scared at the same time. It was unbelievable."

"I used to go down there a lot then, whether I had a slight injury and was left behind with the team, if the team went on the road, or I had a day off," O'Reilly recalls. "I was always at the Garden looking for ice, when we skated with some of the bullgang members [Zamboni drivers, ice men] and played pickup hockey. Even when I was coaching we were playing two-pass, you know, with anybody that wanted to come on the ice. We'd have our morning skate and then I would have the black aces stay out, the guys that weren't gonna dress. Sometimes it would be Jay Miller, or [Lyndon] Byers. We usually had an extra forward or an extra defenseman, so they needed to be out there and do some extra skating. We made them play two-pass with us.

above:

O'Reilly turned himself into a great hockey player and became strong on his skates due to constant practice and use of ice time. His work ethic was as relentless as his desire to win.

"The other place I loved to go was the carpenter shop; that was one of my favorite places in the old Boston Garden," Taz continues. "It was just...I knew the guys, Paul, he was one of the top carpenters there at the time, and I'd go down and watch what he was working on and fixing up. I learned a few tricks from him and it was just a nice room. The carpenters' room was down in the corner, right by where the ramp came up and it had 8- or 10-foot-tall windows all around the two sides of it. So it was probably the brightest room in the building; it was like a solarium. So it was a nice place to go and hide for a little while."

O'Reilly's interest in carpentry continues today. He designed and helped rebuild his home on the North Shore, a multi-unit, five-story building, and most of the cabinetry within.

Since another taste of the NHL coaching ranks as an assistant with the Rangers from 2002 to 2004 after a 13-year hiatus, it would appear O'Reilly's desire to be involved has waned. He says he's looking to relax and enjoy retirement outside of Boston.

below:

O'Reilly gets the best of Mike McEwen of the New York Rangers. Not that it was the case here, but if someone beat him in a fight, he'd fight 'em again.

"I know when he went into New York, he has spoken of this, how difficult it was being an assistant coach on a team that had guys that he didn't think were giving it their all, and didn't care enough about playing this great game," confides Andy Brickley. "He felt like his hands were tied, that he couldn't approach them the way he would have been able to had he been a head coach in that situation."

right:

Blackhawks goaltender Tony Esposito being screened by O'Reilly and Chicago defenseman Keith Magnuson

"I don't think the basic ingredients change a lot, but since I have been out of the game so long, except for the short stint in New York," O'Reilly explains, "I don't know the players anymore. I played for 12, 13 years before I coached the first time, and I knew the personnel in the whole League. The only ones I had to become familiar with were the draft picks that came up, and I was in the same boat as everybody else. But you know, there's a whole new breed of hockey player now, and with the new rule changes, I think there is more to the coaching than in the days of old when there was more of an emotional key to it. I think that's why Don Cherry was such a good coach. I think the right balance is somebody that's a good emotional motivator and somebody that can read personalities and the mood of the team, and somebody that's a real X-and-O technician. In my turn at the bat I had John Cunniff, and he was a great tactician. He just had the answers for everything—power play, penalty killing—and once we established our system, I was the guy that maintained the level, the level of input that we put into it."

Via humility, O'Reilly mentioned only Cherry as a solid emotional leader. The man he left off that short list was himself.

"He was my coach for one year," recalls Brickley. "Obviously I saw him play. Amazing that he would, from the very first minute of his NHL career to his last minute of his NHL career, he never stopped fighting. I don't mean dropping the gloves all the time. I mean fighting for every inch on the ice that he thought was his. And to have played for him as a

left:

O'Reilly became captain of the Bruins in 1983-84 and held the honor for two seasons.

coach, I mean, we had a great room. It was hard to get a word in edgewise with all the characters we had in our room, but Terry O'Reilly was our emotional focal point. That's unbelievable for a head coach. I mean he was so intense as a head coach, I can't imagine what he was like as a player. I didn't have that good fortune of playing with him. I did play against him, but he was our emotional leader as the head coach in the locker room and that's rare."

"As a coach, he was the same: passionate, passionate man for the sport of hockey and the will to win," adds Rick Middleton. "I watched some old clips not too long ago with him coaching and banging the glass. I always felt bad for the fans sitting in the first row because all of a sudden out of nowhere he'd just bang the glass, and they'd all jump."

I had the privilege to watch Terry as a player and I had the privilege to play under him when he was coach," adds Bob Sweeney, for six years a Bruins forward. "I thought Terry and John Cunniff as coaches were a great team, a great tandem. Terry was one of the best motivators that I ever came across. John Cunniff knew the game better than any coach that I ever played with. It was a great combination of motivation and tactics that I think brought the most out of us. That's the reason why in 1988 we went to the final. We may not have been the most talented team, but we were the best prepared team, we were the best conditioned team, and that's the reason we went all the way to the final."

left:

"Emotional leader as the head coach ...and that's rare," describes Terry O'Reilly as the coach of the Bruins for almost three full seasons beginning in November 1986.

above:

Steely determination. O'Reilly and Maple Leaf defenseman Ron Ellis.

O'Reilly's regular season coaching record finished up with 115 wins, 86 losses, and 26 ties. In the postseason, his teams lost in the first round, lost in the Stanley Cup final, and then lost in the second round.

For all of his efforts as a player and a coach and for his dedication to the "Black and Gold," O'Reilly received the ultimate honor on October 24, 2002: jersey retirement. Fittingly, he entered the event by wading through the fans in the stands, and then through the penalty box.

He was so intense as a head coach, I can't imagine what he was like as a player.

"It was a fantastic honor," O'Reilly recalls. "I had mixed feelings. It's a great honor to have my number up there, but I look at the guys that are up there—Bobby Orr, Phil Esposito, Ray Bourque, Cam Neely, Milt Schmidt—there's some amazing players up there. So I... sometimes I look up and think that I snuck in, and I look at some players that I played with—Brad Park, Rick Middleton, Wayne Cashman, you know, great players in their own right. And I don't see my career as being superior to theirs. In fact, they were my teammates and friends. So I wish everybody that I played with could be up there. But I'm not going to complain!" he chuckles.

"He's one of a kind. They threw the mold away," proclaims former Lunch Pail Gang teammate and tough guy John Wensink. "Talk about covering up for one another and leadership, he was absolutely number one. He's our oldest daughter's godfather and a super guy. Terry and I don't keep in touch that much, I'm not a big phone person. But it's funny. I hadn't seen Taz for a few years, we got together with the alumni in Phoenix, and it was like we never missed a beat. We just carried our conversation like we just had it yesterday, and to me that's a good friend."

above:

Former Bruins coach Don Cherry with O'Reilly, the epitome of the Lunch Pail Gang, at O'Reilly's sweater retirement ceremony.

Besides the wonderful long-term relationships and the jersey retirement, O'Reilly has a not-so-delightful reminder of his career: the pieces of Terry O'Reilly that really aren't Terry O'Reilly.

"Well, the teeth are all paid for," Taz says, laughing. "I did have bilateral hip replacement; it'll be three years in March, and they've been working pretty good, you know. It's amazing that if someone told me that I was going to have both my hips cut out of my body and replaced with metal, that I'd feel as good as I do.... But, it's a fad. Bobby has two new knees, Bobby Orr. Brad Park just had his second knee replaced in November of '07, so he's just getting back on his feet and getting more and more mobile. All just getting ready for the golf season."

The injuries are just another long-term example of Terry O'Reilly paying the price—something his fans and his cohorts will never forget.

below:

Taz looks ahead and leaves Rob Ramage of the Blues in a bind.

"Growing up here, and just watching Terry O'Reilly running around the ice throttling guys, I mean, every kid who grew up a Boston Bruins fan wanted to be Terry O'Reilly," proclaims Billerica, Massachusetts native and 17-year NHL veteran Tom Fitzgerald. "Number 24 was everybody's favorite player really—you take Bobby Orr, Phil Esposito and those guys—but everybody loved the way Terry O'Reilly played, because every time he stepped on the ice he gave it everything he had."

Hall of Fame defenseman and Bruins great Ray Bourque sums up Terry O'Reilly unequivocally: "The toughest player I ever played with and the best coach I've ever played for."

above:

Fitting for "every fan's" favorite Bruin, O'Reilly entered the rink for his jersey retirement through the crowd and then through the penalty box.

right:

October 24, 2002, number 24 heads to the rafters. Evan and Connor, Terry's sons, assist with the effort.

below:

left to right, Don Cherry, Connor O'Reilly, Evan O'Reilly, Bobby Orr, Milt Schmidt, O'Reilly, John Bucyk, and Raymond Bourque.

TERRY O'REILLY (RW) Niagara Falls, ON | #23, 24 | The embodiment of a Bruin

BRUINS REGULAR SEASON STATISTICS	GP	G	A	Pts	PIM
1971–1985	891	204	402	606	2,095
Bruins Postseason Statistics	108	25	42	67	335

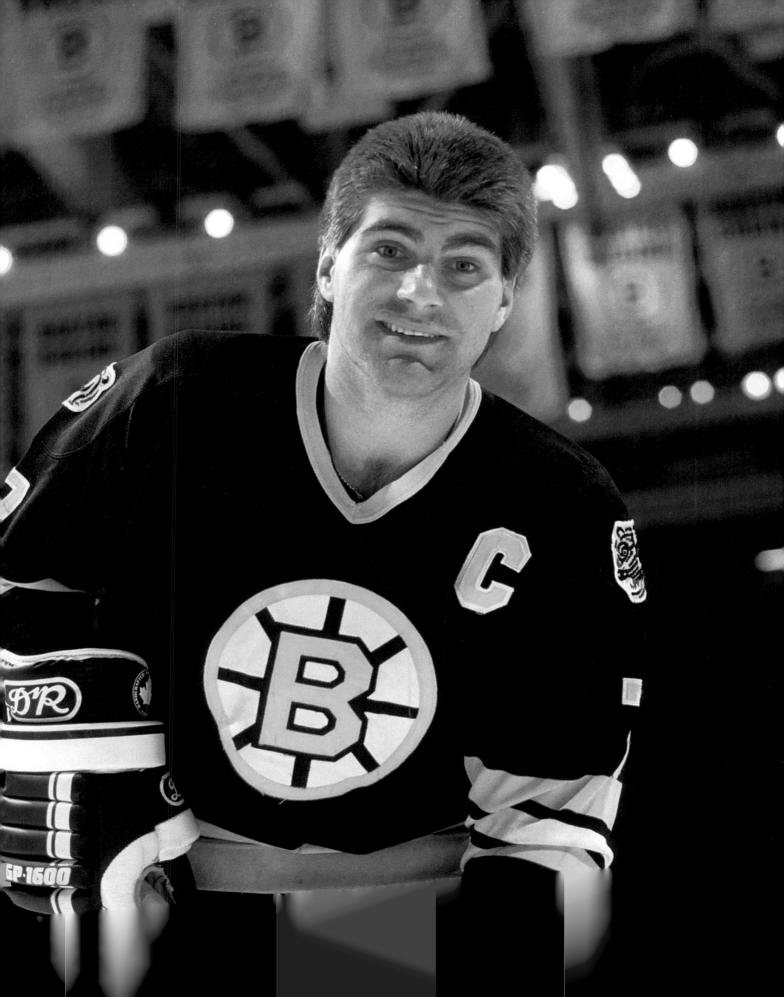

CHAPTER

BRUINS LEGEND:
RAY BOURQUE

above:

A rare image of Ray Bourque wearing number 29, his training camp number prior to his rookie season in 1979-80.

left:

Bourque right after being named captain, still number 7, below the B's banners at the old Garden. Bourque was Bruins captain from 1985 to 2000, the longest tenure in team history. He shared the honor the first three seasons with Rick Middleton.

Just three years after the departure of Bobby Orr, Bruins fans found themselves staring at a baby-faced teenager from Saint Laurent, Quebec. Ray Bourque, drafted eighth overall by the Bruins in 1979, would develop into the NHL's next iconic defenseman. There were many great D-men in the '80s, but Ray Bourque was in a league by himself.

For 21 seasons, Bourque donned the Spoked B, and Steve Babineau was on hand to capture all of the great moments.

"I've lost track of the records and of the record-breaking moments," Babs points out. "I have to check the old calendar and match things up all of the time. Let's see, was that the assists records photo, was this when he broke the Bruins scoring record, I remember this one, I remember that one. It goes on and on."

There is one simple way to summarize the various records. Ray Bourque is the all-time leading scorer among NHL defensemen: in assists (1,169), in goals (410), and in points (1,579).

"Those are the obvious things that people, fans, and everybody came to appreciate about Raymond," points out Don Sweeney, a longtime teammate and D partner. "He was an elite player, but they didn't necessarily realize the behind-the-scenes things he did day-to-day for his teammates—his approach to the game, his preparation, his commitment, every

left:

Bourque playing in his first NHL game on October 11, 1979, against the Winnipeg Jets at the Garden, being pursued by winger Larry Hopkins. Bourque scored in his first game.

shift. When your best players are your hardest working players, it sets a precedent; it really sets a foundation for your organization. That's what he was. He was an absolute cornerstone. When you go to build a franchise you think about a few players, and he fits that bill."

In 1998, prior to leaving Boston and winning a Cup in Colorado three years later, Bourque was rated as the 14th greatest player of all time by *The Hockey News*, in its definitive list. The accolades had stacked up. A five-time Norris Trophy winner as the NHL's best defenseman, Bourque was voted to the mid-season NHL All-Star Game a record 19 consecutive seasons. He retired with the second-most assists in NHL history. Bourque remains the Boston Bruins all-time leading scorer.

> God knows if I was going to make the team or not, but if you were Bruins property, you were treated great by all the players.

"You also look at the unannounced things that he would do when a young kid would come to training camp," Sweeney continues. "He'd be the first one to walk over. Rather than have the kid look at his toes as he walked past, Ray would be sticking out his hand or inviting him over to dinner. It didn't matter—if you were wearing the sweater he was wearing, then you were a friend to him and a teammate. To me, those are the things that stood out an awful lot."

"One of the biggest pleasures for me was walking into my first training camp and having Ray Bourque walk up to me and say...and actually introduce himself," former Bruins defenseman Bob Beers describes. "I'm looking at him, thinking, 'I know who you are; you don't need to tell me who you are.' And it was tough to get over...being in awe of the guys around you."

above:

Two practically identical poses, a decade apart. Bourque in 1986-87, and Bourque in 1995-96. Teammates are different, jersey number is different, the building is different, the helmet brand is different, and his stick blade is up as a veteran. Early shot: Keith Crowder is to the left. Later shot: Alexei Kasatonov is photo right.

The common trait for Bourque and the other great Bruins players: an unconditional devotion to the Spoked B.

"It's tradition—a winning tradition—and pride," Bourque states emphatically. "I came here in 1979, and the year before they had lost the semi-finals to Montreal in overtime. They were a great team that had some great runs throughout the whole '70s and late '60s. They were really one of the dominant teams, a team rich in tradition and character and all the things you talk about with winning traditions: guys sticking up for each other, being one big family, really feeling for one another. From day one when I got here, I just remember walking into that locker room or meeting the guys just before camp and them making me feel like I was already part of the team. God knows if I was going to make the team or not, but if you were Bruins property, you were treated great by all the players. That started with the captain—that was Wayne Cashman back then—Gerry Cheevers, Jean Ratelle, Terry O'Reilly. Brad

Park was incredible with me. So many great players who had great careers, but that was just passed on from generation to generation. When you got here you felt that, and it was definitely something you passed on, and you tried real hard to make other players coming in feel that, because not all organizations have it."

Longtime Bruins public relations man Nate Greenberg witnessed some of that continuity firsthand.

"I didn't see Eddie Shore, but I did see a lot of Orr. He was with us for a few years, and I remember thinking how the Bruins were blessed with great defensemen," Greenberg recalls, "and then along comes Bourque. I always said Orr was the greatest player I ever saw—he revolutionized the game—but Bourque is certainly high up on the list. He was a horse from day one. He played great, and he played as much or more than any player ever. No one played more, no one influenced the game more, and he was right there in the mix. From the day he stepped on, to the day he finished, how many games did he miss to injury? He blocked shots, he did it all, and just kept playing. Especially near the end, he didn't have some of the great players other Bruins defensemen had, and he didn't win any Stanley Cups with the Bruins, but I'd put him up against any defenseman in the '80s and '90s."

above:

Bourque celebrates a goal early in his first season with teammates Peter McNab, Mike O'Connell, and Rick Middleton.

"Bourque shot the puck from the point like Orr shot the puck from the point," Babineau states. "They got open and they cranked it. Other guys cashed in."

Kevin Paul Dupont, who has covered the Bruins for the *Boston Globe* for 30 years and continues to do so, offers up possibly the ultimate praise a Bostonian can offer.

above:

Bourque one game after losing three front teeth during the 1999-2000 season.

"As I say, if you want to make a case, and I have before, better than Orr," Dupont starts, "better in that it was longer, and that it was damn near perfect every time. And to the last drop. I haven't seen anyone's career in any sport like that. Great from day one, great right to the end, and look at the years. To me, I hate to use 'body of work'; it was that entire dossier, every day. Even hurt, which was minimally... he virtually never missed, his conditioning incredible—our doctors at Mass General will tell you he blew out all aerobic testing—add dedication and a total professional. The entire length, the entire portrait, I've never seen anyone like that."

Bourque also handled his other team leadership responsibilities with patience and fortitude. As captain, he was available to the media every day after practice or a game, bar none.

"He would laugh at himself, saying he was the most boring man in North America," Dupont adds, "but that said, he had a sense of when to say something, never controversial, never with a lot of edge to it, but every game, every practice, he'd accommodate the question. We've all heard the stupid questions, we've all asked them, but he'd take the time to answer it all. Absolute professional."

It's said that there is no greater honor than the honor bestowed upon one by his peers. The respect and fame earned in the game by Bourque was rarified. Babineau recalls instances where teammates and opponents alike, hockey players yet hockey fans at the same time, were in awe of Ray Bourque's career and his presence.

"I was working between the benches when Rob Ray of the Sabres leaned over and said, 'Try to get a picture of me and Ray on the ice,'" Babineau recalls.

It was late in Rob Ray's career, and late in Bourque's Boston existence.

"Rob Ray hadn't played all night," Babineau continues. "So I said, 'When? How?'"

"I'm going out in two shifts," Rob Ray answered.

"You'll probably have to hit 'em," Babineau suggested.

"I will, I will."

During the shift, Bourque carried the puck down the right wing boards to the Buffalo blue line just as a teammate stepped offside. The whistle blew and a moment later, Rob Ray ran into Bourque.

"I was following [Rob] Ray around in my lens, panning him," Babineau remembers. "The whistle went, and a good second or two later, [Rob] Ray comes over and pushes Bourque into the glass. A scrum, kind of melee, ensued, but I got his photo or two for him."

above:

Bourque holding the Prince of Wales Trophy after defeating New Jersey in the conference finals in 1988.

below:

New Jersey Devil and future Bruin Bill Guerin with the big hook on Bourque as they race for a puck at the Fleet Center.

above:

Bourque leading the offensive charge at the Garden with center Tom Fergus.

After the game, Babineau revealed the truth to the legendary defenseman while having some fun.

"Ray, what was the deal with Rob Ray? What was that all about?" Babineau asked, knowingly.

"Yeah, what the hell *was* that? I don't know," Bourque answered.

"I'll tell you what it was: he had set it up. He was trying to get me to take a picture of him with you."

"You're kidding me," Bourque responded with a grin.

Dave Shaw, who had played with Boston, and was later with Tampa Bay, did the same thing.

> To see his whole career unfold… when we first started shooting him, nobody knew that young Raymond Bourque was gonna turn into Ray Bourque, Hall of Famer.

"Hey Babs," Shaw said as he leaned by the bench, "get a shot of me and Bourque together, would you? Right after the commercial is over."

"But Dave, you're a defenseman, he's a defenseman, you're on the opposite ends of the ice," Babs replied.

"Don't worry about it. Now, before the draw," Shaw said. "I'd love a picture."

Sure enough, Shaw immediately skated over, leaned over to Bourque and said, "Ray, look at Babs; he's taking our picture."

Players as fans, like little kids, around a legend.

"To see his whole career unfold…when we first started shooting him, nobody knew that young Raymond Bourque was gonna turn into Ray Bourque, Hall of Famer," Babineau reflects. "He became that special guy, the core of the team.

Here's a guy who I was friends with as a rookie, becoming a star. He saw my family grow up and I saw his family grow up simultaneously. When he first came to my house, he didn't have any kids. He saw my kids, and then I watched *his* kids grow up."

During Bourque's rookie year, he and his wife, Christiane, spent two hours one afternoon looking at slides in Babineau's living room. It was the start of a two-decade-long dream for the photographer.

"One weekend there was a casual day at the Garden," Babineau brightens up, "and I got to skate with the team after practice. We were screwing around. Ray was a rookie. He sent me in on a breakaway against Rogie Vachon and I top-shelfed it. To this day, it's a highlight in my life. I didn't know much about him then, but I still have memories of that moment.

"The relationship I had with Bourque and his whole career was cool, number 7 with the A, to number 7 with the C, to number 77," Babineau continues. "I could ask him to take a picture anytime, anywhere, with anybody, and he'd say yes. It was unbelievable."

"Well, I'd like to say he [Babineau] was a kid, but he was a just a little older than me," Bourque points out. "He was taking pictures at every game, and I remember going to his house on more than one occasion, just to go through all of the pictures he had taken of me, for me to pick the ones I wanted to have, to sign for people, or just to collect. I went even for other pictures, action shots with other players, that I was looking for, to have for myself. Just an incredible amount of pictures, The stuff that he's taken was truly remarkable, and he shows you the other stuff, the other pictures from the other sports, and being a sports buff, it's pretty impressive. I couldn't imagine now, you know, going through all of his stuff."

One of the most memorable moments for both men occurred in 1996, when Boston and the new Garden (then called the Fleet Center) hosted the NHL All-Star Game. The Eastern Conference won the game 5-4 on Bourque's game-winning goal, and Ray was named the game's Most Valuable Player.

above:

Ray Bourque waves to the berserk Bruins faithful after winning the All-Star Game MVP honors at the Fleet Center in 1996. One of his most memorable and emotional moments for Bourque in his career, and for photographer Babineau in his 35 years.

below:

Photographer Steve Babineau with Ray Bourque during a practice scrimmage at the Garden during Bourque's rookie season.

"To be the All-Star photographer, me and my son Brian hired by the League, and to have Ray win the MVP—it was fantastic," Babineau smiles. "Chris Bourque [Ray's son], then a young teenager, was in the room after the game. It was another moment for both our families, a family tie."

"He's got many, many pictures of me. I know that," Bourque adds. "I remember after my first year or two, having grown up in Montreal, trying to get some pictures that Guy Lafleur and Larry Robinson would be in. I found a great picture of Guy Lafleur and I crossing sticks on the ice. Babs is the one who took that and I've got that one on my wall."

Another fellow French-Canadian who enjoyed a big night at the Garden: Mario Lemieux.

"Mario's first game in the NHL was at the Garden and I shot that," remembers Babineau, "and his last regular season game the first time he retired was at the Garden as well. For 'Mario Night,' Ray presented him with a big lounge chair, and a seat from the old Garden. It was a special moment for Ray and it was definitely cool for me."

With any long-term relationship, be it professional, personal, or otherwise, familiarity doesn't necessarily breed contempt; it simply breeds more familiarity.

Bourque with two of his French-Canadian favorites:

above:

Ray with childhood hero Guy Lafleur.

right:

Ray with long-time friend and contemporary superstar Mario Lemieux.

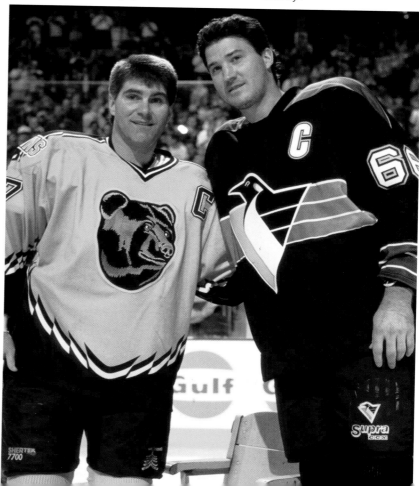

"They, the mainstays of the club treated me like a piece of furniture," Babineau points out. "I was always around. The conversations would go on whether I was standing there or not. It was relaxed, it was casual, and I had full access. If I had an idea, or needed an unusual photo, I'd just go up and say, 'Hey, can we do this photo?'

"I remember the last game during a non-playoff year," Babs continues, "We wanted to get the players getting dressed and doing their routine in the locker room. I wanted shots during the game, during the intermission. I sat in the dressing room right up until the guys went out. Don Sweeney was hurt, so I sat in his stall, next to Ray. I got Ray taping his stick, some of the other guys getting ready. I shot the equipment guys. Ray had a routine; he did his stick, did a heating pad, and then came into the room. I'm in the room with Sammy [Sergei Samsonov] and Joe Thornton. Bourque walked in."

"OK Babs, let's get going, big game, let's get going, come on, big one!" Bourque mocked. "Gotta get the shots off! Gotta take some good ones."

above:

A fisheye lens view of Ray Bourque and his teammates on the Bruins bench. That's assistant coach Jacques Laperriere behind him, to the left of Don Sweeney's stick, and team trainer Don DelNegro to the right of it.

"He was bustin' chops, having a good time, and treating me like one of the guys, and that was cool," Babs concludes.

Staged photos, or ones taken in a controlled environment, were common. However, a great majority of Babineau's Bourque shots were taken in the completely uncontrolled environment of a real game.

"Bourque got his teeth knocked out near the end of his career," Babineau says with a grin. "He looked like hell. Lost his top chops. I was sitting there at the end of the bench, and he looks over and gives me a big smile. He knew I was there and he made this big face and smiled at me. He'd skate by every once and a while, smile, and make a face. He was so comfortable on the ice, having a good time."

above:

Ray Bourque skated his way to five Norris Trophies, given each season to the NHL defenseman with the greatest all-around ability. Only three other players have won it more times than Bourque.

Without a doubt, Bourque experienced a very successful and enjoyable career in Boston. The only thing lacking was a Stanley Cup victory. Twice, the Bruins came close. Bourque's and Babineau's first final: 1988.

The Bruins lost Games 1 and 2 in Edmonton to the Oilers by scores of 2-1 and 4-2. Boston hosted Games 3 and 4.

"The biggest disadvantage was we were playing hockey in June," Babs points out. "No air conditioning, no ventilation, they were playing the games in a fog. I mean, both teams had to deal with the same thing, but from a photographic standpoint it was a nightmare, and I'm sure it was tough for some of the fans."

The Bruins lost Game 3 6-3 and were temporarily spared a Stanley Cup final sweep by the summertime conditions at the Garden. The power went out with the score tied 3-3, and the electricians couldn't get it up and running again. The photographers thought it was their fault. Some believed the electronic strobes, strung throughout the building to act as "flashbulbs" for the photographers, commonly utilized then and today, may have pushed the energy situation to the brink.

"We thought we had done something with the strobes," Babineau remembers. "We had strobes set up in the ceiling and there were a lot of photographers. Turns out it was a generator outside. Too many generators running, the ice pack, the whole thing, they couldn't get the lights back on. Although the individual player statistics were tallied and counted, the game was scrapped. The teams moved back to Edmonton where the Oilers completed the series with a 6-3 win."

above:

Classic shot of the captain putting on the brakes behind his net at the old Garden for a quick change of direction.

Two years later, Bourque led his team to the final again, against the same representative from the West (Clarence Campbell Conference). Again, the B's lost. This time, the series started in Boston.

"Unbelievable atmosphere," Babineau reminisces excitedly. "Everyone was wearing yellow T-shirts, and screaming their heads off. It was the ultimate way to experience a hockey game in Boston, although it was super hot in the building."

The generators held up; in fact in Game 1, they worked overtime…triple overtime.

below:

One of the most famous set of jerseys in hockey history. Bourque third jersey at top, Garden style white 77 on left, All-Star jersey from Pittsburgh on right, and an old Bourque number 7.

"We were still shooting film at that time, actual film, not digital," Babs points out, "and I was literally running out of it. The game kept going and going and I was down to my last few snaps. Petr Klima, who doesn't play at all in the game, shows up on the ice. He's gung ho and has his 'jet skis' well rested. He comes out and kills us."

Klima, who had 25 goals for Edmonton in the regular season after being acquired in early winter from Detroit but had sat on the bench most of the night, came off the pine and scored the game winner (3-2) 115 minutes and 13 seconds into the marathon.

"[Glen] Wesley had a chance to score—a glorious chance he shot over the net [in the first OT]—and we fell short," remembers then Bruins head coach Mike Milbury. "We still had a really good feeling about ourselves. But I think part of it was [goalie] Andy Moog just couldn't recover from the Game-1 loss. In Game 2, [Bill] Ranford was younger and more athletic and at one point I looked up at the board and the shots were 16-4 in the middle of Game 2, and we were down 3-2. We had our chance, but in the end they grabbed the momentum by the horns, in particular their kid line in [Martin] Gelinas, and [Adam] Graves, and [Joe] Murphy, and damaged us in the later parts of the series. We lost to a team that just grabbed it and beat us. If we win Game 1 it becomes a different series, maybe not a winning series, but at least a much longer and closer series. Anything could have happened."

The Bruins lost Game 2 at home, won Game 3 in Edmonton, and then lost the next two, and the series, four games to one.

It marked the last Stanley Cup final for Ray Bourque with the Bruins.

below:

Ray Bourque celebrates a goal against the Edmonton Oilers in the 1990 Stanley Cup Final.

A decade later, with his career in its latter stages and the Bruins not a serious contender, Bourque requested a trade for a final legitimate opportunity at winning the Cup. Harry Sinden and the Bruins honored the request, and on March 6, 2000, Bourque and Dave Andreychuk were sent to Colorado, in exchange for Brian Rolston, Martin Grenier, Sammy Pahlsson, and a first-round draft pick. On June 9, 2001, after what turned out to be his last game, Bourque and the Avalanche hoisted the Cup.

"Everyone in Boston was happy for Ray," Babineau concludes. "I know I was happy for him, and now he's living back here again. This is home."

Four years ago, Babineau had a chance to close the circle with Bourque so to speak, to tie their careers all together, from his point of view. During a charity event, the annual Bruins Wives' Carnival, Steve had his wife, Anita, approach Ray for an autograph on a framed photograph. The shot had Bourque and Babineau standing together in front of a goal—the day rookie Raymond Bourque sprung Babineau for the breakaway.

"He was speechless, dumbfounded; he didn't know what to write," Babs recalls fondly. "He couldn't believe that photograph. Understandably, given everything he's done and been through, they forget this stuff. I'll never forget it."

above:

These four Bruins all won the Calder Trophy as NHL Rookie of the Year. Left to Right: Derek Sanderson (1968), Bobby Orr (1967), Sergei Samsonov holding the Trophy (1998), and Raymond Bourque (1980).

below:

Bourque returned to Boston to face the Bruins as a member of the Colorado Avalanche on March 24, 2001, in a 4-2 Colorado victory. That's Steve Babineau getting shots of Bourque at ice level.

right:

Phil Esposito returns the favor, handing Bourque his number 77 for retirement on October 4, 2001, 14 years after Bourque took number 7 right off his own back and delivered it to Espo for retirement.

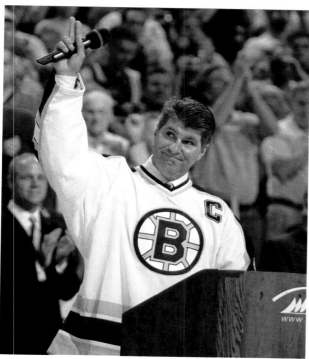

above:

Bourque in his sweater, acknowledging the crowd prior to making his jersey retirement speech.

right:

Number 77 begins its journey skyward. Left to right: Ray's wife Christiane, and kids Melissa, Ryan and Chris, watch dad as he unveils the banner.

Ray Bourque (D) Montreal, QC | #7, 77 | The NHL's all-time greatest scoring D-man

BRUINS REGULAR SEASON STATISTICS	GP	G	A	Pts	PIM
1979–2000	1,518	395	1,111	1,506	1,089
Bruins Postseason Statistics	180	36	125	161	151

CHAPTER

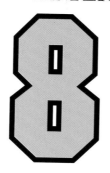

BRUINS LEGEND: CAM NEELY

above:

Neely in his first season in Boston. He arrived via trade with Vancouver along with a first round draft pick (Glen Wesley) for Barry Pederson June 6, 1986.

left:

Cam Neely, inducted into the Hockey Hall of Fame in November 2005, named Vice President of the Bruins in September 2007.

June 5, 1986: the Bruins trade Barry Pederson to the Vancouver Canucks for Cam Neely and a first-round draft choice, which turned out to be Glen Wesley. One could maybe see where Vancouver was coming from at the time; they were picking up a veteran forward who averaged 39 goals a season in the four years he was healthy in Boston. Meanwhile, in the prior campaign, as a Canuck, Neely had 14 goals and 126 penalty minutes in 73 games, and no points in three playoff games.

The change of scenery obviously served Neely and the Bruins very well. No one knew at the time that his number 8 would one day be hoisted to the rafters.

"I wore number 12 growing up [near Vancouver]," Neely says. "I liked Stan Smyl. I actually played with him in Vancouver where I wore number 21, 12 backwards. I had 21 in juniors in Portland, as well."

Neely's Winter Hawks team won the Memorial Cup, major junior's ultimate prize, in 1983, with Cam contributing 20 points in 14 playoff games.

"When I came to Boston I was handed number 8," Neely adds. "I asked if I could switch to 21 and they said no. 'Harry likes you in 8; you're wearing 8.'"

"Neely turns out to probably be my best move," ponders longtime Bruins general manager Harry Sinden. "I made some good ones, I made some bad ones, but that one turned out pretty darn good. I give the credit to the scouts; they told us to get him."

Barry Pederson chuckles when he gets mentioned as the "other side" of the deal.

"Well, it worked out very well for the Bruins here, not only with Cam as an individual but their team," Pederson says. "They played well late-'80s, early '90s, and he was a huge part of that. He took his game to the next level when he got here, and I didn't when I went to Vancouver. That's kind of where that broke down. But it was a losing environment there, and they [the media] took a lot of shots at the players who didn't get it done, and I didn't really, and that was fine." A classy and understanding mind-set from Pederson, who went to a bad team, while Neely arrived to one beginning an upswing.

above:

Neely crashes the net of Florida Panthers goalie Mark Fitzpatrick. The spinning puck has risen high above the crease on end, the width of the puck covering the first "e" in Reebok.

"I think part of the reason Cam turned into a great player was because of the playmakers the Bruins put around him," states Steve Babineau. "He was a great player, a typical bruising Bruins player, but he played with [Craig] Janney, and Dave Poulin, and then the ultimate playmaker in Adam Oates.

Flying down the wing became powering down the wing, and into the corners, and in front of the net.

"When I showed up, they put me with good players," Neely agrees, "and the old Garden was suited for my style of play."

"I had a chance to play with Cam when he showed up," recalls Rick "Nifty" Middleton. "He played with me and Thomas Gradin. Gradin was a very good centerman, a great playmaker. All Cam and I had to do was get open and he'd get us the puck. I just remember Cam flying down the wing."

Flying down the wing became powering down the wing, and into the corners, and in front of the net.

The Garden's small ice surface didn't leave much room for the faint of heart.

"He kind of reminds me of a cross between Terry O'Reilly and Mike Bossy," observes Babineau. "Prior to Cam, O'Reilly was the ultimate Bruin. Both of them could turn a game around with a body check and both of them were relentless. For Cam, though, add Bossy's scoring touch. He'd be deeper in the slot than Bossy, getting pummeled, but he could still control the puck and score. He had Bossy's finesse, but in much worse traffic. Throw in a Johnny-Bucyk-like hip check, a Bobby-Hull-like slapper and release, and leadership. He was the super-Bruin. Players would sit and watch him and then go out for their next shift."

below:

Neely fires a shot while being whacked by Devils defenseman Tommy Albelin. Bruin Greg Hawgood charges on the left behind backchecker David Maley (#8).

Comparing him to a handful of players melded together might be fair, but comparing him to just one other guy probably isn't. His enforcer teammate and pal off the ice Lyndon Byers concurs.

"One of a kind," states Byers. "I think one of the biggest misconceptions, one of the biggest mistakes reporters and hockey people and fans make is they try to compare people to Cam, they try to compare Cam to people. There will never be another power forward in the game that scores 50 goals in 44

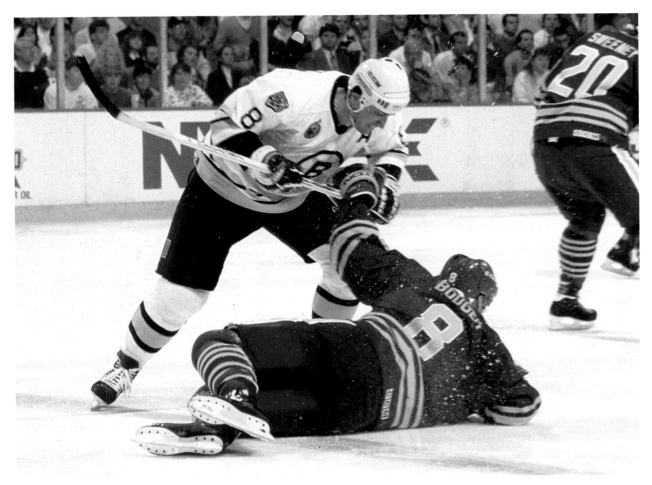

games. I still don't think he gets the accolades. We all respect him and we all know what he does, but there are all-stars and there are superstars, and so often it's 'he was a perennial all-star and tough as nails.' But I really and truly believe he is on a plane with the Gretzkys, the Messiers, the Lemieuxs, the Crosbys, the Orrs, and all those guys, as someone who reinvented—didn't reinvent—he *invented* superstar power forward. He was it. He's by himself; he's on a plateau by himself. It's pretty simple."

above:

Neely was the consummate power forward, here disposing of, and following up on Doug Bodger of the Buffalo Sabres. That's Bob Sweeney (#20) photo right.

"He hit me a few times in practice," former defenseman Mike Milbury remembers, "and he'd just explode into you. I hadn't played with a guy who hit like that."

Neely's nickname became the appropriate "Bam Bam." He also later became known as Seabass, for his role in the 1994 film *Dumb and Dumber*, directed by his acquaintances the Farrelly brothers. These names set aside his original NHL moniker, "Tricky Dicky Hambone," given to him early in his career by Canucks centerman Gary Lupul. That nickname shortened to "Bone." Glove manufacturers used to stamp a dog bone-shaped emblem on his glove cuffs.

"Cam was immensely strong and had great puck skills," former teammate Gord Kluzak adds. "People said he wasn't that great of a skater, but he'd always get there. They said he'd fit very well in the Boston Garden and boy did he ever."

The Garden was legendary for its small ice surface and its tight corners: no place to run, no place to hide. The hits, the chances, the goals came quickly.

Neely scored 36 goals his first season in Boston, then 42, then 37. By 1989–90, he powered his way to 55 goals and 92 points plus 117 penalty minutes. He actually became the super Bruin, every New England hockey fan's hero. Similar to Gordie Howe in his time, Neely was the best scorer and the most feared physical player on the ice as well.

below:

Canadiens defenseman Eric Desjardins battles "Bam Bam" for a loose puck in front of goaltender Patrick Roy. Bruin Craig Janney is behind the net.

In 1988, in just his second season in Boston, Neely endeared himself to Bruins fans another way: by helping the organization end a four-and-a-half decade long playoff drought against the Montreal Canadiens. The Bruins' last postseason series win against Montreal came in 1943, four games to one. Forty-five years later, after years of heartache at the hands of the Habs, the Bruins polished them off again in five games.

"That ended a long string of frustration against Montreal," points out Middleton. "I was still nervous when we were up 3-1 in that last game, but when Neely put us up 4-1, I knew we had it."

"I really didn't understand the full impact of beating them for hardcore, longtime Bruins fans, until we actually won the game," Neely thinks back. "And what it meant. When we showed up at Logan [Airport] and there were two to three thousand fans waiting, it was pretty special to be part of a team that could create that atmosphere, that we'd get that from a second-round win."

above:

Ulf Samuelsson (middle) being restrained by linesman Kevin Collins after yet another tussle with Neely. Samuelsson, who delivered a devastating open-ice knee-to-knee hit to Neely, along with countless other cheap shots, refused to drop the gloves. For this, Neely had little respect for his arch-enemy. That's Penguin Joe Mullen and Ray Bourque to the left.

The Bruins made it to the Stanley Cup final, only to be swept by the Edmonton Oilers. Despite the loss, Neely had established himself as a bona fide scorer and a physical presence.

He would pummel people, and be pummeled; or at least opponents would try.

As the next few seasons unfolded, to slow down Neely, and to prevent the strong winger's physical domination from being one-sided in his favor, opponents stooped to cheap shots. The most notorious perpetrator: Pittsburgh defenseman Ulf Samuelson, who nailed Neely with an open-ice knee-to-knee hit that led to one injury, and who sparred with him countless other times. Their battles in the 1991 postseason, in a Conference final where the

I never really respected a guy who played a certain way and didn't want to answer the bell.

Bruins led two games to none at one point but was won by the Penguins, are infamous. A collision between the two late in the series led to Neely's chronic hip condition. Meanwhile, the fact that Samuelson consistently delivered cheap shots while wearing a visor, and the fact he'd never answer the bell and drop the gloves, drove Neely's old-time mentality crazy.

Neely expressed his dismay during an interview with NESN, produced at the time of his Hall of Fame induction.

"If you do not want to handle what is going to come because you chopped a guy, you slashed a guy, you cross-checked a guy; you know, you stuck a glove in the back of his head, his helmet, and pushed his helmet into his face," Neely starts, "then if you don't want to turn around and drop the gloves when the guy challenges you, then you shouldn't play that way. You know. He's got a face shield on. You play a certain way; I don't think you should wear a face shield if you're not going to back up what you're doing. You look at a lot of hockey players who play tough…if they get somebody mad, if somebody wants to go and drop the gloves, they're going to answer the bell. I never really respected a guy who played a certain way and didn't want to answer the bell."

Neely answered every bell, and overcame devastating knee and hip injuries to continue his career. Over two seasons, from 1991 through 1993, he played in only 22 games. He returned in 1993–94 and played as tough as ever, while essentially taking every other game off to rest his knee. He reached the 50-goal mark in 44 games played.

below:

The Bruins score on Sean Burke of the Devils as Neely and New Jersey defenseman Randy Velischek head to the net, taken from the catwalk in the old Garden.

"It would be difficult in the history of the League, to find someone who combined what he did so effectively," Bruins president Harry Sinden was quoted as saying. "And that was scoring goals and being so powerful and the aggressive forward that he was. We've had a lot of great goal scorers who couldn't really live up to the other part. Cam had it...he had it all."

Rick Middleton adds, "Not many players could play that way—score and physically dominate."

And he did it on a knee and with a hip that was never again one hundred percent.

"His rehab was a lesson in perseverance I won't forget," Sinden states.

On top of "legend" status, Neely earned the Masterton Trophy in 1994 for his efforts. Each season, the Professional Hockey Writers' Association delegates the award to the NHL player who "best exemplifies the qualities of perseverance, sportsmanship, and dedication to hockey." That year's decision would fall under the "no-brainer" category.

Babineau remembers being in awe of some of the battles Neely went through.

above:

The many images of Neely, inspired by his jersey retirement, designed as a collage poster by Brian Babineau, using dad's photos, and sold through their company Sports Action Images.

below:

Knee and hip problems ended Neely's career prematurely at age 31 in September of 1996. Here, he goes knee to knee with Edmonton's Kevin Lowe.

"He'd be getting the hell beaten out of him in front. He'd lose his cool on occasion but mostly he'd keep his cool. Sometimes I'd pull the camera away just to watch the battle.

It was laughable sometimes—elbows, high sticks."

Tongue in cheek at the time, Babineau would warn Neely of the other side effect of his fracases.

"Don't get hit in the head or face, because you'll have to wear a shield. Those shield photos aren't going to sell," Babineau would say with a grin.

Because of a broken nose or an eye injury, maybe an average of once every year or two, Neely would actually have to don the shield for a couple games. He couldn't wait to take it off.

When asked which photograph of himself he liked best, Cam netted an unusual request.

"Goal, hit, or fight? Maybe all three 'mooshed' together in a collage or something like that. That would be cool," Neely says. "I remember Babs always being around, lurking in the corners. I remember him standing on that huge ladder taking the team pictures.

"It's hard to get those photos of those physical plays," Neely adds.

Babineau managed to get them, and he managed to get plenty of them.

"I think players should request certain kinds of shots ahead of time, instead of 'let me see what you have,'" Neely suggests. "There is one shot, where I'm celebrating a goal; I've got my stick in the air... that one stands out. It shows a lot of emotion." The Bruins used the image on a poster.

For Neely, as a Bruin, emotion stemmed from pride, and pride stemmed from tradition. Those two elements went hand in hand with old-school accountability.

"Original Six, so much history, so much pride to wear that jersey," Neely says with a smile. "It's expected that you embrace that tradition. When I walked in, we had guys like Ray Bourque, who led by example. He worked really hard. The best guy in the League day in and day out, and he had the work ethic. There's a correlation between working hard and having a great career.

"Bobby Orr was around and he'd sometimes walk into the dressing room and that was really cool," Neely adds. "Johnny Bucyk was around. They'd always come in and you'd always feel proud to be a Bruin."

"Neely was the consummate player, the toughest guy I ever played with," reflects Ken Hodge Jr., who joined the Bruins in 1990. "I was fortunate. I remember coming to my first game. I was number 10 at the time, and I saw 8 [Neely] next to me and Carpenter's number, I can't remember the number, but that was the line. 'Who am I playing with and what am I doing?!' I remember Cam saying to me, 'I don't want the puck in the defensive zone; I want the puck in the offensive zone. That's the only thing you have to remember.' 'OK, Mr. Neely,'" he remembers with a smile. "But Cam was a great guy, and we see him quite a bit, at the golf tournaments and involved now, and it's nice to see him able to do well."

above:

Best way to break a horse? Ride 'em or rope 'em. Calgary Flames defenseman Dana Murzyn wraps and rides a power forward next to the net.

"My favorite games were afternoon games on Saturday," Neely told NESN. "Get up, eat, get dressed, and go to the rink and play. Night games, you have the morning skate, you eat, you sleep, there's so much time to think of the game. Afternoon games at the Garden were the best, and an opportunity for people to bring their kids to the game. I loved the atmosphere."

"When I first played in the League with Calgary, I played against Neely so I really don't think I truly saw really what a great player he was," says former Bruins forward Tim Sweeney.

above:

Ottawa goaltender Don Beaupre disappears under the weight and power of Neely. Senators' defenseman Sean Hill turns for the puck.

"I saw him score a lot of goals and I saw him score a lot of goals on one knee too, because I was there for the end of his career and he was terrific—your prototypical power forward that really worked hard on and off the ice. It was a privilege to play him, but you really noticed it in Boston when you saw him doing it day in and day out."

Twice Neely played in the Stanley Cup final with Boston, the second time in 1990. They lost to the Oilers in five games.

"Game 1, triple overtime loss took some wind out," Neely said years later. "We were definitely better in '90 than '88. It's frustrating to this day that we didn't have a better series there."

After the '91 Conference final, Neely's Bruins would never again advance past the first round. Five years later, the damaged inflicted to his limbs was irreversible; there would be no more incredible rehabilitations.

"My right hip injury is a permanent disability which will prevent me from ever returning to professional hockey," a choked-up Neely announced on September 5, 1996.

Neely finished with 344 goals in 525 games with Boston, and is the franchise's all-time leading playoff goal scorer.

above:

Cam Neely: A picture speaks a thousand words.

left:

A warrior rests in the penalty box. Neely's pounding style led to 921 PIM with Boston, to go with 344 goals, and 590 points.

Between his physical retirement and his jersey retirement in January of 2005, Neely devoted his time to starting a family, and to helping those in the community less fortunate than himself. He had remained single until after his playing days.

"At home it was get up and think about hockey, and on the road it was get up and think about hockey. That's what I liked," Neely asserts. "As a player, I saw early on, guys were married and missed a lot of family stuff. When I wanted to start a family, I wanted it to be after the career, because I didn't want to miss [all of the] 'firsts.'"

Meanwhile, tragedy affected the Neely family as well. Cam lost both his parents, Marlene and Michael, to cancer. In 1995, Cam started the Neely Foundation, an effort he oversees with his brother, Scott. The basic mission statement: "Dedicated to helping patients and families deal with cancer."

Aside from raising funds and awareness for the Cancer Center at Tufts-New England Medical Center and its Floating Hospital for Children, Neely continues to expand the Neely House, a 15,000-square-foot, 16-apartment living area within the walls of the medical facility. It's a home away from home for families of cancer patients, particularly adolescent patients. Since 1997, thousands of people have stayed as guests,

"The best part about Cam, he's a better human being than he is a hockey player," maintains Lyndon Byers. "He takes care of his family, he takes care of his friends, and he takes care of strangers."

Byers's sentiment, and Cam's philosophy of "giving first," are best exemplified in Neely's Hall of Fame induction speech from November 2005. Excerpts focus as much or more so on

left:

High scoring linemates Adam Oates and Neely celebrate a goal against Quebec Nordiques defenseman Craig Wolanin and goaltender Stephane Fiset.

below:

Adam Oates and Cam Neely. This photo ended up on the cover of the Bruins yearbook and on a Beckett hockey card magazine.

being thankful and being a generous giver than they do on being a legendary hockey player.

"...I loved playing it [hockey] as a mite, a pee wee, a bantam, winning the Memorial Cup with the Portland Winter Hawks as a junior, and right through my time as a professional. However, there was that one brief instant in my life, a moment of misguided youth, when I actually wanted to quit hockey. I was 15 years old, playing my first year of midgets, all of my teammates were 16 and they were driving cars to and from games, while there I was heading home with Dad after games. I felt so out of place, I told my dad I wanted to quit, and my dad gave me one of life's great lessons: He said, 'Cam, you know what, you tried out for this team, and you made it. You took someone else's spot,

I remember well the gift of giving by the fans; their support extended beyond the game.

and I want you to honor your commitment and finish the year.' He continued, 'If you don't want to sign up next year, that's your choice.' No yelling, no screaming, just a valuable opportunity to grow up and make my own decision. To say the least, I'm very glad that I continued and I'm profoundly indebted to my dad for that great lesson in life on commitment. To my brother, Scott, [and] sisters, Christine and Shaun, you deserve an enormous amount of thanks for the support you have given

right:

Cam and younger brother Scott pose with the Prince of Wales Trophy in 1988 after the Bruins advanced to the Stanley Cup finals. The brothers presently work closely in handling the family's charitable endeavors, including the Neely Foundation for Cancer Research.

below:

Neely celebrates a goal at the Garden.

me over the years. My mother and father, my biggest supporters, I know you're watching today and are here with us today. I love you and I miss you. Their gift of giving is another life lesson, which is very much an important aspect of my life to this day. I thank them from the bottom of my heart.

"...They also gave me the opportunity to work hard every day, compete toward a common goal, and honor the tradition of all who wore the Bruins jersey. My teammates and I all knew that the name on the front meant a lot more than the name on the back. My memory of these gifts and opportunities mean the world to me, especially on a day like today. I remember well the gift of giving by the fans; their support extended beyond the game. I will never forget their compassion during my personal battles, with the illness of my parents, or with my professional battles with injury. I thank them deeply and sincerely. While I'm gratified today to be recognized for hard work and achievement, I also know this was part of my life's work. As we examine our lives, and certainly we all come from different walks of life, different parts of the world, we do share a common humanity. We believe that life's purpose is to give to others whenever possible. Sometimes it's an event that reaches deep within us that causes us to give back. Personally, after I lost both my parents after their courageous battles with cancer, a direction in my life became abundantly clear. I realized many more things about my life in my parents' passing. As a professional athlete, I have been given so much, but today, I have satisfaction from giving back. I want to give back to those who have helped me, who stoked my dreams. I want to give back to family and friends and others that have

encouraged me. I want to give back to those who I may have the privilege and responsibility to help in their time of need. Many have helped me along the way, and it's my honor and responsibility to return the favor. As you all know, and I have learned well from you, there is no better gift than giving. I thank you again for this terrific lesson, I will never forget it..."

"The Bruins didn't send me to his induction," recalls Babineau, "but I do remember being in the dressing room with him before his jersey was retired. The current Bruins at the time all came over and shook his hand and then he led them out on to the ice. He skated out, which was rare for one of those jersey retirements. It was cool; he took a lap around the ice while the team followed him and went to the bench. It was a big night for a guy who represents the ultimate Bruin."

In September 2007, Cam Neely was officially re-introduced into the Boston hockey community as a Bruins vice president. Neely works closely with the general manager and the hockey staff to evaluate players and their performance. He once again finds himself the face of the franchise, a responsibility he welcomes, with a chance to restore and re-affirm dedication to, and the tradition of, the Spoked B.

left:

Left to right: Wife Paulina Neely, daughter Ava, and son Jack, Bruin Shaone Morrisonn leaning over (obscured), Jeff Jillson, and Cam.

above:

Hollywood celebrity and friend Michael J. Fox toasts Cam on his jersey retirement night, January 12, 2004. Bruins on the bench left to right: Glen Murray, Nick Boynton, Andrew Raycroft, and Joe Thornton. Standing are equipment manager Peter Henderson and assistant coach Norm Maciver.

left:

Cameron Michael Neely's number 8 gets hoisted.

CAM NEELY (RW) Comox, BC │ #8 │ Heart, more than stats, earned him the Hall					
BRUINS REGULAR SEASON STATISTICS	GP	G	A	Pts	PIM
1986–1996	525	344	246	590	921
Bruins Postseason Statistics	86	55	32	87	160

THE LUNCH PAIL GANG

above:

After winning the Bruins Seventh Player Award for the 1977-78 season, Stan Jonathan gets an appreciative peck from head coach Don Cherry.

left:

Bobby Schmautz celebrates his game winning goal in overtime of Game-4 against Montreal in the 1978 Stanley Cup final on May 21st. The goal tied the series, but the Canadiens went on to win in six games.

Even after Steve Babineau had become the Bruins' official photographer in 1977, he had never been in the team's dressing room. That changed suddenly one afternoon after practice at the Garden, midway through his first season.

The short little assistant equipment manager nicknamed "Tattoo," after the Fantasy Island character from the '70s, found Babineau standing near the glass along the far boards.

"You Steve Babineau?" he asked Babs.

"Yeah."

"Coach wants to see you in his office," came the demand.

"Oh my God," Babineau thought to himself, "what could this be all about?" The same interjection entered his mind again as the dressing room doors swung open, which for Babineau was like opening the doors to a shrine. He stared at the player stalls and then moved cautiously through the room.

"Coach, I'm Steve Babineau, the team photographer," Babs introduced himself as he stepped into the coach's office.

Head Coach Don Cherry, nicknamed "Grapes," had seen Babineau's blown-up, framed Bruins photographs lining the walls of the new season ticket holder social area, the Boards and Blades Club. He wanted copies of a few of those photos and he wanted to see others.

"Sure thing," Babineau agreed.

The two arranged to meet the next Sunday afternoon at Babineau's apartment in Medford. When the day arrived, Cherry and his wife, Rose, pulled up in a huge, black Lincoln Continental.

"The car seemed to take up the whole block," Babs recalls.

Cherry spent a few hours going through dozens, maybe even a couple hundred photos. He also told stories about his players, and did imitations of the way they skated.

During the 1970s, the Big Bad Bruins gave way, or morphed themselves, into the Lunch Pail Gang. The gang was still "bad," with guys like Stan Jonathan, Terry O'Reilly, and John Wensink, but they also had a collective team work ethic like none other. Coach Cherry loved his grinders as much as he had loved watching Bobby Orr. Character players like Mike Milbury, Bobby Schmautz, and Al Secord made his team complete. The Bruins flew around the ice and, more often than not, ran into anything that moved. They were tough, intimidating, and successful.

"It was great. Don Cherry was definitely a players' coach," points out Gary Doak, a Bruins defenseman for much of 14 seasons. "It was different than the Cup teams. We had a lot of guys that worked hard; we had 20 guys that would stick their nose in and do whatever Don wanted us to do. Back then it was rough and tough. We all chipped in and we played that style of hockey, and that's how it was back then. We had Jonathan and Wensink, Wayne Cashman, Schmautz, and we also had players that could score goals, like Peter McNab and Rick Middleton. So we had a solid all-around team back then. It was great playing for him; a great coach and a great person."

"We played hard for him because he always had us ready to play," states 5-foot-8-inch, 175-pound battler Stan Jonathan. "We had good leadership with Chief and Wayne Cashman, and we believed in one another. Part of it was the guys, part of it was Don, but we didn't take s— from anyone!"

Jonathan scrapped his way to 751 penalty minutes for the team, with all of his 411 NHL games coming in Boston. A smaller man with a big heart, the prototypical Lunch Pailer, Jonathan was a player coach Cherry adored.

"Grapes was a guy who'd go out and have a beer with you," remembers former defenseman Milbury. "He used to make me drive to the rink with him, from Andover, where we lived about a half-mile apart. He'd pick me up in the morning of the game, we'd ride in, and he'd practice his pre-game speeches. I knew exactly what he was going to say before he said it because I had heard it four or five times on the way in. I took some grief for riding with the coach, but I really had no choice—he insisted that I ride with him. We'd ride back after the skate on the day of the game and he'd stop and have a couple of Budweisers, order some Chinese food—the specials for him, his wife, and his son—and then he'd go home and have a little Chinese food and a nap."

Cherry's gang came together in a variety of manners. Schmautz came in a trade from Vancouver in February of 1974. Jonathan came via the 1975 draft, as a sixth rounder, 86th overall. Mike Milbury was a non-drafted college player who signed as a free agent in November of 1974. Harry Sinden was the general manager at the time, the man responsible for building this prototypical working class Boston club.

below:

Don Cherry coached exactly 400 regular season games for the Bruins. His team won or tied 295 of them.

Wensink's initial pro deal involved a three-year contract with St. Louis. For a portion of that time, he was assigned to Rochester, New York, in the AHL, where Cherry was coach. After a back injury his second season, Wensink had spinal fusion surgery and missed a year of hockey. Potentially considered damaged goods, he didn't get re-signed by St. Louis. The Bruins picked up Wensink as a free agent in October 1976. Midway through his fourth overall season, he was called up to the Bruins. Wensink is forever grateful to Grapes.

"He was my first pro coach, and the way I played and the way he coached, obviously that was the perfect marriage," points out Wensink. "He just was a good guy, a players' coach. He was also the one who gave me the shot when he was with the Bruins and I was in the minors. For me, I know management at that time, ownership [probably had their doubts], and I had just come off a year of not playing after having spinal fusion done. The Bruins ended up signing me and it was sometime early January they called me up. Grapes was the one who made the call. He said, 'Get that guy up here.' I was fortunate enough to stay."

Rick Middleton, meanwhile, took some time getting out of Cherry's doghouse. Acquired for Ken Hodge in the spring of 1976, the long-haired goal scorer with an early-career propensity for ignoring the back end gradually learned his lesson and gained ice time.

above:

Cherry and his Gang follow the action. Players left to right: Jim "Seaweed" Pettie, Dwight "Dewey" Foster, Al "Rocky" Secord, John "Wire" Wensink, Stan "Little Chief" Jonathan, Bobby Miller, Don Marcotte, Rick "Nifty" Middleton, Mike "Dooner" Milbury, Jean "Ratty" Ratelle, Bobby Schmautz, Al Sims, Dennis O'Brien.

below:

Head equipment guy Dan Canney and "Wire."

"It was my third year in the League, but I didn't think I'd be coming to Boston and stepping into a lineup that was very solid, especially on the right side," says Middleton. "I mean, Cashman, Schmautz, O'Reilly. I wanted to play, I thought they would play me, but I also realized I had so much more to learn. I never really learned in New York; no one ever taught me about the complete game. That's why I always thank Don, because he did it by forcing me to either make it or break it, because if I didn't learn, I wouldn't have been playing. I ended up watching these guys [teammates] as he wanted me to, and then applying it on the ice, and it worked out.

He just was a good guy, a players' coach.

"Not always, though," he continues. "I remember one time in Buffalo, I went back to watch my point—he used to say, 'Watch your point, kid'—I watched my point and my defense-man [to cover] was Bill Hajt, who scored two goals a year. The other guy was Danny Gare, who scored 50 goals a year. So I went to Gare, and he puts it back to Hajt, and he gets one of his two goals a year, and I didn't want to go to the bench, 'cause I knew what was coming. For the most part, after that I didn't make too many errors and when Don left, he had really set the groundwork for me to continue and to excel at the whole game, so I thank him for that."

"Grapes was a great coach. I loved playing for him," claims the Chief, John Bucyk, who finished his 21-year Bruins career in 1978. "He stood up for his players and he was a great guy to play for. He never took the credit. If we won, it was because the players played well; if we lost, he'd take the blame and say it was the coach's fault. He never took credit and [always] treated us well."

"Cherry's mantra was 'them against us,'" says PR guy Nate Greenberg. "It worked out quite well. He had a terrific team, obviously, and I think it was safe to say he was the right coach at the right time. He had a lot of veteran players, and he coached them, treated them like veterans—the perfect coach for them. He knew how to mold them, and the whole "Lunch Pail" thing worked. It was a little bit of a misnomer. You think of a lunch pail gang, you think of hard workers that do it all with maybe no talent, but these guys worked hard, and had quite a bit of talent. They had some damn good players and he [Cherry] did a terrific job. The right time and place for him."

Boston Globe writer Fran Rosa is credited with coming up with the "Lunch Pail" moniker.

above:

Cherry at home in his basement, checks out photos from his playing days in Rochester.

"It seems to me I was talking to someone about them and said, 'They're like working stiffs—get up and go to work and then go home,'" remembers Rosa. "And they said, 'Like a lunch pail guy,' and I said, 'Yeah, just like that.' I added gang because they were a team, and they were very much a team. It's funny because some of the players, I don't remember who exactly, almost resented the fact that I called them that, because they thought it implied that they had no talent; that they were just a bunch of working stiffs. It wasn't true. They had talent on those Cherry teams; the nickname just described the work they did."

"The four years I was in Boston, it was the case of 20 guys, or however large the roster was, 20 guys wanting to back each other up," states Wensink. "I knew as an individual, if you were called to go out for the next shift or whatever, you went over the boards not wanting to let any of the other 19 guys down. I think that said a lot for our togetherness. It wasn't always fancy, we didn't try to entertain always, but we wanted to get a job done. I know myself, and I think a lot of the other guys would say the same thing, you didn't want to let the other guys down. We had some talent, guys like Middleton, Park, and Ratelle, these guys knew how to handle the puck and wheel and deal, but we also had a core group of guys... with limited talent and a great work ethic."

In his five seasons as coach, Cherry went 231-105-64. His winning percentage is the best in team history among coaches who handled the job for more than three seasons. Only Tom Johnson (two-plus seasons) and Armand Guidolin (two seasons), his immediate predecessors with the Big Bad Bruins, had better winning percentages in team history.

below:

New York Ranger Phil Esposito having a difference of opinion with Bruin Brad Park. The two were swapped for one another in a multi-player deal in 1975. Others involved from left to right: Mike Milbury, Terry O'Reilly, and Ranger Don Murdoch.

In the postseason, Grapes was almost as impressive. His record was 31-24 in overall games. His problem: the Gang never won the big one. Twice the team reached the Stanley Cup final, in 1977 and 1978, only to be swept in four games and then lose in six, both times to the Canadiens.

"It's enough to make a grown man cry," states Terry O'Reilly, referring to Cherry's last crack at it, the 1979 playoffs, when the Bruins lost a semi-final series they were moments away from winning, once again to Montreal.

O'Reilly refers to the infamous too-many-men-on-the-ice penalty late in Game 7. After Middleton scored to give the Bruins a 4-3 lead with about four minutes remaining in the game, a screwed-up line change led to the infraction at 17:26 of the third period.

Goalie Gerry Cheevers, sitting on the end of the bench that evening, recalls the play and the discussions that followed.

"There were only nine guys on the ice there," Cheevers jokes. "Johnny D'Amico made the call, the linesman. I saw him in the summer and I said, 'John…,' and he stopped me right away and said, 'I didn't want to call it after six, after seven, and then after nine I had to call it.'

"I was injured. I didn't play that game," Cheevers adds. "Gilbert played it and it was so frantic and the pace was so frantic, everyone got caught up in the game. I don't know who

above:

On the bench with Don Cherry, Rick Middleton, Peter McNab, Terry O'Reilly and John Wensink.

above:

The whole gang joins Wayne Cashman and Peter McNab (at top) in celebrating a goal against the Montreal Canadiens.

[caused the penalty]. Even if I knew who, I wouldn't say anything, but when players came to the bench they had their position, center, left wing, right wing, and the guys were so caught up they didn't know who was up next and I think two or three guys jumped on."

O'Reilly believes the entire late third-period scenario could have been avoided much earlier.

"Well, I remember that game…we went into the dressing room at the end of two periods with a 3-1 lead," Terry recalls. "But I think, if I remember correctly—I've never gone back and looked at the video—I remember a play near the end of that second period where Peter McNabb passed it over to me. I think he was in the left corner of the Montreal end, he passed it out, and I took it and snapped it and hit the goalpost dead center. Ugh, I mean, if it hit the inside of the post it went in and we've got a 4-1 lead going into the third period. It hit the post dead center, came right back out to Don Marcotte, and he blasted it and it went right into Dryden. So we had two opportunities to extend our lead, but we didn't and they came back, as Montreal often did in those days. And Guy Lafleur scored a goal with a slap shot. I think the puck was on the blue line. He was just stepping into our zone and if I looked at the video again you'd see his stick in the back swing came so close it almost touched the boards. That's how far…he was so far over to the side, so far back, but you could not fault [goalie Gilles] Gilbert for that goal. It was a perfect shot, it was like a laser, two inches off the ice, right off the inside of the far post."

Lafleur, in reality, a bit closer to the top of the face-off circle, ripped the power play goal home with a minute and 14 seconds left in the third. Yvon Lambert scored the game winner at 9:33 of overtime on a feed from Mario Tremblay, and the Habs advanced to beat the New York Rangers in the Cup final.

So the playoff jinx against the Canadiens continued—a jinx that may have simply been a match-up issue, seen often in the regular season as well.

"We were in Montreal one time; we couldn't ever win there, so Grapes said, 'Hey, we're gonna change things up,'" remembers Milbury. "The night before the game, he says, 'You're coming with me,' so we go around the corner from the hotel to a little tavern and a few of us sit and drink beer and tell stories for about five hours. The next night we got the crap kicked out of us. He just laughed about it and said, 'At least we tried. We had to do something different.'"

"It was great," chimes Cheevers. "I think more than any time, you'd go out of your way to go to the rink because every day was a new adventure with Grapes. We had fun. The dressing room was fun, everything was very positive. I was maybe the only guy who had played with him in Rochester, so when he started barking, I kind of knew what he was really like. Every day was an adventure."

"They [the Bruins] never had much of a power play, and there was a game over in Minnesota, and I think the Bruins had something like eight power plays, and were zero for eight," remembers beat writer Rosa. "So after the game I went down to the dressing room to get a few quotes as we always did, and Cherry looks at me and says, 'Damn you!' And I said, 'What?' And he said, 'I'm trying to pay attention to the game, and all I can think about is that Rosa is going to come down and ask me what I'm going to do about the power play.' I said, 'Well Don, you had little to do if you were thinking about what I was going to ask you.' And Don said, 'What do you want me to do, go out

below:

left to right: Gary Doak, John Wensink, Dwight Foster, Al Sims, Terry O'Reilly, Peter McNab (standing and cheering), Rick Middleton, Mike Milbury (standing on bench cheering), Bobby Schmautz, Stan Jonathan, Bob Miller, and coach Cherry behind the last two players.

above:

Stan Jonathan clocks Bob Murdoch of the Los Angeles Kings. LA goalie Rogie Vachon follows the puck.

and shoot myself?' And I said, 'No…try practicing it.'

Rosa wrote the conversation into his story for the next morning and Cherry then talked about it on the radio.

"I guess he ripped me up a little bit," Rosa says, "I didn't hear it. So I went to practice at the Garden the next day and [I was a little worked up and] I said to Don, 'Were you giving me the business on the radio?' And he said, 'Yeah, sit down and I'll tell you why we don't practice it,' which he did. It was funny. How could I get mad?"

Humor on and off the air became a foreshadow for Cherry, a man who has developed into one of Canada's most popular, controversial, and talked-about persons because of his comments on the "Coach's Corner" intermission segment on the CBC's *Hockey Night in Canada* weekly telecast.

"It's like the basic fan on the street…When I go up to Canada and I run into my buddies, people up in Canada, they either like him or dislike him," points out Wensink. "Funny

thing is, everybody watches him. The ones who like him watch him, because they're great followers of him; the ones that think he's off the wall, they want to listen and they do watch to hear what he has to say, to agree with him or disagree with him.

"The thing about it with him is, he may get a little carried away sometimes, no question, but the bottom line is, if you know the game at all or follow the game at all, he's not wrong. The way he gets there might be a little off-board sometimes, but he's right about pretty much everything he says. It may not be right at that moment—it may take a year or two—but eventually everyone says, 'Hey, that's exactly how it turned out.' He's not wrong very often, believe me."

More often than not, the controversy is somewhat playful and harmless. On other occasions, Cherry says something he's forced to take back. Nate Greenberg remembers one such occasion from Cherry's coaching days.

"He probably wanted it back after he said it, but one of the most controversial things…," recalls Greenberg. "We had played the Blackhawks where there was a stick deal, an incident, and the quote from Cherry was, 'The next time we're here we're gonna send Stan Mikita back to Czechoslovakia in a pine box.' He got all kinds of heck for it, and deservedly so, and he backed off of it later. [Then NHL president] Clarence Campbell called him and I think he recanted. He was always jousting with other teams."

above:

Don Cherry wearing his Scottish red plaid, acknowledging the Garden faithful at the Last Hurrah in October 1995.

Cherry, a relative unknown when he arrived from coaching in the minors, remains one of a kind, a promoter and a personality the NHL has lacked on the bench or on the ice since.

Stirring the pot was just another way to bring attention to himself and to his hockey team. Cherry, a relative unknown when he arrived from coaching in the minors, remains one of a kind, a promoter and a personality the NHL has lacked on the bench or on the ice since.

"When he left Boston he went to Colorado, and the first time he came back to Boston coaching another team, I think it might have been in the first period, he took his time out," recalls Rosa. "He took his time out to sign autographs around him. I said it was outrageous [at the time]."

above:

"Media savvy" doesn't do enough to describe coach Cherry, a showman in every sense of the word. He's a fixture on Hockey Night in Canada *on CBC television and considered one of Canada's most influential countrymen. Here, interviewed by Gail Granik of WBZ-4 Sports.*

"You never knew what was going to come out or what he was going to do," adds Greenberg. "Plus, he dressed then like he does now, almost, he had that unique style, and he was a show unto himself some nights. He really was, plus the team was successful. The act may not have gone over as well if the team was lousy. But it was perfect. He was a character and the team was good."

"Yeah, we were a very close team for quite a few years," says O'Reilly. "Wonderful place to play hockey. You know, it was a place where you look forward to going to work."

"Most of the guys on the team could call Grapes a friend," states Milbury. "We just had a ton of fun. Everyone around him realized they were enjoying a special time, and it wasn't just Grapes, it was the players, because he didn't have the same guys when he got tripped up in Colorado. But it was a pretty neat time and a great group of guys, all in all."

"Craziest guy?" responds Bucyk when asked. "Probably Bobby Schmautz, he was a bit whacky, and Cashman, he wasn't crazy but he was a team player and he would protect you. Yeah, Grapes had his moments, too."

"Grapes was a players' coach," adds Milbury. "He was no tactician. Our breakout play was to fire it around the boards and get it to our big wingers and we'd run over their defensemen. And it worked pretty effectively.

"He was with you or against you," Milbury continues. "If he was against you, chances are you weren't going to last very long. He was demanding in a sense that he wanted guys in good shape—we had some tough practices—and that you committed yourself physically. Beyond that, there wasn't a lot of high tech. Of course, it was a different era, too; there wasn't a lot of high-tech coaching going on either. You played hard or he was going to give it to you."

below:

Wayne Cashman with time for a smile while being pinned to the boards by Toronto's Ian Turnball.

above:

Casual spontaneity for the Lunch Pail Gang after practice at the Garden at the suggestion of coach Cherry: Left to right, those not totally obscured: Gary Doak in white, John Wensink craning his neck in back, Dick Redmond in black, face in back is Dennis O'Brien, moustache in front Dwight Foster, black helmet Al Sims, tall Tom Songin obscured in back, shorter face is Jim Pettie, stick blocking face of Bobby Schmautz, goalie Gerry Cheevers, white helmet above is Mike Milbury, Rick Middleton holding up the mouse ears, Al Secord in Spoked-B, Terry O'Reilly alone in front, behind the kid (Don's son Tim Cherry) is Stan Jonathan, Brad Park immediately behind, and Peter McNab behind them, coach Don Cherry with the hat on, Gilles Gilbert in front of him, tall Bill Bennett in back, Rick Smith, Jean Ratelle in white, and Bobby Miller.

"He's a great guy and if he likes you, he'll go to the end of the world for you," Wensink adds. "As a coach that's how he was, too. If he liked you, unless you did something stupid, you were going to play.

He really is a great friend of mine, I wish him the best, and he's obviously done real well for himself. He's a good guy."

"It would have been nice to have been able to win one in the late '70s, and there was a couple there that could have been taken," concludes Cheevers. "We didn't take them, and it's disappointing in that respect, but there were other good teams. I think that's what happened a couple of those years."

Video highlights of the Lunch Pail Gang remain a consistent feature of the Bruins pre-game video presentation on the huge high-definition scoreboard above center ice to this day. A new generation of Boston supporters is constantly reminded of the personality and the work ethic of Cherry's Bruins. Meanwhile, the coach himself still publicly pulls for his old organization while on national television in Canada—all the result of a rare and enduring love affair between hockey players, a coach, and their fans.

CHAPTER

10

COACHES

above:

During Babineau's tenure as team photographer, Harry Sinden twice filled in as interim coach, replacing Fred Creighton for the last seven games of season in 1979-80 and shown here, finishing the 1984-85 season after relieving Gerry Cheevers.

left:

Former Bruins coach Don Cherry presents Bruins head coach Pat Burns with the Jack Adams Award for NHL Coach of the Year in 1998. Cherry had won the award in Boston 22 years earlier.

Including the legendary Art Ross, who ran the bench starting back in 1924, there have been 28 head coaches in the history of the Bruins. Steve Babineau has photographed and worked with 18 of them. Many of them had direct ties with the club as former players, while others came from outside the Bruins "family."

Considering all of the talents, personalities, and success stories tied into the Bruins coaching list the past 35 years, it may seem as though picking the most prominent bench-boss would be a difficult task. In reality, the selection is easy. Despite only coaching twice as an interim during that time period, for portions of two separate seasons, Harry Sinden commands the list. Maybe it's because as a hands-on general manager and Club president during most of the last three decades, his influence was often felt directly in the coach's office and in the dressing room. Or perhaps it's simply because of the vast depth of hockey knowledge he brought to the organization, as a former world championship player, Stanley Cup coach, and Hall of Fame executive.

"I have a great deal of respect for Harry—the longevity here in Boston, what he did for the Bruins and for the organization," states Ken Hodge. "We won a Stanley Cup. We won it with Harry. He was really the maestro of that team; he put the lines together. Granted, Milt Schmidt went out and made the trades then—that made everything possible—but Harry put everybody together in the right positions at the right time and right places. A tremendous coach and I have a great deal of

left:

Former Bruins defenseman Mike Milbury coached the team to the 1990 Stanley Cup final against Edmonton, a series Boston lost in five games. Replaced after the 1991-92 campaign, Milbury won 63 percent of his regular season games.

respect for him as a coach and a general manager and you've gotta respect what he's done for hockey here in New England and what he's done for the National Hockey League."

"The absolute best coach I ever played for was Harry," insists Mike Milbury. "I never had him very long, because he only pinch-hit on occasion when he fired a guy, but you could tell he was totally in charge. He knew what he was doing and it was a great learning experience to be a player with him and to later be a coach for him. He had so much experience going into it."

"Harry Sinden was the best coach I ever had in pro hockey," proclaims Phil Esposito, a man not very fond of Harry as a GM. "He really was. He recognized that I could score, and I remember him saying to me very early in my time with the Bruins, he said he was going to get me two wingers to get me the puck, and here's where he wanted me to play, by the hash marks, slot area, and he said they won't be able to get you there because you've got Orr at the point, and that's where I want you to be. That's sure worked best for me."

Oddly enough, it was Sinden's success as a coach that probably led him to have a quick hook as general manager. He had himself, his knowledge and expectations, to compare with everyone else. The coaching position, particularly in Sinden's latter years in charge, became a bit of a revolving door.

"I had four different coaches here," remembers former defenseman Frank Simonetti. "Gerry Cheevers, Harry Sinden, Butch Goring, and Terry O'Reilly. And that was over a time span of four years. The recipe isn't always right, every time. I think in coaching, the lifespan, and you still see it now, is two or three years if you're doing OK, but often times not longer than that. Gerry Cheevers had a three- or four-year run and

above left:

Hall-of-Fame goaltender Gerry Cheevers never enjoyed coaching as much as playing, despite good success during a nearly five season run. "I don't know if there's a best part about it," Cheevers states.

above right:

Cheevers with Gary Doak.

the team kind of stagnated—then Harry came in and coached for the rest of the season—then he selected Butch, a former player who lasted a couple seasons—and then they brought in Terry. To find the right player and coach combination isn't easy and certainly the Bruins can attest to that the last couple years and in the past."

Since Don Cherry, who actually played one playoff game for Boston in 1955, there have been 15 head coaches besides interim Sinden. Of the five with the most longevity, four were former Bruins players. This wasn't an unusual phenomena for the traditional clubs, to recruit and to stick with those with organizational ties. However, as coaching becomes more modernized, more technical and video oriented, and some would argue more generic, the emotional element becomes less of a factor around the League. The Bruin's latest GM Peter Chiarelli, with no previous ties to the club, has hired two head coaches with no previous ties. Bringing success and passion to the coaching position within an organization, simply because one possessed those elements as a player, no longer seems to matter as much over time.

Goring took over the head coaching job in Boston the next season after wrapping up his 16-year NHL playing career in 1985. He played his final half season in Boston, after he was better known as an LA King, and well known as a New York Islander. He coached the Bruins for a total of 93 games.

"That's a good word for it—brief," Goring laughs. "We had a real good first year, and we had a lot of young guys over the two years that I did coach. It was my first coaching job. I had come right from playing, and I had a lot of fun with it. I was involved with Ray Bourque, which was a lot of fun. He was a great player and a great practice player. I was able to get Cam Neely's career going with him coming here, so that was a good experience for me. It was a tough ending for me because I was just getting started. I did learn some things along the way. I enjoyed the Boston Bruins when I played for them, and I certainly enjoyed the city. It was the start of a coaching career for me."

General manager Harry Sinden replaced Goring 13 games into Butch's second season, in November of 1986.

"I liked Harry then and I still like Harry today," points out Goring. "You know, he was a tough general manager because he was very much hands-on, but when we got together and talked hockey, he was always a pleasure to be with and I always respected what he needed to do. That was part of his job. I don't have to agree with it or like it, but I understand what he did. We've still maintained a friendship to this day. I always got along with Harry; he's a great hockey guy."

above:

Robert "Butch" Goring left the ice and immediately headed behind the bench in 1985. He coached 93 regular season games and three in the playoffs.

We had just beaten Montreal and eliminated them from the playoffs for the first time in 50 or 55 years.

above:

O'Reilly and John Cunniff were a dynamic coaching duo. A South Boston native, Cunniff was a Boston College All-American, the Beanpot MVP twice, the eventual head coach of the New Jersey Devils, and a long-time coach and developer of talent for the United States national team. He died of throat cancer in May, 2002.

below:

Needham native, high school scoring phenom, and Former WHA scoring star Robbie Ftorek coached the Bruins for almost two full seasons. His tenure ended in March of 2003, when he was replaced on an interim basis by GM Mike O'Connell.

Sinden went from firing one passionate hockey man to hiring the ultimate in passionate Bruins: Terry O'Reilly.

"Butch Goring was the first coach [for me] for a brief stint," recalls then defenseman Al Pedersen. "That's when Terry O'Reilly and John Cunniff came on board, and then after that was Mike Milbury along with Gordie Clark and Ted Sator."

Many ex-players would agree with Pedersen's assessment of O'Reilly and Cunniff, a dynamic hockey duo.

"They were both old school," says Pedersen. "It's sad that John's not with us anymore. He lived…everything he did was hockey, that guy. He was amazing in terms of being dedicated to the game. Terry's just Terry; he was a fair, intense guy. When you played for him you wanted to make sure you left it all out on the ice."

"Terry was my first professional coach here in Boston," remembers longtime Bruins defenseman Don Sweeney. "There was no more inspirational leader than him. He coached the same way he played. His emotions were right there in front of you; you knew what was required of you each and every night: go out and play for the [name on the front of the] jersey and not the name on the back. He bled Boston Bruin hockey. To me, being the player I was, being a player that had to

above:

For almost three full seasons, Terry O'Reilly coached with practically the same intensity with which he played, a leadership trait that has all but vanished from the modern game. "Terry was our emotional focal point," states a former player.

left:

Fiery competitor Brian Sutter coached 2-and-a-half seasons for the Bruins beginning in 1992 and won 61 percent of his games. The former NHL player was one of six Sutter brothers from Viking, Alberta, to play in the League. Assistant Coach Tom McVie on left.

compete each and every night, he was probably the perfect coach for me. He took the things that I could do and had me work on the things that I couldn't do. He really helped me learn how to pass the puck at the NHL level, and just on being a competitive guy each and every night, and that's what he expected of all his players."

"He worked very hard as a coach," adds Hall of Fame forward Cam Neely. "He certainly knows the game. I know guys would certainly try to be accountable for him, because if you didn't give anything but that, he'd let you know."

O'Reilly's feather-in-the-cap coaching moment came in 1988 when his team beat the Montreal Canadiens in the second round of the playoffs, to end a lengthy head-to-head drought.

"When we beat Montreal, we had a two-goal lead and I was looking up at the clock and there was 24, 30 seconds left, and I was still worried, because in my career we had never beaten Montreal in the playoffs," O'Reilly recalls. "And it got down to nine seconds, and I was standing there on the bench as the head coach, thinking, 'They can't score two goals in nine seconds.' Maybe I was getting over-confident. The clock ran down and I remember jumping on the ice, realizing that we had just beaten Montreal and eliminated them from the playoffs for the first time in 50 or 55 years."

O'Reilly's Bruins lost in the Stanley Cup final that year to Edmonton, just as head coach Mike Milbury's Bruins would lose two years later. The two had that unfortunate result in common, and a coaching intensity in common as well.

"They had their own ways of motivating," remembers goalie Reggie Lemelin, who played for both. "They were players' coaches in that they wanted you to succeed. They were on your side, and they were great guys."

Often, it's not a single game or series that defines a coach, it's a single moment—a fact best represented by Steve Kasper. Nine years a forward for Boston, Kasper took over the coaching reins in 1995. He finished his first season nine games above .500. The next season the Bruins finished 19 games below .500. Along the way, Kasper left an unfortunate benchmark by benching Cam Neely and Kevin Stevens during a game in Toronto. It's what he's remembered for.

Chapter 10

above:

Mike Sullivan was victimized by the organization's post-lock-out decisions in 2005-06. A division champ' the year prior to the work stoppage, a completely revamped roster finished last in the division the following season of play. A change at general manager brought an end to Sullivan's tenure after his second season.

left:

It's believed Steve Kasper was only following orders from above when he benched Cam Neely and Kevin Stevens in a game versus Toronto, a move he's remembered for, and which overshadows an excellent career as a Bruins centerman in the eighties.

"I was on the team when Neely got benched, and Kevin Stevens, too," recalls then Bruins forward Tim Sweeney. "I think Kasper—he was a new coach—was trying to gain a little bit of respect by saying no one is playing very well, you guys aren't playing very well. I think what really struck me that was really weird about that was, not only did they dress to play, but then they never played. I think that's what really irked a lot of people because, hey, it's one thing to sit them

above:

Pat Burns won the Jack Adams Award as top NHL coach three times with three different Original Six teams, including Boston in 1997-98. He's the only three-time winner of the Award.

in the stands, but it's another thing to sit them on the bench the whole game." [Was the benching actually ordered by Harry Sinden? If so, the coach never spoke up, took the heat, and eventually lost his job.]

Kasper was replaced by Pat Burns in the spring of 1997, the same year a young Swede began his lengthy playing career as a Bruin in Boston.

"I think all of them [coaches] have had an effect in one way or another," states Bruins forward P.J. Axelsson. "I had Pat Burns when I first got here. He helped me to prepare to play every night. It was different coming from Sweden where you play 36 games or 40 games to 82 games so that was different, and he helped me out with that. The Swedish League was real defensive, so the coach that we had in Sweden before I got here was really defensive minded, so that helped me a lot, especially coming over and having Pat Burns as coach, because he was really defensive."

"I was really intimidated by Pat Burns that first season I was allowed to shoot between the benches," recalls Steve Babineau. "He had this stare, a really intense stare. I had to take his photo from between the benches for the yearbook and I finally had to just go up and ask him, because I didn't want to snap his picture without asking. I had an experience in Toronto when he was coaching the Leafs where he yelled at me for taking strobe pictures during practice, so I was a little cautious with him."

Often, it's not a single game or series that defines a coach; it's a single moment.

Burns's tenure in Boston ended as the new millennium began. A string of six, semi-rapid-fire coaching changes have followed. Inconsistency in a position as important as head coach can be challenging not just for a hockey club's players, but for its front office staff as well. Every personality brings new quirks, rules, and temperaments to the organization.

above:

"Iron" Mike Keenan replaced Burns eight games into 2000-01 and lasted just the one season. As of June 2008, he's held the head coaching position with eight different NHL teams.

"We've been really lucky—I think Claude Julien is the 13th or 14th coach since I've been here and they've all treated me well," says Heidi Holland, who joined the club's media department in the mid-80s. "For a PR person they've all been great. You know, some [media people] have issues with Mike Keenan, but he never met a microphone he didn't like, so for a PR person that was great. Brian Sutter had his Western Canadian farm boy ways and thoughts. Some of his quotes would make you think twice, but I was very lucky with all of the coaches over the years. They were great to deal with. Kasper was good to me. Obviously, media wasn't his favorite thing to do, but he knew the Boston market and he knew the Boston media from playing here for so many years, and he was fine."

"It was easy with guys like Kasper, O'Reilly, Cheevers, and Milbury because they had been players, they all knew me, and they always saw me around the room," points out Babineau. "They knew what I had to do; they understood what I was up to. I could even get pretty good set-up shots from them. Although they were coaches with the team, they were still players in my mind.

"Keenan was a little different. He took down all of the archive photos in the dressing room—Orr, Shore, stuff like that," adds Babineau, "and he even had a weird thing about the team picture. I had taken about 25 of these things, and right after I had everyone set up that year for the photo, he stood up and

above:

Dave Lewis earned renown as an assistant in Detroit under Scotty Bowman, helping to win three Stanley Cups. As Bowman's successor with the Wings, he didn't meet with similar head coaching success. In 2006-'07 in Boston, his team finished six games below .500 and failed to make the playoffs.

below:

Armand "Bep" Guidolin took over with 26 games remaining in the 1972-73 season for legendary Canadiens and Bruins defenseman and defending Cup winning coach Tom Johnson. The former Boston Braves (AHL) coach found the act too tough to follow, or more accurately, his players did.

started critiquing the set-up and where everyone was sitting. It became a joke after that. Every time I had a set-up photo of any sort, I'd laugh and say, 'Did Keenan approve this?'"

Two factors most often affect coaches more than anything else. The first one can prevent a career from burgeoning: a former player realizes that coaching, aside from the competitive element of compiling wins and losses, isn't the same as playing. The camaraderie vanishes, or at least is completely different, and the pressure and the frustration of not being able to control matters on the ice becomes overwhelming. Coaches are hired to be fired, and very few retire on top.

"I don't know if there is a best part about it," states legendary Bruins goalie and former coach Gerry Cheevers. "I figured it out after I took the job, that every year, there were all but one who failed. The only guy that succeeded was the guy who won the Cup. There was one success and however many failures. As a player, you could shake off a loss and prepare yourself for the next game. As a coach, to me it was a much tougher deal. I wouldn't be playing the next game. Playing, I'd jump right back in. As a coach, I took it harder, and I don't think I was programmed for it. Instead of dealing with it yourself, you're looking at it through 40 eyes."

The other factor that can't be controlled is being hired after a legend or a huge success has moved on.

The first example would be former Bruins player Armand "Bep" Guidolin, who followed the last two coaches to win Cups in Boston, the combination of Harry Sinden and then Tom Johnson.

"Bep used to whistle," exclaims Esposito. "He used to whistle at us, and one night he was whistling and I wouldn't come off the ice. And he got angry at me and he said, 'Don't you hear me?' I said, 'I'm not a dog so don't whistle. I'm not going to answer to a whistle. My father used to whistle and I'd come a-runnin', so I'm not answering to a whistle no more.' He and I really didn't get along all that much. I really didn't think he was that great a coach."

Was Bep actually a bad guy or a bad coach? Maybe the new face, the adjustment, contributed to Espo's, and other players' potential dislike. Guidolin coached 104 games in Boston and 21 more in the playoffs. He moved on despite winning more than 73 percent of his games.

Example two is Fred Creighton, who had an impressive winning percentage as well (63.7), one that would earn a coach a lengthy stay anywhere else. Unfortunately for him, Creighton replaced the irreplaceable: Don Cherry.

above:

Fred Creighton had the disadvantage of following larger-than-life Don Cherry as the head coach of the Bruins. He lasted seven games short of a full season despite an excellent winning percentage.

"What I remember about Fred Creighton is that he was kind of a quiet guy. I kind of remember that," says then Bruins forward Al Secord. "I think the toughest part was following the act of Don Cherry. Don was the kind of guy…he approached it as a very simple game. What I liked about the guy [Cherry] was, he let the older guys run the team. The older guys knew when to cut loose and have a good time; they knew when to shut it down. They kept the younger guys in line, and they taught you how to be a team player all the time. The team was very close, they took care of each other, and we didn't have any problems. If a guy created a problem and it got all the way to Don, he was shipped out pretty quick.

"I think after Don Cherry being such a character, and I think also [because] he was the best coach I ever had, I think [for Fred] it was such a tough act to follow. I mean, he took over pretty much right after Cherry was fired, and I think that was the thing—it just wasn't the same thing," Secord adds.

Timing of tenure is uncontrollable, more a matter of circumstance than an actual element to the job.

For fans in Boston, regardless of when a bench boss is hired, physicality must be part of the coaching formula. Even in this most modern incarnation of the rules and game, the elements that mean the most to Bruins fans are pretty straightforward: Combine winning with toughness. Rough 'em up on the ice, while you're roughing 'em up on the scoreboard. Simple advice for any Bruins coach.

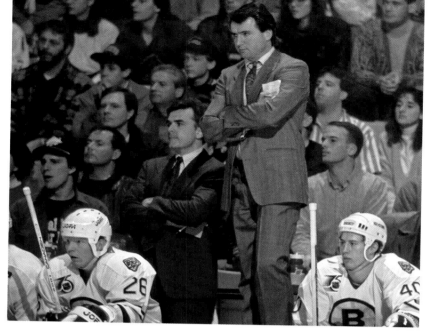

right:

It may be unfair to state Rick Bowness is a better assistant coach than he is a head, although in nine different seasons with five different clubs, he's only led a team to the playoffs once. That was in his lone Boston season, 1991-92, when the B's were swept by eventual Cup champ Pittsburgh in the third round. He was replaced by Brian Sutter after the one season.

Coaches whose tenures included or began after 1973-74, the season in which Steve Babineau took his first professional photo at a Bruins game.

REGULAR SEASON STATISTICS	GP	W	L	T/OTL	W%
Rick Bowness | 1991–1992 Fired after 1992 playoff sweep at the hands of the Penguins	80	36	32	12	.525
Pat Burns | 1997–2000 Coach of the year in three cities: Montreal, Toronto, and Boston	254	105	103	52	.516
Gerry Cheevers | 1980–1985 Reluctant to coach despite success behind bench	376	204	126	46	.604
Don Cherry | 1974–1979 Now considered one of Canada's most famous and influential persons	400	231	105	64	.658
Fred Creighton | 1979–1980 Simple problem of following a larger-than-life legend	73	40	20	13	.637
Robbie Ftorek | 2001–2003 High school star in Needham; 1972 U.S. Olympian	155	76	52	27	.577
Butch Goring | 1985–1986 Straight from the ice to the bench	93	42	38	13	.522
Armand "Bep" Guidolin | 1972–1974 Started as a player at age 16 in NHL; still youngest ever	104	72	23	9	.736
Claude Julien | 2007–2011 Four straight playoff appearances, a Jack Adams Award, and a Stanley Cup	328	179	103	46	.635
Steve Kasper | 1995–1997 Disliked for benching Neely & Stevens in Toronto	164	66	78	20	.463
Mike Keenan | 2000–2001 "Iron Mike"; hired by Sinden, fired by O'Connell	74	33	28	13	.538
Dave Lewis | 2006–2007 Won multiple Cups as an assistant coach in Detroit, but didn't translate	82	35	41	6	.463
Mike Milbury | 1989–1991 Last to coach Bruins to the Stanley Cup Final	160	90	49	21	.628

REGULAR SEASON STATISTICS	GP	W	L	T/OTL	W%
Mike O'Connell | 2003 Brief stint to figure out Sullivan was replacement for Ftorek	9	3	3	3	.500
Terry O'Reilly | 1986–1989 Coach when Bruins snapped 45-year playoff drought to Canadiens	227	115	86	26	.564
Harry Sinden | 1966–1970, 1980, 1985 Greatest GM never to win Stanley Cup; won as coach in 1970	327	153	116	58	.557
Mike Sullivan | 2003–2006 Victim of poor post-lock-out financial strategies of team hierarchy	164	70	56	38	.543
Brian Sutter | 1992–1995 Fired the same day the Celtics fired Chris Ford	216	120	73	23	.609

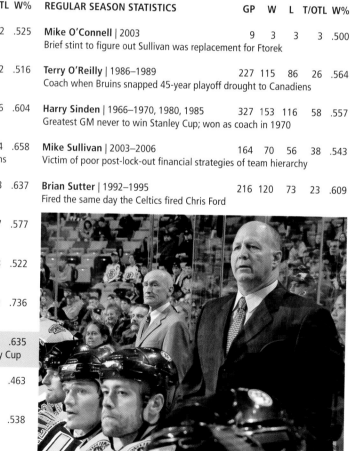

CHAPTER

11

MASKED MEN

above:

Gerry Cheevers's stitch-art is arguably the most famous mask design in hockey history. Simplistic yet barbaric, the stitch marks indicate where the goaltender would have been hit. "That would have been my face," laughs Cheevers.

left:

A focused Andy Moog makes a glove save. Acquired from Edmonton in March of 1988, Moog backstopped the Bruins to the Stanley Cup final in 1988 and 1990.

Of the goaltenders on the Bruins Hall of Fame list, an overwhelming majority made just a brief stop in Boston. Names like Harry "Apple Cheeks" Lumley [78 games with Boston], Jacques Plante [8 games], Terry Sawchuk [102 games], and Bernie Parent [57 games] are all more readily identifiable with other organizations. Only Cecil "Tiny" Thompson from the 1920s and '30s, Frank Brimsek from the 1930s and '40s, and Gerry Cheevers from the 1960s and '70s are legitimate black-and-gold Bruins. Cheevers is the only post-expansion netminder, and the only one from photographer Steve Babineau's era, to earn his way into the Hall.

The list of Bruins netminders who "stole the show" is short: Many simply held down the fort while a talented and feisty group of skaters in front of them, particularly defensemen, commanded much of the attention. Part of it may just be a coincidence, part of it may be impatience with development, or part of it could be the physical, low-risk style of play, which prevented goaltenders in Boston from consistently having to stand on their heads. For whatever reason, goalies fall behind blueliners and forwards in the Bruins annals of greatness.

When listing prominent Bruins netminders, mainly because he manned the crease for Boston's last two Cups, Cheevers's name first comes to mind.

His crease partner for those title runs, veteran Eddie Johnston, is the last to play every game of his team's season [all 70 in 1963–64], but as the Bruins climb into Cup contention in the late '60s, Cheevers emerged as the choice.

CHAPTER

11

MASKED MEN

"He was very consistent," states former teammate John "Pie" McKenzie. "He helped win some very important games for us, a championship goalie."

"'Cheesie' was a big-game goaltender," proclaims Babineau. "When the game was on the line, he was there. He never wanted to practice; he'd take as few shots as he could. He didn't want to stand there and take slapshots, but in the game he was huge."

One could argue that Cheevers is not only the greatest Bruins goalie of the modern era, but the greatest goalie of all time. Only Frank "Mr. Zero" Brimsek, for two stints beginning in 1938, with one more win and nine more shutouts, has similar numbers. Cheevers had several fewer losses and a similar goals-against-average.

"Cheesie was fading out at the beginning of my career," adds Babineau, "but I remember from watching just as a fan and as a photographer what a great goalie he could be. Then of course, there's the mask."

Cheevers's mask artwork, made up of simple black stitch marks on the spots where the puck had made contact, has to

Cheevers's mask artwork, has to be hockey's greatest ever. "That would have been my face," states Cheevers.

be hockey's greatest ever. Despite the simplicity, it remains unforgettable and sends a strong message. It was assistant trainer John "Frosty" Forristall who first put the magic marker to Cheevers's mask.

"That would have been my face," states Cheevers, who began his career sans protection.

The goaltending carousel in Boston has been consistent throughout the years, thus making Cheevers an exception to the rule. Only five other men's names pop up when one thinks of decent consistency during the last three-and-a-half decades. The acrobatic Gilles Gilbert [277 Bruins games played] played a prominent role with the Lunch Pail Gang. Byron Dafoe [283 games] nailed down 25 shut-outs as a

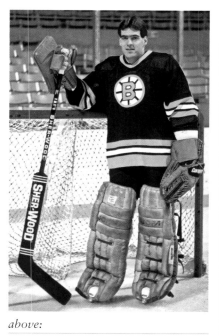

above:

Pete Peeters posing without his mask.

right:

Pete Peeters was the last Bruins goaltender to win the Vezina Trophy as the League's best keeper. To the goalie's left, that's a glimpse of former Bruin Peter McNab with Vancouver, seeking a scoring chance.

Bruin at the turn of the millennium and was runner-up for the Vezina Trophy behind Dominik Hasek in 1999. But his teams only passed the first round of the playoffs once. Reggie Lemelin [183 games] had some big playoff wins and helped the team to the final twice. Andy Moog [261 games] fell into place right along with Lemelin, while the 1982-83 Vezina Trophy winner Pete Peeters [171 games] was the next closest thing to goaltending greatness.

In his fourth year in the League, his first in Boston after a trade from Philadelphia, Peeters put together a 31-game unbeaten streak, which fell one short of the NHL record of 32, set in 1971–72 by Cheevers. Peeters's streak ended on February 16th in Buffalo.

"Gerry was our head coach, and late in the game when we knew we were going to lose in Buffalo, he sent all of the guys off the bench out to me, to congratulate me and such," Peeters remembers. "That was a special moment and a great gesture I thought. He was a pretty special coach. As a former goalie, he helped me with the mental aspects, how to deal with the trials and tribulations.

Peeters and the Bruins made it to the conference finals that playoff season before bowing out to the eventual Cup champs, the New York Islanders.

These days, Peeters continues to take Cheevers's advice one step further, as the goalie coach for the Edmonton Oilers.

above:

Gilles Gilbert was a fixture for the Bruins as a tandem goaltender. After arriving in 1973 he was the number one, then shared time and played behind Cheevers from 1975 to 1980. Toronto's "Cowboy" Bill Flett is looking for the rebound while Bruin Daryl Edestrand approaches. The photo is from the 1974-75 season.

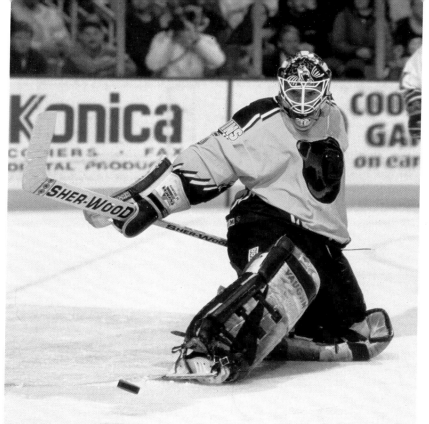

right:

Bill Ranford had two stints in Boston a decade apart. He was first drafted by the B's in 1985 as the 52nd overall pick. Both times he was traded, a goalkeeper came the other way as part of the deal, Andy Moog from Edmonton in March 1988, and Jim Carey from Washington in March 1997. Here, Ranford dons the B's "Bear-head" third jersey, referred to by some jokingly as the "Pooh jersey." Less than ferocious, the image wasn't based on the lovable character obviously, but on a bear painting that hung behind Harry Sinden's desk.

left:

Gerry Cheevers departed Boston for the start-up World Hockey Assocation after the 1972 Cup. He returned in 1975. Here, Cheevers recovers from a save, with Cleveland Baron J.P. Parise on the doorstep.

"I try to emphasize lateral motion; it's something I learned from [the late goaltending coach] Warren Strelow in Washington," Peeters says. "When things go south for a goalie, when he gets deep in his crease, when he goes in the tank, it's usually because he's lost his lateral motion. I wish I had understood that much earlier. When I played, I got traded every time I went in the tank."

Peeters had great years in Philly, Boston, and Washington, but remembers the Bruins with the most fondness.

"Our [Edmonton's] AHL affiliate is in Springfield [Massachusetts] now, so as goalie coach I'm able to sneak back to Boston now and again," Peeters says. "I have flashbacks of the great times, the people, the fans, and playing for Cheevers."

While Cheesie's career may be the Bruins' benchmark, and Peeters's single season is almost unmatched, the same can't be said for Cleon Daskalakis and his efforts. A Boston native who produced All-America numbers at Boston University, Cleon's pro career wasn't "all that." Cleon played a grand total of 12 NHL games for the Bruins, and as a local, he still gets teased by the other alumni about his career stats. Cleon remains a fixture in town, as the president for Celebrity Marketing, which handles philanthropic endeavors for pro athletes, and represents Hall of Famer Bruin Ray Bourque and other pro athletes.

"It was the fulfillment of a dream," states Daskalakis. "I grew up in Canton, Massachusetts. There's pictures of me when I'm 10 and 11 years old with a Bruins jacket on, and I always aspired to be Gerry Cheevers: that was my goal. I idolized him and Bobby Orr. When I was a kid, I dreamed of being the Bruins goaltender. In my high school yearbook under class predictions, they predicted that I'd be goalie for the Bruins. So, when the opportunity came, I was a free agent, the Bruins showed interest, and it worked out. I think it's almost hard to believe, hard to think about the dream of playing for the team you grew up with, but then to have that happen! I wouldn't change a thing—even though I didn't play much—to play in Boston.

"A lot of my friends were guys that were hurt a lot," Cleon continues. "Being a second or third goaltender, I'd spend time hanging out with the hurt guys, training at the same time, taking practice shots when they were recovering. That's part of the reason why Gord Kluzak and I are such good friends. He had injuries quite a bit while I was there."

Defenseman Kluzak was Daskalakis's best man at his wedding in Greece: the ultimate symbol of camaraderie on the ice—and off the ice.

While a number of position players from New England have had a huge impact on the Bruins' success over the years, it's simply not the case for goaltenders. The region has produced solid NHL netminders, but very few who have helped the Bruins. In fact, the list is short. For example, Jim Stewart, born in Cambridge, played one game for the B's, and Matt DelGuidice, from Connecticut, played 11. Only Olympic Gold Medalist Jim Craig and Dorchester native Jim Carey had definitive impacts, and the impacts were felt elsewhere or outside the NHL.

above:

This photo was taken by amateur photographer Steve Babineau from his obstructed view seat in the stadium section of the old Garden. Netminder Eddie Johnston retired prior to Babs getting his press credentials and becoming a professional shooter. Based on ticket stubs, Babs believes he took this photo during the 1970-71 season.

Dorchester native Jim Carey came from Washington in a trade that sent Bill Ranford to the Cap's in 1997. After Carey had won a Vezina Trophy in DC, his career slowly fizzled, it's believed mostly due to his lack of interest in playing the position.

Jim Craig returned to his home town to sign with the Bruins in 1980-81 after playing just four games at the end of the previous season for the Atlanta Flames. The former Boston University Terrier won Gold with Team USA in 1980 with the "Miracle" team, but then his pro career was short. He played 23 games in all for Boston.

Possibly, the goaltender who best represents Boston ideals is one of Boston's most recent. Tim Thomas isn't a New Englander—he's from Flint, Michigan—but he does represent the concepts of perseverance and hard work as well as anyone. By chance, Thomas ended up in the region playing college hockey at the University of Vermont. With teammates and future NHLers Martin St. Louis and Eric Perrin, Thomas helped lead the Catamounts to their first NCAA Frozen Four. From there, he was drafted by Quebec (Colorado), but was released by the Avalanche. After a brief stint in the Edmonton organization, Thomas headed overseas and played in Finland and in Sweden. After catching the eye of NHL scouts, he was signed by the Bruins as a free agent in 2001. By then he was already 27 years old.

"They decided to give me a chance," Thomas remembers, "and I had a really good camp. But when they broke camp, they kept two other goalies in Providence, including Andrew Raycroft, and I was under contract to the Bruins, headed back to Finland."

After a season there, Thomas returned to the Boston organization in 2002–03, where he was called up to the NHL for the first time, playing four games (three wins, one loss), including a win in his first start in Edmonton.

"I was very emotional coming off the ice [after] the first game," admits Thomas, smiling, "and *Hockey Night in Canada* pulled me aside for an interview, so I had to put on a straight face right away and pretend I wasn't that emotional."

The next blip for Timmy: the NHL lockout. He went back to Finland to become league MVP one season, and then came back to the Bruins, only to be shipped to Providence once again. Finally, midway through 2005–06, due to injuries in the lineup, Thomas earned a full-time gig. He signed a three-year contract that season after single-handedly helping the team stay in the playoff race in the weeks prior to the Olympic break.

"After getting called up in January, I ended up winning a lot of games and ended up winning the [Bruins] Seventh Player Award, so it was a season of highs and lows, that's for sure," says Thomas.

A new benchmark came in 2008, when he was named to the NHL Eastern Conference All-Star team. Thomas played the third period and ended up winning the game.

"I've hit a few milestones that I'm proud of," says Thomas, "but hopefully we can hit a few more."

Not bad for a kid whose childhood dream was to play for his local pro team, the Flint Generals of the IHL.

above:

Andrew Raycroft looked like a world beater in 2003-04 before the NHL work stoppage, winning the Calder Trophy as rookie of the year. After the lockout he was a contract hold-out, he suffered an injury, and his time in Boston went downhill before being dealt to Toronto in the summer of 2006.

One thing Thomas hasn't experienced on a regular basis is the thrill and intensity of the NHL playoffs. Aside from Cheevers, one of the Boston goalies whose seen more than most is Reggie Lemelin. Lemelin was the netminder in 1988 when the Bruins beat the Canadiens in the playoffs for the first time in 45 years.

"The whole playoffs were great," states Lemelin. "To me, it didn't mean the same as it did to the team, and some of the players, and to the organization. It was my first year in Boston, so I didn't feel the same thing that these guys felt playing Montreal—what it meant. I had played for Atlanta/Calgary for nine years. I hadn't been part of this rivalry and I came in with a different attitude and view. Beating Montreal was great, because I felt for the other guys on the team, and the management and the fans. I was happy for that part there, but as far as I was concerned, we hadn't won the Cup—we had beaten Montreal in the second round. It didn't mean as much to me, although it was an important step. For all of the fans around, it was as if we'd won the Stanley Cup. It was incredible."

> For all of the fans around, it was as if we'd won the Stanley Cup. It was incredible.

The Bruins would go on to earn a chance at the Cup that season against Edmonton in the finals and again two seasons later, both times with Lemelin as one of the backstops.

"We had a better chance in the '90 series than we did in the '88," Reggie points out. "Nineteen eighty-eight—a lot of things happened along the way. It was crazy. It was the year of the doughnut thing with the ref [after a tough loss to Boston, New Jersey coach Jim Schoenfeld called referee Don Koharski a pig and told him to "have another donut"], the year the lights went out, and it was also the year we finally beat Montreal in the second round. Nineteen ninety—I thought we had a better hockey club, they [Edmonton] had lost Gretzky, they had lost Fuhr, some of their core players. The first game, we played a pretty good game. Glen Wesley [Bruins defenseman] missed the [wide open] net in the overtime. We were all

below:

Along with Gilbert/Cheevers, the Reggie Lemelin/Andy Moog goaltending tandem was arguably one of the best two in Bruins history.

above:

On January 24, 1987, Steve Babineau, using flash strobes, snapped a photo of Reggie Lemelin of the Calgary Flames during pregame warm-up as Lemelin looked up at the ceiling of the Garden. Lemelin noticed the strobes, was spooked, and early in the first period asked the referee to tell Babs to stop taking pictures. He signed with Boston the next season and forgot the incident, much to the relief of the team's nervous photographer.

standing on the bench thinking it was over; then it goes three overtimes and we lose. Then the next night, they had gained so much confidence they won the game pretty bad. From that point on we just never recovered. I really believe if we win that first game we're in good shape and it's maybe [a] different series."

During that playoff season, Lemelin experienced one of the goaltending quirks, or realities, of postseason hockey: when a coach [Mike Milbury] sticks with the goalie who won the most recent game. With Captain Ray Bourque injured and out of the lineup, Lemelin was replaced in Game 4 of the opening series against Hartford with the score 5-2 for the Whalers. Andy Moog came in, the Bruins scored four unanswered goals to win the game. Boston would go on to win the series in seven.

"He took over in that game and won, and we won again, and we went on to the next round against Montreal and we won in five games, and then we played Washington and won

in four, and he was playing well, and we kept going, and that stuff happens," explains Lemelin. "He and we kept winning, so we go with it."

Most recently, Lemelin is a goaltending coach in the NHL for the Philadelphia Flyers. This, after a 15-year NHL career and 236 regular season wins.

"Toward the end, no question about it, I was always talking to the younger players. I didn't view the younger players as a threat to my career at that point, so I was always trying to help them by showing them the tricks and discussing the game with them," Coach Lemelin states. "I think that's why Andy and I had such a good relationship. He was six years younger than me when he joined the Bruins and I actually helped him out. It was my first year with the Bruins and he came in at the deadline, and we went all the way to the final, and we had a very healthy relationship. Two or three years later he took over."

If only Cleon Daskalakis had had Reggie as a teammate.

"I backed up Pete Peeters, Doug Keans, Pat Riggin, and Bill Ranford," lists Cleon. "One of my favorite goaltenders

above:

Doug Keans played 154 games in net for the Bruins, a solid back-up during the mid-1980s. Here, Keans plays the puck up the boards, away from Montreal Canadiens Captain Bob Gainey.

that I didn't get to play with was Reggie Lemelin. He was the type of goaltender…me as a young guy, I really could have benefited from him. He's so intelligent about the position, about the game, not only the physical elements but also the mental aspects of the game. He always jokes with me and says, 'You'd have had an amazing career if I was around,' and I know that. He had an ability to break things down, and teach, and had perseverance. He's the one goalie I wish I had played with. I think he would have made a difference in my career. I didn't miss him by that much, maybe a couple years."

Lemelin responds with laughter. "I've seen him play some alumni games and I started to play some alumni games and several times I'd say to him, 'How did you not make it big? You've got a lot of good stuff in your game.' I'm not sure if I could have helped him—I wasn't there then—but maybe."

below:

Sussex, England, native "Lord" Byron Dafoe manned the crease for the Bruins for five seasons beginning in 1997. He lost only 104 of the 283 games he played in Boston, and tallied 25 shut-outs.

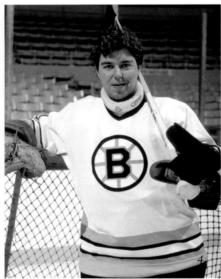

1. Robbie Tallas   2. Vincent Riendeau   3. Cleon Daskalakis   4. Pat Riggin   5. Blaine Lacher   6. Dave Reece   7. Jim Pettie

8. *John Grahame*   9. *Ken Broderick*   10. *Craig Billington*   11. *Marco Baron*   12. *Daniel Berthiaume*

left:

Surfer dude [now minister] John Blue from Huntington Beach, California, and the more successful veteran Jon Casey from Grand Rapids, Minnesota, gave it their best effort for the B's during the 1993-94 campaign. Both moved on right after, the flopper Blue played 5 more NHL games, Casey played 43 more.

Goalies whose careers included or began after 1973-74, the season in which Steve Babineau took his first professional photo at a Bruins game.

BRUINS REGULAR SEASON STATISTICS	GP	W	L	T/OT	GAA	SO
Alex Auld—Thunder Bay, ON	23	9	7	5	2.32	2
#29 | 2007–2008 | Two-career shut-out losses, in shoot-outs						
Scott Bailey—Calgary, AB	19	6	6	2	3.42	0
#39 | 1995–1997 | Victimized by a four-goal Mario Lemieux night						
Mike Bales—Prince Albert, SK	1	0	0	0	2.40	0
#30 | 1992–1993 | Scored goal two seasons ago in German pros						
Marco Baron—Montreal, QC	64	31	24	5	3.40	1
#31, 33 | 1979–1983 | Pro debut in same game as Jim Stewart						
Yves Belanger—Baie Comeau, QC	8	2	0	3	3.48	0
#31 | 1979–1980 | Cheevers injury opened the door for him						
Daniel Berthiaume—Longueuil, QC	8	1	4	2	3.16	0
#31, 50 | 1991–1992 | 2-17-1 in Ottawa's inaugural season						
Craig Billington—London, ON	35	15	14	3	3.35	1
#1 | 1994–1996 | 15-year NHL career as the ideal back-up						
John Blue—Huntington Beach, CA	41	14	16	7	2.94	1
#39, 45 | 1992–1994 | Face injury with surfboard one summer						
Ken Broderick—Toronto, ON	20	9	8	1	2.61	1
#31 | 1973–1975 | Team Canada; '64 Olympics; no medals						
Ross Brooks—Toronto, ON	54	37	7	6	2.64	4
#30 | 1972–1975 | Tied NHL mark with 14-game win streak, '73–'74						
Jim Carey—Dorchester, MA	29	8	15	1	3.52	2
#30 | 1996–1998 | Vezina in Washington; didn't like his job						
Jon Casey—Grand Rapids, MI	57	30	15	9	2.88	4
#30 | 1993–1994 | Dubbed "Technicolor 5-hole" by writer						
Gerry Cheevers— St. Catharines, ON	416	229	101	74	2.89	26
#30 | 1965–1972, 1975–1980 | Two Stanley Cups and a legendary mask						

BRUINS REGULAR SEASON STATISTICS	GP	W	L	T/OT	GAA	SO
Tim Cheveldae—Melville, SK	2	0	1	0	3.23	0
#31 | 1996–1997 | Goal partner in Detroit named Alain Chevrier						
Jim Craig—North Easton, MA	23	9	7	6	3.68	0
#30 | 1980–1981 | Hero of Team USA Olympic Gold in 1980						
Byron Dafoe—Sussex, England	283	132	104	40	2.30	25
#34 | 1997–2002 | "Lord Byron" Vezina finalist in 1999						
Cleon Daskalakis—Boston, MA	12	3	4	1	4.86	0
#35 | 1984–1987 | Better known as Ray Bourque's PR man						
Matt DelGuidice—West Haven, CT	11	2	5	1	3.87	0
#33, 70 | 1990–1991 | East Haven Comets; then University of Maine						
Manny Fernandez—Etobicoke, ON	32	18	10	3	3.62	2
#35 | 2007–2009 | Arrived from Minnesota grumpy with a bad knee						
Brian Finley—Sault Ste. Marie, ON	2	0	1	0	3.05	0
#60 | 2006–2007 | Sixth overall pick in 1999, Nashville						

BRUINS REGULAR SEASON STATISTICS	GP	W	L	T/OT	GAA	SO
Norm Foster—Vancouver, BC #29, 36 | 1990–1991 | Won 1986 National Title with Michigan State	3	2	1	0	4.57	0
Gilles Gilbert—St. Esprit, QC #1 | 1973–1980 | Traded for fellow goalie Rogie Vachon in 1980	277	155	73	39	2.95	16
John Grahame—Denver, CO #30, 47 | 1999–2003 | Won Calder Cup in 1999, Ron's son	76	29	30	9	2.77	4
Ron Grahame—Victoria, BC #31 | 1977–1978 | Traded to LA for '79 draft pick, Ray Bourque	40	26	6	7	2.76	3
Jeff Hackett—London, ON #30 | 2002–2003 | Goalie coach with Avalanche	18	8	9	0	3.21	1
Doug Keans—Pembroke, ON #31 | 1983–1988 | Took over starting job from Pete Peeters	154	83	46	13	3.33	4
Blaine Lacher—Medicine Hat, AB #31 | 1994–1996 | '92 Lake Superior State National Champs	47	22	16	4	2.80	4
Reggie Lemelin—Quebec City, QC #1 | 1987–1993 | In net to beat Habs in '88 to break jinx	183	92	62	17	3.09	6
Joey McDonald—Pictou, NS #31 | 2006–2007 | March win in NJ kept brief playoff hopes alive	7	2	2	1	2.68	0
Mike Moffat—Galt, ON #30 | 1981–1984 | Won the Buffalo series in 1982 playoffs	19	7	7	2	4.29	0
Andy Moog—Penticton, BC #35 | 1987–1993 | On 3 Cup winners in Edmonton	261	136	75	36	3.08	13
Pete Peeters—Edmonton, AB #1 | 1982–1986 | Won '83 Vezina, with 31-game unbeaten streak	171	91	57	16	2.99	9
Jim Pettie—Toronto, ON #31 | 1976–1979 | Prominent role in Plimpton book *Open Net* in '77	21	9	7	2	3.68	1
Felix Potvin—Anjou, QC #29 | 2003–2004 | "Felix the Cat" fought goalie Ron Hextall	28	12	8	6	2.50	4
Bill Ranford—Brandon, MB #30 | 1985–1987, 1995–1997 | Won Smythe Trophy with Edmonton vs. Boston	122	52	49	14	3.19	6
Tuukka Rask—Savonlinna, Finland #40 | 2007–2011 | "Finnish Flash" obtained from Toronto for Raycroft	79	36	27	8	2.25	8

BRUINS REGULAR SEASON STATISTICS	GP	W	L	T/OT	GAA	SO
Andrew Raycroft—Belleville, ON #1 | 2000–2006 | Calder Trophy hold-out; then injury	108	43	46	10	2.62	3
Dave Reece—Troy, NY #29, 30 | 1975–1976 | Sole victim of Darryl Sittler's 10-point game	14	7	5	2	3.32	2
Vincent Riendeau—St. Hyacinthe, QC #37 | 1993–1995 | First North American NHLer to jump to Russia	29	10	12	2	3.00	1
Pat Riggin—Kincardine, ON #1, 30 | 1985–1987 | Started career with Atlanta Flames	49	20	16	9	3.36	1
Roberto Romano—Montreal, QC #1 | 1986–1987 | Arrived from Pittsburgh for Pat Riggin	1	0	1	0	6.00	0
Philippe Sauve—Buffalo, NY #35 | 2006–2007 | His goalie father Bob a B's archrival in Buffalo	2	0	0	0	5.85	0
Paxton Schafer—Medicine Hat, AB #1 | 1996–1997 | 10 minor league teams; 3 NHL games	3	0	0	0	4.68	0
Steve Shields—Toronto, ON #31 | 2002–2003 | Journeyman; wore Cheevers's testimonial mask	36	12	13	9	2.75	0
Jordan Sigalet—New Westminster, BC #57 | 2005–2006 | Played goal with multiple sclerosis	1	0	0	0	0.00	0
Peter Skudra—Riga, Latvia #35 | 2000–2001 | NHL for eight seasons, then to Russian League	25	6	12	1	3.33	0
Jim Stewart—Cambridge, MA #31 | 1979–1980 | Called up same day as M. Baron; started; lost	1	0	1	0	15.00	0
Don Sylvestri—Sudbury, ON #30 | 1984–1985 | ECAC 1st-Team All-Star with Clarkson	3	0	0	2	3.53	0
Robbie Tallas—Edmonton, AB #35 | 1995–2000 | Heart attack while playing in Finland	87	26	35	10	2.85	3
Tim Thomas—Flint, MI #70, 30 | 2002–2003, 2005–2011 | "Tank" won Conn Smythe Trophy at age 37	319	161	102	44	2.50	44
Hannu Toivonen—Kalvola, Finland #33, 54 | 2005–2007 | Ankle injury sidetracked progress	38	12	14	5	3.33	1
Rogie Vachon—Palmarolle, QC #1 | 1980–1982 | End of career with B's; had three Cups with Habs	91	44	30	12	3.47	2
Kay Whitmore—Sudbury, ON #31 | 2000–2001 | 26th overall pick for Hartford in 1985	5	1	2	0	5.32	0

12

BLUELINERS

above:

In a photo taken at the Hartford Civic Center, Brad Park skates away from Hartford Whaler forward Jordy Douglas. "Park is the best defenseman never to win the Norris," touts photographer Steve Babineau.

left:

Boston defensemen Garry Galley and Don Sweeney celebrate a goal. Galley came via free agency in 1988 and stayed three-and-a-half seasons while Sweeney was a near lifer, spending all but 63 of his 1,115 NHL games in Boston. He later moved to the Bruins front office.

The characteristics that define most Bruins defensemen over the years are somewhat generic: play hard, hit, fight. Characteristics New Englanders would want in any hockey player. Or maybe so many Boston defensemen simply seem generic, because for so long, five or six of them on the roster would be residing in a shadow of greatness—greatness which, intended or not, took the spotlight off everyone else.

Eddie Shore, Bobby Orr, Ray Bourque: the first blueliners to pop into everyone's mind the moment the words "Bruins" and "defenseman" are mentioned in the same sentence. Believe it or not, there have been many other fine defensemen working the blue line for the Bruins over the past 35 years.

Brad Park for example played 501 games with Boston, 1,100-plus in the NHL, and his plaque resides in the Hall of Fame.

"Basically, Park was hated by the Bruins fans for a time there when he played for the Rangers," remembers Steve Babineau. "He and Orr were rivals. I remember them fighting one night. Until Bobby got hurt and Park came in as the savior replacement, Boston fans didn't like him. They did actually

left:

In his first year with the team, Brad Park is shown wearing a B's road jersey with the 1976 U.S. bicentennial patch on the shoulder. Taken at the Montreal Forum on one of Babineau's first road excursions, the man back right is legendary bilingual Habs PA Announcer Claude Mouton.

overlap for about a dozen [ten] games. I remember them working together at the point on the power play. Back and forth, back and forth, and finally one of them blasted it home."

"Brad was a great teacher, mentor, and a guy who showed us how to play the game, and how to handle ourselves outside the game," states Ray Bourque.

"Park was an unbelievable passer! Just unbelievable. He'd get it up to the blue line and then he'd make a seeing-eye pass to someone up-ice," Babineau says. "I remember him making passes to Jean Ratelle and Bobby Schmautz. Park's remembered for having that big goal against Buffalo [Park scored a game-7 overtime winner on April 24, 1983, against Buffalo to win the division final]. He was like a professor. It seemed like he was able to slow the game down."

Park spent eight seasons with the Bruins. He and the other Hall of Famers weren't the only D-men to enjoy lengthy, prosperous careers in Boston.

> I remember them working together at the point on the power play. Back and forth, back and forth, and finally one of them blasted it home.

Maritimer Don Sweeney played all but 63 games of his 16 NHL seasons in Boston as a steady partner to Bourque and others.

"I came in at a time with some guys that had been around this organization for a while," says Sweeney, "and [they] felt like the Spoked B was tattooed on their ass, so to speak. That's how I learned, and I carried that with me."

above:

It's believed Hall-of-Fame defenseman Ray Bourque spent more shifts during his career with Don Sweeney than with any other defenseman. Here, the two lace up in the "new" Garden Bruins dressing room.

Since Sweeney entered the League in 1988, just 20 years ago, the attitude and devotion surrounding a team and its emblem has changed dramatically, probably more so than anything else because of the money involved and the level of free agency. It's a tendency that can be overcome.

"With the changeover and some of the younger players coming in, some of those things go by the wayside," Sweeney explains. "The onus is on older players to make guys understand and appreciate what it means to wear that [sweater], and point to the guys that have done it before them. For a period of time there, I thought that had waned a bit, but now being involved with the organization in a different capacity [Director of Hockey Operations and Player Development], and seeing Cam back here, and knowing the direction the GM wants to take things, *is* going to take things, and the way the

left:

The Bruins selected Glen Wesley 3rd overall in the 1987 draft out of Portland of the Western League. He spent seven seasons with Boston before being traded to the Hartford/ Carolina organization in the summer of 1994. He won a Cup with the Hurricanes in 2006 and retired in May, 2008 after 21 NHL seasons.

right:

The Bruins were looking for another great defenseman when they chose big Gord Kluzak of the Western League Billings Bighorns as the first overall pick in the 1982 draft, ahead of forward Brian Bellows, and ahead of future Hall-of-Fame defensemen Scott Stevens and Phil Housley. Knee problems shortened Kluzak's career to 299 games.

coach handles things day to day, I think guys are starting to garner a greater appreciation for that. For me, that says an awful lot about where our organization is headed."

Sweeney played college hockey at Harvard, making him well aware of the Bruins' tradition, via osmosis across the Charles River.

I remember walking into the locker room for the first time at training camp, and to see all of those sweaters hanging there!

Meanwhile, many others obtained a love, devotion, and respect for the Spoked B simply by growing up near Boston. Not unlike Ontario natives playing for the Maple Leafs, certain Quebec natives playing for Montreal, or a kid from Windsor playing for the Red Wings, the hockey hotbed that is New England produces an endless list of Bruins fans who become Bruins.

"It was extra special for me and for any kid growing up in Boston to play locally," says 1980s Bruins defenseman Frank Simonetti. "To have an opportunity to play for your hometown team it was—certainly to play in the NHL was a treat—but to play for your hometown team was extra special."

Regional connections, college ties, and simple respect for hockey history affected others.

"It was a dream come true," admits Mike Milbury. "I played at Colgate and I really didn't have any anticipation of a professional career. I didn't get drafted. They used to have what they called a negotiation list, and each team could put four players on their negotiation list. They could drop a name, add a name; it was another one of those quasi-slavery rules. So after a tournament in Syracuse, Boston put me on their list. At the end of my senior year I got called up to the old Boston Braves and played a few games with them, and based on how I did there, they [the B's] gave me a tryout. My first day of training camp, eight o'clock practice for the veterans and I was on at ten. I was there two hours ahead to be ready."

"My childhood years were through the '70s, and I watched the Bruins, and that's when they were the Big Bad Bruins and I loved watching them," says Pennsylvania native Bob Beers, who spent 77 games as a defenseman with Boston. "So to have the ability to put that jersey on...I remember walking into the locker room for the first time at training camp, and to see all of those sweaters hanging there! I never got to play in any exhibition games that year. When I actually got to play in my first game it was down in Hartford and I walked into the locker room and you see all the sweaters hung nicely, the equipment guys did everything right; you walk in there and you see that, and you see that jersey and that was...it really hit. The feeling was unbelievable, and then you start to see the guys filter into the locker room...you realize it's for real."

below:

Mike Milbury, out of Colgate University and fresh off two years with Rochester in the American League, joined the Lunch Pail Gang and head coach Don Cherry in 1976. He went on to play more than 750 games as a Bruin.

above:

Gary Doak, known as "Sammy" because according to teammate Eddie Johnston, when they first came up, Doak had a nose like rat-packer Sammy Davis Jr. As is often the case in hockey, the name stuck in perpetuity. Doak, who won a Cup with the B's in 1970, is being chased by Canadiens left wing Yvon Lambert.

"Boston was the greatest place to play," says longtime D-man Gary Doak, who like Sweeney, Milbury, Simonetti, and Beers, remains in the area. "I played in Vancouver, Detroit, and New York, but out of all those cities, Boston is a big city, but it's also a small city you can get around easy. We'd go to the North Shore, be at the rink in 15 minutes. We practiced up on 114 at the Danvers twin rinks. Everything was pretty unique. The people and fans of New England, you won't find a better group of fans than right here in Boston."

"I think being on an Original Six team is special in itself," states 333-game Bruins' defenseman Al Pedersen. "Not only at home but on the road, people come to see the Original Six teams. To be a part of the history of Boston sports...there's definitely more pressure playing in a town like Boston, but it made you better, and it made you appreciate the sport and the city that much more."

Pride in city, pride in team, and pride in emblem were characteristics shared by Pedersen and Sweeney, whose careers in Boston overlapped.

"I always felt this was going to be a difficult place for teams to come in and steal two points from," Sweeney points out, "and you knew when you went into certain buildings that you were in for a tough night. That's what it stood for to be a member of the Boston Bruins. We had a pack mentality and [coach] Mike Milbury described it as a pack mentality. It was a team mentality; it wasn't ever about one guy. You were able to call out teammates, and the pride and the heart, for me, stood out first and foremost."

Sweeney played more of his games with Ray Bourque than he did with anyone else. He shares the aforementioned common appreciation for one of the game's all-time greats.

"A lot of young players got a chance to play with Raymond, but it seems like more of a crutch, because obviously he can

below:

Strike one on Bourque, with Sweeney playing catcher. How this puck ended up where it did, with Ray trying to grand slam it out of the zone while Don is standing right next to him is anyone's guess. Goalie Andy Moog is poised behind them.

dominate the game and you can just kind of play off of that, and he could cover up for a lot of your mistakes," Sweeney explains. "I did get the opportunity to play with him for an extensive period of time and after that, where I was acclimated into the League, I felt like I was contributing rather than just being on the ice just to take up time as a young player. That was a real pleasure because we were matched against the top lines and he took that to heart. That challenge to him—he knew he'd put up points, he knew he'd be on the power play—was to come out of the night as a plus against the top lines in the League. That was a challenge I think both of us really, really enjoyed. That was probably the highlight for me, that period of time, getting to play with him exclusively."

> That challenge was to come out of the night as a plus against the top lines in the League.

"By that point [with me], 30-plus minutes a night, he [Bourque] played with everybody," Pedersen adds. "Unselfish. I thought he was the epitome of team player. To see a guy play with the energy and passion that he did night in and night out, it was just amazing. I was fortunate to be a part of that, to play with one of the best players of all time."

left:

Al "Beach" Pedersen, known as an excellent shot-blocker, about to go down on two knees to do just that. Big and fearless; two qualities Al used to make it his forte. His sarcastic nickname came from being pale in comparison to most.

right:

A high priced free agent acquisition in 2006, Zdeno Chara immediately became the Bruins captain. A Norris Trophy finalist in 2008, Chara brings size, skill, and a temper to the Bruins blueline, a triple threat Boston fans love.

below:

Reed Larson came to Boston following ten seasons as a Red Wing. His wicked hard, high slap shot made goalies nervous. He had 77 points in 141 Bruins games.

Pedersen, who wrapped up his NHL playing career in 1994, was a Bruin who had a tight relationship with the Bruins photographer. Pedersen also had one of the team's great nicknames.

"Babs was like part of the team," Pedersen says. "He was there such a long time. What I liked about him, he went about his business very professionally; you didn't really know he was around, but he was always around. He's a class act."

"My nickname was 'Beach,'" Pedersen continues. "Back in Medicine Hat in juniors when I came up I was a skinny bugger, 6-foot-3, 165 pounds, and white as a ghost. The older guys, tough guys, 19- or 20-year-olds, they used to call me 'Casper' and all that, but then they started calling me Beach because they said I'd never been to one. It stuck. People still call me Beach."

Pedersen is obscure compared to Bourque, to most everyone except Bourque himself. To Ray, and the same could be said for Bobby Orr, the names Pedersen, Beers, Hawgood, Larson, Simmons, and others, all meant as much as the names Bourque and Orr. Each man went to battle wearing the Spoked B; each man protected his net, his zone, and his teammates. Therein lies what it means to be a Bruin, and to man the Boston blueline together.

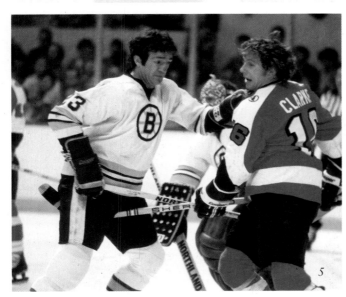

1. Andrew Alberts   2. Al Sims   3. Bob Beers   4. Left to right, back row: Mike Milbury, Gord Kluzak, Assistant coach Gary Doak, Randy Hillier, Jim Schoenfeld. Front row: Mike O'Connell, Ray Bourque, Guy Lapointe wearing number five (briefly). 5. Rick Smith   6. Brian Leetch

7. *Left to right, back row: Jim Wiemer, Gord Kluzak, Al Pedersen. Front row: Garry Galley, Assistant coach Ted Sator, Glen Wesley.* 8. *Dick Redmond* 9. *David Shaw* 10. *Carol Vadnais* 11. *Brad McCrimmon* 12. *Frank Simonetti*

Defensemen whose careers included or began after 1973–74, the season in which Steve Babineau took his first professional photo at a Bruins game. A handful of defensemen have been moved to the enforcer list.

above:

The Euro Connection from left to right: Alex Kasatonov, Mats Thelin, Michael Thelven, and Mattlas Timander.

BRUINS REGULAR SEASON STATISTICS	GP	G	A	Pts	PIM
Johnathan Aitken—Edmonton, AB	3	0	0	0	0
#49	1999–2000	One of the three 1st round picks for Wesley					
Andrew Alberts—Minneapolis, MN	184	1	18	19	231
#41	2005–2008	Four years at BC; work in progress					
Bobby Allen—Weymouth, MA	50	0	3	3	12
#38	2006–2008	On BC National Championship—2001					
Matt Bartkowski—Pittsburgh, PA	6	0	0	0	4
#43	2010–2011	Former Panthers 7th rounder came in Seidenberg trade					
Bob Beers—Pittsburgh, PA	77	3	11	14	53
#22, 34, 43	1989–1992, 1996–1997	Bruins radio color commentator					
Bryan Berard—Woonsocket, RI	80	10	28	38	64
#34	2002–2003	Unlikely career after blinded in right eye					
Nick Beverley—Toronto, ON	82	1	10	11	28
#6, 27	1966–1967, 1969–1970, 1971–1974	NHL Captain, head coach, GM, and scout					

BRUINS REGULAR SEASON STATISTICS	GP	G	A	Pts	PIM
John Blum—Detroit, MI	169	5	22	27	443
#33	1983–1986, 1987–1988, 1989–1990	Big hitter at Michigan; fought a lot early in NHL					
Andrew Bodnarchuk—Drumheller, AB	5	0	0	0	2
#65	2010	Played junior hockey in Halifax; NHL debut against Toronto					
Paul Boutilier—Sydney, NS	52	5	9	14	84
#34	1986–1987	Survived fight with Nilan during bench-clearer					
Johnny Boychuk—Edmonton, AB	121	8	23	31	88
#55	2008–2011	Earlier played for 5 different AHL teams plus the Av's in NHL					
Nick Boynton—Etobicoke, ON	299	22	62	84	399
#44	1999–2006	Two-time 1st round draft pick					
Rich Brennan—Schenectady, NY	7	0	1	1	6
#59	2002–2003	Hockey East 1st team at BU, 35 goal Junior year					
Sean Brown—Oshawa, ON	81	1	6	7	164
#23	2001–2003	B's 1st rounder in '95; last playing in Germany					
Zdeno Chara—Trencin, Slovakia	388	68	164	232	484
#33	2006–2011	Tallest player in NHL history; climbed Kilimanjaro with the author					
Denis Chervyakov—Leningrad, Russia	2	0	0	0	2
#43	1992–1993	One of 1st Russians B's allowed on club					
Paul Coffey—Weston, ON	18	0	4	4	30
#74	2000–2001	Hall-of-Fame career wound down in Boston					
Mark Cornforth—Montreal, QC	6	0	0	0	4
#40	1995–1996	Now wins World Pond Hockey titles					
Alain Cote—Montmagny, QC	68	2	9	11	65
#26, 33, 37, 40	1985–1989	Had Milbury's number until Mike unretired					
Kevin Dallman—Niagara Falls, ON	21	0	1	1	8
#58	2005–2006	Never drafted; regular shifts in LA					
Albert T. DeMarco—Cleveland, OH	3	0	0	0	0
#19	1978–1979	"Ab" played for 7 NHL teams; B's last					

Nathan Dempsey—Spruce Grove, AB — 17 0 1 1 6
#29, 21 | 2006–2007 | One of Chiarelli's ex-Senators

Gary Doak—Goderich, ON — 609 20 81 101 656
#25 | 1965–1970, 1972–1981 | Would block slap shot with face to help team

Dale Dunbar—Winthrop, MA — 1 0 0 0 0
#45 | 1988–1989 | BU'er, knee injury ended career in Finland

Darryl Edestrand—Strathroy, ON — 215 8 37 45 195
#6 | 1973–1978 | One of few to win decision in fight with Orr

Dave Ellett—Cleveland, OH — 136 3 26 29 92
#44 | 1997–1999 | Owns a team in the Central League

Andrew Ference—Edmonton, AB — 253 6 51 57 197
#21 | 2006–2011 | Activist visited Africa with Right to Play charity in '07

Mike Forbes—Brampton, ON — 32 0 4 4 15
#6 | 1977–1978 | Oilers took him from B's in expansion draft

Garry Galley—Montreal, QC — 257 24 82 106 322
#28 | 1988–1992 | Spectacular O.T. winner vs. Habs in 1990

Hal Gill—Concord, MA — 626 20 77 97 588
#75, 25 | 1997–2006 | Jaromir Jagr's personal nemesis; good on PK

Jonathan Girard—Joliette, QC — 150 10 34 44 46
#55, 46 | 1998–2003 | Prospect career cut short by car accident

Sergei Gonchar—Chelyabinsk, Russia — 15 4 5 9 12
#55 | 2003–2004 | Pre-lock-out deadline deal; then gone

John Gruden—Virginia, MN — 59 0 7 7 28
#29, 36 | 1993–1996 | Not the coach of the Tampa Bay Buc's

Doug Halward—Toronto, ON — 65 3 9 12 14
#26, 29 | 1975–1978 | Puck mover with knee and phlebitis issues

Ken Hammond—Port Credit, ON — 1 1 0 1 2
#55 | 1990–1991 | RPI National Champions' Captain in 1985

Greg Hawgood—Edmonton, AB — 134 27 51 78 160
#35, 38, 39, 40 | 1987–1990 | "Hawgy Hockey"; puck rusher

Matt Hervey—Whittier, CA — 16 0 1 1 55
#43 | 1991–1992 | Schooled in '92 playoffs by Jagr

Randy Hillier—Toronto, ON — 164 3 30 33 253
#23 | 1981–1984 | Heavyweight body checker

Shane Hnidy—Neepawa, MB — 111 4 13 17 88
#34 | 2007–2009, 2010–2011 | 3 regular season & 3 playoff games in Cup campaign

Marty Howe—Detroit, MI — 78 1 11 12 24
#27 | 1982–1983 | Son of "Mr. Hockey"; brother of Mark

Matt Hunwick—Sterling Heights, MI — 164 13 32 45 76
#48 | 2007–2011 | With Colorado, delivered hit that ended Marc Savard's season

Gord Hynes—Montreal, QC — 15 0 5 5 6
#47 | 1991–1992 | Played 12 playoff games in '92; 3 points

Al Iafrate—Dearborn, MI — 12 5 8 13 20
#43 | 1993–1994 | "The Planet" with hardest shot in hockey

Richard Jackman—Toronto, ON — 2 0 0 0 2
#43 | 2001–2002 | Part of a revolving door period for B's

Jeff Jillson—North Smithfield, RI — 50 4 10 14 35
#23 | 2003–2004 | Drafted by the Sharks at the Fleet Center

Milan Jurcina—Liptovsky Mikulas, Slovakia — 91 8 6 14 74
#68 | 2005–2007 | "Jerky" gassed by Dave Lewis

Tomas Kaberle—Rakovnik, Czech Rep. — 24 1 8 9 2
#12 | 2011 | Won Cup after a six-year drought without a playoff game

Steven Kampfer—Ann Arbor, MI — 38 5 5 10 12
#47 | 2010–2011 | Played four years of college hockey for his hometown Wolverines

Alex Kasatonov—Leningrad, Russia — 63 3 14 17 45
#6 | 1994–1996 | Twilight years after greatness in Russia

Chris Kelleher—Cambridge, MA — 1 0 0 0 0
#48 | 2001–2002 | Freshman for National Title at BU, 1995

Gord Kluzak—Climax, SK — 299 25 98 123 543
#6 | 1982–1991 | First overall pick in 1982; knee problems later

Pavel Kolarik—Vyskov, Czech Rep. — 23 0 0 0 10
#72 | 2000–2002 | 10 seasons including title; Czech League

BRUINS REGULAR SEASON STATISTICS	GP	G	A	Pts	PIM
Jarno Kultanen—Luumaki, Finland	102	2	11	13	59
#64	2000–2003	"B's best D-man"—Keenan					
Zdenek Kutlak—Budejovice, Czech Rep.	16	1	2	3	4
#39	2000–2001, 2003–2004	Big lefty; happy playing at home					
Guy Lapointe—Montreal, QC	45	2	16	18	34
#5, 27	1983–1984	Caused uproar by wearing Clapper's number 5					
Reed Larson—Minneapolis, MN	141	25	52	77	196
#28	1985–1988	The wickedest of high slapshots					
Matt Lashoff—East Greenbush, NY	46	1	7	8	22
#49	2006–2009	Plays a mean blues guitar					
Dominic Lavoie—Montreal, QC	2	0	0	0	2
#37	1992–1993	Accomplished fighter elsewhere					

	GP	G	A	Pts	PIM
Jay Leach—Syracuse, NY	2	0	0	0	7
#48	2005–2006	Posed on cover of *Rhode Island Magazine*					
Grant Ledyard—Winnipeg, MB	69	6	15	21	39
#36	1997–1999	Undrafted; played for nine NHL clubs					
Brian Leetch—Corpus Christi, TX	61	5	27	32	36
#22	2005–2006	Ended Hall-of-Fame career with bad knee					
Ray Maluta—Flin Flon, MB	25	2	3	5	6
#23, 27	1975–1977	Unenviable task of filling Orr's shoes/skates					
Paul Mara—Ridgewood, NJ	59	3	15	18	95
#23	2006–2007	Belmont Hill trained, 7th overall pick, 1997					
Brad McCrimmon—Dodsland, SK	228	17	37	54	325
#29	1979–1982	As Red Wing, almost strangled Lazaro					
Dan McGillis—Hawkesbury, ON	90	5	24	29	75
#6	2002–2004	Hockey East 1st Team twice at Northeastern					
Kyle McLaren—Humboldt, SK	417	34	90	124	370
#46, 18	1995–2002	Second youngest player in NHL as rookie					
Adam McQuaid—Charlottetown, PEI	86	4	12	16	117
#54	2009–2011	One of three Canadian Maritimers on the Cup winner					
Larry Melnyk—Saskatoon, SK	75	0	12	12	123
#33	1980–1983	On ice with Park for Game-7 winner vs. Buffalo					
Mike Milbury—Brighton, MA	754	49	189	238	1,552
#28, 26	1975–1987	Led Walpole in scoring; then D at Cornell					

BRUINS REGULAR SEASON STATISTICS	GP	G	A	Pts	PIM
Steve Montador—Vancouver, BC	13	0	1	1	18
#23	2008–2009	After two seasons in Buffalo signed with Chicago in 2011					
Ian Moran—Cleveland, OH	55	2	6	8	40
#18	2002–2006	Renowned yapper with chronic knee problems					
Derek Morris—Edmonton, AB	58	3	22	25	26
#53	2009–2010	Has spent 14 seasons with 3 teams in Western Conference					
Shaone Morrisonn—Vancouver, BC	41	1	7	8	18
#28	2002–2004	B's 1st rounder; 19th overall in 2001					
Gord Murphy—Willowdale, ON	106	8	20	28	126
#28	1991–1993, 2001–2002	Broke an ankle falling down some stairs					
Anders Myrvold—Lorenskog, Norway	9	0	2	2	4
#14, 41	1996–1997	Norwegian trailblazer in NHL					
Graeme Nicolson—North Bay, ON	1	0	0	0	0
#29	1978–1979	Played 41 games with the Colorado Rockies					
Jeff Norton—Acton, MA	3	0	1	1	2
#33	2001–2002	Cardinal Cushing Academy; then Michigan					
Dennis O'Brien—Port Hope, ON	83	4	11	15	138
#28	1977–1980	Solid 6th defenseman					
Mike O'Connell—Chicago, IL	424	70	198	268	312
#20	1980–1986	As GM, traded Joe Thornton to San Jose					
Sean O'Donnell—Ottawa, ON	232	5	47	52	275
#27, 21	2001–2004	Went on to win Cup in Anaheim					
Brad Park—Toronto, ON	501	100	317	417	553
#22	1976–1983	Best defenseman never to win the Norris Trophy					
Allen Pedersen—Fort Saskatchewan, AB	333	4	31	35	408
#41	1986–1991	Personal friends with team photographer					
Jeff Penner—Steinbach, MB	2	0	0	0	0
#62	2009–2010 / Free agent out of college hockey in Fairbanks, Alaska					
Peter Popovi—Koping, Sweden	60	1	6	7	48
#23	2000–2001	Gentle giant; ended with five seasons in Sweden					
Petr Prajsler—Hradec Kralov, Czechoslovakia	3	0	0	0	2
#52	1991–1992	Hradec Kralov's greatest Bruin ever					
Stephane Quintal—Boucherville, ON	158	8	19	27	219
#21	1988–1992	Bruins picked him so Quebec couldn't					
Dick Redmond—Kirkland Lake, ON	235	36	79	115	124
#6	1978–1982	Brother of 50-goal scorer Mickey					

	GP	G	A	Pts	PIM
Stephane Richer—Hull, QC #25 | 1992–1993 | The other Stephane Richer	21	1	4	5	18
Barry Richter—Madison, WI #46 | 1996–1997 | Member of B's last worst overall team	50	5	13	18	32
Jamie Rivers—Ottawa, ON #31 | 2001–2002 | Piled up points in Sudbury, before seven NHL teams	64	4	2	6	45
Gord Roberts—Detroit, MI #14 | 1992–1994 | Beat B's with Minnesota North Stars in 1981	124	6	18	24	145
Jon Rohloff—Mankato, MN #38 | 1994–1997 | Turnover in NJ led to 1995 playoff loss	150	7	25	32	129
Jim Schoenfeld—Galt, ON #13 | 1983–1984 | As rookie with Buffalo, started brawl with Cashman	39	0	2	2	20
Dennis Seidenberg—Schwenningen, Ger. #44 / 2009–2011 | 2nd German to win Cup; also won Calder Cup in Philly in '05	98	9	32	41	47
Jeff Serowik—Manchester, NH #49 | 1994–1995 | Runs hockey academy in Boston area	1	0	0	0	0
Yevgeny Shaldybin—Novosibirsk, USSR #62 | 1996–1997 | Softer than butter sittin' in the sun	3	1	0	1	0
David Shaw—St. Thomas, ON #34 | 1992–1995 | Won Memorial Cup with Kitchener in 1982	176	14	27	41	229
Jonathan Sigalet—Vancouver, BC #50 | 2006–2007 | Played with brother Jordan in Providence	1	0	0	0	4
Al Simmons—Winnipeg, MB #26 | 1973–1974, 1975–1976 | Also had one game with California Golden Seals	10	0	1	1	21
Frank Simonetti—Melrose, MA #21 | 1983–1988 | Shoulder injury shortened career	115	5	8	13	76
Al Sims—Toronto, ON #20, 23, 29 | 1973–1979 | Bobby Orr's partner during Al's rookie year	310	22	48	70	172
Jiri Slegr—Jihlava, Czech Rep. #71 | 2003–2006 | Cup winner, Olympic Gold, World Champ	68	9	26	35	83
Brandon Smith—Hazelton, BC #53 | 1998–2001 | A favorite of coach Pat Burns; strong work ethic	30	3	4	7	10
Dallas Smith—Hamiota, MB #8, 20 | 1959–1962, 1965–1977 | 7th Player Award winner; "strong as an ox"	861	54	248	302	936
Rick Smith—Hamilton, ON #10, 23 | 1968–1972, 1976–1980 | Scored 1st goal of Final Game 4 in 1970	513	36	125	161	391
Steve Staios—Hamilton, ON #48 | 1995–1997 | Cup Final run with Edmonton in 2006	66	3	8	11	75
Paul Stanton—Boston, MA #25 | 1993–1994 | Back-to-back Cup wins with Pittsburgh	71	3	7	10	54
Brad Stuart—Rocky Mountain House, AB #6 | 2005–2007 | Wife wanted him "elsewhere"	103	17	31	48	62
Mark Stuart—Rochester, MN #45 / 2005–2011 | Captain of USA World Junior Champs in 2004	283	13	27	40	284
Don Sweeney—St. Stephen, NB #32 | 1988–2003 | Bourque's long-time defensive partner	1,052	52	210	262	663
David Tanabe—White Bear Lake, MN #55 | 2005–2006 | Slowed by wrist injury	54	4	12	16	48

	GP	G	A	Pts	PIM
Mikhail Tatarinov—Angarsk, USSR #28 | 1993–1994 | Top offensive D-man in Russia	2	0	0	0	2
Mats Thelin—Stockholm, Sweden #27 | 1984–1987 | Swedish "goon"; played with an edge	163	8	19	27	107
Michael Thelven—Stockholm, Sweden #14, 22 | 1985–1990 | Versatile; knee injury hurt career	207	20	80	100	217

	GP	G	A	Pts	PIM
Mattias Timander—Solleftea, Sweden #47, 37 | 1996–2000 | Best season with Flyers in 2004	146	2	23	25	52
Patrick Traverse—Montreal, QC #63 | 2000–2001 | Involved in rare Boston-to-Montreal trade	37	2	6	8	14
Carol Vadnais—Montreal, QC #10 | 1972–1976 | Added for Cup run in February, 1972	263	47	134	181	433
Darren Van Impe—Saskatoon, SK #45, 20 | 1997–2001 | Distant relative of "Bully" D-man Ed	220	15	56	71	216
Dennis Vaske—Rockford, IL #29 | 1998–1999 | Captain of '99 Providence Calder Cup Champs	3	0	0	0	6
Terry Virtue—Scarborough, ON #71 | 1998–1999 | Providence '99; beat them with Hartford '00	4	0	0	0	0
Philip Von Stefenelli—Vancouver, BC #41 | 1995–1996 | BU, Detroit Viper with Samsonov	27	0	4	4	16
Aaron Ward—Windsor, ON #44 | 2006–2009 | Two Cups with Detroit and one in Carolina	150	9	17	26	116
Eric Weinrich—Roanoke, VA #27 | 2000–2001 | Came in deal from Montreal; traded for Traverse	22	1	5	6	10
Glen Wesley—Red Deer, AB #26 | 1987–1994 | The "Buckner" of missed empty nets, '90	537	77	230	307	421
Dennis Wideman—Kitchener, ON #6 | 2006–2010 | Scored Bruins franchise's 18,000th goal	256	38	61	99	165
Jim Wiemer—Sudbury, ON #30, 36 | 1989–1994 | Solid 5th or 6th defenseman	201	11	47	58	259
Andy Wozniewski—Buffalo Grove, IL #53 | 2009–2010 | Swiss League after cups of coffee with Leafs, Blues & Bruins	2	0	0	0	0
Jason York—Nepean, ON #25 | 2006–2007 | Part of the GM Peter Chiarelli Ottawa connect	49	1	7	8	32
Joe Zanussi—Rossland, BC #29 | 1975–1977 | Went with Phil Esposito to NYR in trade	68	1	8	9	38
Rick Zombo—Des Plaines, IL #34 | 1995–1996 | Comic book artist; shares birthday with author	67	4	10	14	53

13

SCORERS

above:

To the most modern generation of Bruins fans, "Jumbo" Joe Thornton was the face of the franchise from the time he was drafted 1st overall by the Club in 1997, to the time he was traded in November of 2005. He tallied 454 points with the Bruins.

left:

From 1992 to 1997 Adam Oates led the Bruins in scoring during four of his five full seasons in Boston and also led them in scoring in four of their five playoff runs. He's the Bruins 13th all-time leading scorer.

As exhibited by our list of legends, it would appear that just being a talented scorer in Boston isn't enough. One also needs to be tough as nails, and as physical as possible. Johnny Bucyk's hips, Cam Neely's fists, Terry O'Reilly's entire body: testaments to the key combination of grit and "game." Phil Esposito by the way, was no pushover in his day, at 6-foot-1, 205 pounds. Even a more recent scoring machine, the man who found his way to San Jose, Joe Thornton was known as "Jumbo Joe." He didn't necessarily use his size as others have or would have, but his big body and skill were well respected. To the latest generation of Bruins fans, his trade away in November of 2005 from the team that drafted him first overall in 1997, remains the benchmark moment of trauma. Thornton is a potential Hall of Famer.

If not physically dominant, another way to earn a quick trip into the hearts of Bruins fans is to simply use what one has in the most aggressive way possible. Fearless, reckless at times, and feisty, are all qualities readily appreciated.

Ken Linseman originally earned his nickname "the Rat" for his bent-over skating style, but getting into opponents' faces, playing with an angry streak, and lighting the lamp all the while, didn't hurt his cause or seem inappropriate to his moniker. Linseman was a scoring forward with an attitude.

"Bobby Clarke gave me the nickname when I started in Philly because I scurried around the ice, I darted around, plus I was a disturber," Linseman points out. "Clarke had a nickname for everybody, and I did skate bent over quite a bit, like I was on four legs."

left:

Ken Linseman's nickname "The Rat" and his reputation as a shift disturber probably leaves him under-rated as a point producer. He scored 807 points in 860 NHL games. He spent six seasons in Boston in the late-eighties.

The former 1st round pick of the Flyers spent four years in Philly, two years in Edmonton where he won a Cup, and then the next six seasons in Boston.

"I was a second line center wherever I went; then I'd get bumped," Linseman points out. "In Edmonton, Gretzky was the number one center; I was two. When they moved Messier to center, I became expendable. I wasn't a third line guy because our line usually scored quite a bit. So I became the second line center in Boston. I was happy to get back to the [United] States, and was fortunate to play with three really good teams."

I grew up playing street hockey every day that I wasn't on the ice.

These days, the former "hockey rodent" with 256 NHL goals and 1,700 penalty minutes is now a "wet rat." In his spare time, Linseman travels the world surfing with his friends and with his son.

Realistically, despite physicality being the preferred characteristic for Bruins fans, an overwhelming majority of great goal scorers and playmakers are not going to have a nasty streak and rack up penalty minutes. Most will use speed, skill, and guile.

Boston's poster-boy for craft and talent as a goal scorer is Rick Middleton. Middleton wasn't a physical thumper, but he's the former Bruin most often mentioned as the one who should be in the Hall of Fame, but isn't. He was just 17 points short of being a point-a-game man over the course of his entire 1,005-game NHL career. Of those points, 448 were goals, while he added 100 more points in the playoffs. "Nifty" was truly just that, and like so many playmakers and scorers, he learned the game by growing up with a stick in his hand.

above:

Rick Middleton is the best Bruin, and arguably one of the finest NHLers ever, not inducted into the Hockey Hall of Fame. Here he attacks the net on Pittsburgh netminder Greg Millen.

"I think a lot of it started...it was born on the street," explains Middleton. "I didn't grow up on ponds; I grew up playing street hockey every day that I wasn't on the ice. Even taking shots in the summer in the driveway with some buddies, I was in love with the sport, and I was the guy that always called everyone. I grew up in what was a new suburb of Toronto at the time, and it seemed like every boy in the neighborhood was the same age, so we had great teams and great games. If anyone has ever played street hockey with a ball, it's hard to carry the ball, because it sticks. There's nothing worse than a frozen tennis ball, so I learned not to keep it on my stick, you want to keep it ahead of you. I think it just morphed onto the ice for me, and I ended almost liking it better with the puck ahead, bouncing every which way. I felt better than controlling it. I think it was a subconscious thing, but I think street hockey is how I developed a touch with the puck. I never had the big shot from the outside; I always had to work in close. I had to go around defensemen that really didn't like me too much and that was my game. Get in close, score some goals, and make people look foolish. I'm actually surprised I lasted as long as I did."

He lasted 14 NHL seasons, the last 12 in Boston, and like so many others who fall in love with the city and its surroundings, he's still here.

"My kids were born here," Nifty says, "so I felt like I put down some roots. I got a great offer from a buddy of mine to start working ["a real job"] six months after I retired and I just love the area and the people. It's a great sports town, probably greater than any other sports town, particularly right now. I'm from Canada, from Toronto, [so] it's not that far to go home."

One of Middleton's businesses since retiring involves the introduction of his frozen dessert product, "Nifty-16 Dessert Bars," referring to his nickname and his jersey number. He brought the idea from Canada, where Nanaimo Bars, named after the alleged town of their origin—Nanaimo, British Columbia—are popular. He created his own recipe and distributes them to stores himself, and a portion of the proceeds go to area youth hockey programs.

The nickname on the box is from an unknown origin.

"I honestly don't know [where my nickname came from]," Nifty states. "Some players have taken credit for it. Gerry Cheevers said he was the one who gave it to me. I just think it was an adjective given to me, which was put in the paper after I scored a couple of goals and it kind of stuck."

Another of Middleton's businesses is television, where he analyzes the NHL hockey action during Boston Bruins games on NESN. His cohort, and another former Bruins scorer, is color commentator Andy Brickley. "Brick" did a year of radio work after his retirement from hockey prior to joining the TV ranks, where

below:

Middleton in front of the net wearing the captain's C, a distinction he shared for three seasons with Ray Bourque. Middleton, shown battling with future Bruin Rick Zombo, is the 4th all-time leading scorer in Bruins history.

he remains today. A Massachusetts native, being involved with the Bruins organization on and off the ice over the years remains a dream come true.

"I had the advantage of having been a pro for about seven or eight years before I came to Boston, which was huge," Brickley explains. "The reason I bring that up is because I've seen Bostonians that have played for the Bruins early in their career and it's difficult. If you have a certain level of immaturity, to play for your hometown team, the team you idolized growing up, it becomes tough to handle. So I had that going for me, number one, and I also saw other players come to Boston and put that sweater on, and put that emblem on their chest, and it changed the way they played. Garry Galley's a classic example. It just elevates your game. You have the benefit of playing with guys like Bourque and Neely, to see how they prepared and how they got ready—not that you don't have that on other teams, but it was just another level. For me, having grown up in Boston, I idolized the Bruins and everybody that played for the Bruins, whether they were a finesse guy or a tough guy or someone in between. They were all your heroes. So you knew there was a place for you even if you didn't play like Terry O'Reilly.

"Those were the proudest moments, the best four years of my professional hockey career, and this was coming from New Jersey where we had something special happening," Brickley continues. "It was nice to be a part of that, but Boston was a whole newer level of playing the game. I thought it elevated my game, it made me a better player, a more complete player, a more accountable player, because of the tradition that was in place. I think every player should get traded to New York [Rangers] for their salary to go up, and every player should get a chance to play in Boston so their talent level and their understanding of the game goes up."

Sixteen-year NHLer Robert "Butch" Goring, a New York resident, finished his playing career in Boston immediately before his coaching career began here in 1985. He played 39 games, and scored just 13 of his 375 career goals as a member of the Bruins. He previously spent the bulk of career in Los Angeles and then with Cup winning teams on Long Island.

"I enjoyed playing here. Good hockey guys—Kenny Linseman, Bourque, and O'Reilly," says Goring. "It was a little different perspective, playing with them after playing with the Islanders [where he spent five-plus seasons and had won four Cups], but I enjoyed my time here and I was sad to go."

Ken Hodge, another Bruins scorer with a New York connection—he was traded to the Rangers for Middleton in

> Every player should get a chance to play in Boston so their talent level and their understanding of the game goes up.

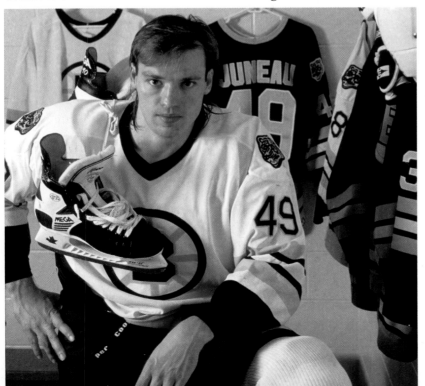

left:

Joe Juneau, originally drafted by the Bruins in the 4th round of the 1988 entry draft, had 70 assists his first full season in Boston, still an NHL single season record for a left wing. Like Adam Oates, Juneau earned All-America honors while attending Rensselaer Polytechnic Institute.

above:

Vancouver Canucks defenseman John Grisdale gives Jean Ratelle the stick. Known more for his time in New York with the Rangers, the classy French-Canadian Ratelle spent his final six NHL seasons with Boston, retiring in 1981.

right:

Boston's 7th all-time leading scorer Ken Hodge battles with Buffalo Sabres defenseman Larry Carriere. Long-time Hodge/Phil Esposito linemate Wayne Cashman skates in the background. The Sabre with the helmet and sideburns is winger Craig Ramsay, who became a Bruins assistant coach in 2007.

1976—returned to Boston in retirement, after beginning to raise a family here during his nine stalwart seasons with the B's.

"What I'm even prouder about is that all three of my boys got a chance to play at the old Garden, which to me is quite an accomplishment," reflects Hodge. "They all played high school and college hockey at the old Garden, which is quite nice."

One of them, Hodge's namesake, actually made it onto the Garden ice wearing the beloved Spoked B.

"For me the thrill was that first game, that first little step," remembers Kenneth D. Hodge. "It was maybe about two inches, [but] it felt like about five miles when I first got on the ice for that first warm-up. It was a thrill just to be there and get the opportunity to play in the Garden and to play where my dad played. That first goal as a Bruin was just an absolute thrill and you couldn't...I didn't care about the paychecks the first couple years; I just wanted to be there.

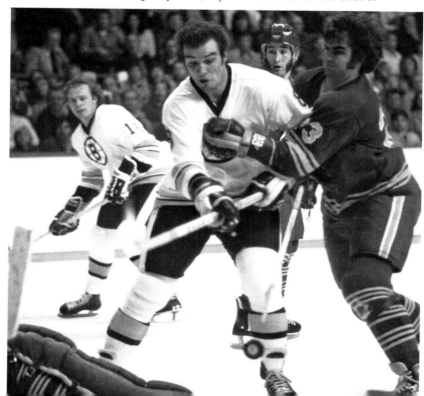

above:

Joe Thornton and Sergei "Sammy" Samsonov were a popular duo in Boston after both being drafted in 1997; Samsonov eighth overall. Both left via trade during the 2005–06 season.

"[The game] was against Quebec and Bobby Carpenter came down the middle of the ice and took a shot and I got the rebound and I was fortunate to get a little bit of a seam," he continues, recalling his first goal. "I think it was Ron Tugnutt, not the game he saved 75 shots, but it was one of his lesser games, and I was able to get that goal and it felt great. I remember going back to the bench and thinking I finally got it. It took me about four or five games to get that goal and it was a relief."

Although not as prolific as Dad in the short term or in the long, Ken did score 30 goals and add 29 assists in his best NHL season, 1990–91.

The younger Hodge played college hockey at Boston College with another Boston scorer with apparent NHL family ties. However, for Tim Sweeney, the assumed direct bloodlines to two other Bruins didn't actually exist. Tim, a prolific scorer in college who ended up earning 291 NHL games, is not directly related to defenseman Don, or to another former B.C. forward, Bob. One would have to return to Ireland to find any family relationship between the Sweeneys.

"My biggest moment as a Bruin actually was the first game I played as a Bruin in the Boston Garden," reflects Tim. "As a

above:

A man with a heavy wrist shot, Brian Rolston scored 101 goals during his four-plus seasons in Boston. He was cut loose and headed to Minnesota via free agency during the Club's lock-out purge.

right:

Unfairly renowned for being part of the trade that brought Cam Neely from Vancouver, Barry Pederson had prolific scoring abilities. Boston's first round, 18th-overall pick in 1980 spent five-plus seasons with the Bruins. He had 76 points in 79 games his first season with the Canucks.

kid growing up in this area, it is probably what a lot of kids dream to do, so I think the first game I ever played in the Boston Garden was probably my biggest moment as a Bruin."

Home grown or not, the aura of the Original Six, the tough old Bruins, and the Garden, proved to be an allure for many a young hockey player. Barry Pederson was born in Big River, Saskatchewan, and played juniors in British Columbia, but the Boston Garden was a magnet.

"The biggest moment for me was the Bruins being able to continue to turn things around after I got here, continue in the right direction," states Pederson, the Bruins first-round pick in 1980. "I had a chance to play with Rick Middleton and it was a thrill to go out there every night and have an opportunity to contribute offensively."

Pederson tallied more than a point a game for the Bruins over 379 games, but is best known to some for being a part of the trade with Vancouver that brought Cam Neely to Boston. For Pederson, now another TV hockey analyst between periods for NESN, it didn't take anything at all off his Original Six experience.

"It was a great thrill. Growing up even in Western Canada, I was a Bruins fan," Pederson states, "a Bobby Orr fan, fan of the Big Bad Bruins. It was a big thrill to be drafted by the Bruins, come into the old Garden, and it was a lifelong dream that I was very fortunate to have lived."

1. *Left to right. Dmitri Kvartalnov, Adam Oates, Joe Juneau*   2. *Anson Carter*   3. *Tom Fergus*   4. *Left to right: Jozef Stumpel,*
Shawn McEachern, Mariusz Czerkawski, Ray Bourque   5. *Jason Allison*   6. *Steve Heinze and Ted Donato*

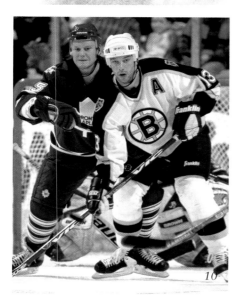

7. Left to right: John Carter, Bob Sweeney, coach Mike Milbury, Bobby Carpenter, Andy Brickley   8. Marco Sturm and Phil Kessel   9. Normand Leveille   10. Bill Guerin   11. Left to Right: Rick Middleton, Barry Pederson, Mike Krushelnyski

Scorers and playmakers whose careers included or began after 1973–74, the season in which Steve Babineau took his first professional photo at a Bruins game.

BRUINS REGULAR SEASON STATISTICS	GP	G	A	Pts	PIM
Rick Adduono (C)—Thunder Bay, ON	1	0	0	0	0
#22	1975–1976	Longevity as a minor/junior league coach					
Jason Allison (C)—North York, ON	301	105	189	294	242
#14, 41	1996–2001	Slow but unstoppable below the dots					
Dave Andreychuk (LW)—Hamilton, ON	63	19	14	33	28
#38	1999–2000	Captain of the Cup winner in Tampa					
Jamie Arniel (C)—Kingston, ON	1	0	0	0	0
#72	2010–2011	His uncle Scott, head coach of the Columbus Blue Jackets					
Ralph Barahona (C)—Long Beach, CA	6	2	2	4	0
#37	1990–1992	Big scorer at Wisconsin Stevens Point					
Shawn Bates (C)—Melrose, MA	135	14	14	28	44
#17	1997–2001	Four Frozen Fours and a title at BU					
Clayton Beddoes (C)—Bentley, AB	60	2	8	10	57
#37	1995–1997	Shoulder injury ended career in Alaska					
Bill Bennett (LW)—Warwick, RI	7	1	4	5	2
#7	1978–1979	One of three to wear Espo's number after Espo					
Paul Beraldo (RW)—Hamilton, ON	10	0	0	0	4
#30, 37	1987–1989	National teamer with Canada and Italy					
Patrice Bergeron (C)—Quebec City, QC	456	121	216	337	142
#37	2003–2011	Missed 72 games in 2007–08 with concussion					
Zdenek Blatny (LW)—Brno, Czech Rep.	5	0	0	0	2
#89	2005–2006	Former Finnish and Czech Leaguer					
Brandon Bochenski (RW)—Blaine, MN	51	11	17	28	20
#10	2006–2007	Half-step too slow as NHL scorer					
Brad Boyes (C/RW) Mississauga, ON	144	39	64	103	53
#26	2005–2007	40+ goals first season in St. Louis					
Andy Brickley (LW/C) Melrose, MA	177	37	76	113	38
#25	1988–1992	Top-rate TV color commentator					

BRUINS REGULAR SEASON STATISTICS	GP	G	A	Pts	PIM
John Byce (C)—Madison, WI	21	2	3	5	6
#42	1989–1992	Played with Mike Richter at University of Wisconsin					
Jordan Caron (RW)—Sayabec, QC	23	3	4	7	6
#38	2010–2011	Bruins first pick in 2009; scored 1st NHL goal vs. Marty Brodeur					
Anson Carter (LW)—Toronto, ON	211	70	73	143	102
#11, 33	1996–2000	No NHL work; headed to Swiss League					
John Carter (LW)—Winchester, MA	185	33	41	74	120
#8, 31, 32	1985–1991	Sinden gave Neely his number					
Bob Carpenter (C)—Beverly, MA	187	63	71	134	175
#11	1988–1992	"Can't miss kid" from high school to NHL					
Stanislav Chistov (F) Chelyabinsk, Russia	60	5	8	13	36
#13	2006–2007	Former 5th overall pick, Anaheim					
Dave Christian (RW)—Warroad, MN	128	44	38	82	49
#27	1989–1991	Hockey stick family; 1980 US Olympian					

BRUINS REGULAR SEASON STATISTICS	GP	G	A	Pts	PIM
Robert Cimetta (LW/RW)—Toronto, ON	54	10	9	19	33
#14	1988–1990	Boston's 1st rounder in 1988					
Gordie Clark (RW)—Glasgow, Scotland	8	0	1	1	0
#28, 29	1974–1976	Executive in Boston, New York					
Geoff Courtnall (LW)—Duncan, BC	259	78	81	159	368
#34, 32, 14	1983–1988	Traded at deadline with 32 goals					

Mariusz Czerkawski (RW)—Radomsko, Poland	100	23	22	45	45
#19, 29	1993–1996, 2005–2006	One of two Poles to play for B's					
Bill Derlago (C)—Birtle, MB	39	5	16	21	15
#14	1985–1986	Fourth overall pick in 1978 draft for Vancouver					
Ted Donato (LW)—Boston, MA	528	119	147	266	297
#46, 21, 40	1991–1999, 2003–2004	Coaches Harvard, his alma mater					
Todd Elik (C)—Brampton, ON	90	17	45	62	56
#20	1995–1997	10 years in Europe after 8 in NHL					
David Emma (C)—Cranston, RI	5	0	0	0	0
#52	1996–1997	Bishop Hendricken School					
Tom Fergus (C)—Chicago, IL	289	98	138	236	138
#28	1981–1985	Made Bruins at age 19 in 1981					
Ron Flockhart (C)—Smithers, BC	4	0	0	0	0
#36	1988–1989	Later coached Reno in the WCHL					
Dwight Foster (RW)—Toronto, ON	252	51	82	133	165
#27, 20	1977–1981, 1985–1987	Bruins 1st rounder in 1977					
Lee Goren (RW)—Winnipeg, MB	35	4	1	5	14
#37	2000–2001, 2002–2003	Spoiled BC's Frozen-4 in 2000, UND					
Thomas Gradin (C)—Solleftea, Sweden	64	12	31	43	18
#10	1986–1987	Neely's first center					
Bill Guerin (RW)—Worcester, MA	142	69	60	129	213
#13	2000–2002	Two-time 7th Player Award winner					
Zach Hamill (C)—Vancouver, BC	4	0	2	2	0
#52	2009–2011	Bruins first rounder, eighth overall in 2007					
Brett Harkins (C)—Cleveland, OH	45	4	15	19	8
#40, 65	1994–1997	"Minor League Mario"					
Eric Healey (LW)—Hull, MA	2	0	0	0	2
#40	2005–2006	Career AHLer after scorer at RPI					

BRUINS REGULAR SEASON STATISTICS	GP	G	A	Pts	PIM
Steve Heinze (RW/LW)—Lawrence, MA	515	131	108	239	275
#45, 23	1991–2000	Career ended by concussions					
Andy Hilbert (C/LW)—Lansing, MI	38	3	3	6	18
#29, 16	2001–2004	Demanded one-way deal; got "go-away"					
Kenneth R. Hodge (RW)—Birmingham, England	652	289	385	674	620
#8	1967–1976	Two-time 50-goal scorer					
Nathan Horton (RW)—Welland, ON	80	26	27	53	85
#18	2010–2011	Clutch performer knocked out of final by Aaron Rome in Game 3					
Ivan Huml (LW)—Kladno, Czech Rep.	49	6	12	18	36
#36	2001–2004	Played in Czech, Swede, and Fin Leagues					
Craig Janney (C)—Hartford, CT	262	85	198	283	44
#22, 23	1987–1992	Clutch goal vs. NJ in '88 playoffs					
Bobby Joyce (LW)—St. John, NB	115	26	38	64	78
#27	1987–1990	Led NHL rook's with 8 goals in '88 post					
Joe Juneau (C/LW)—Pont-Rouge, QC	161	51	142	193	72
#23, 49	1991–1994	Juneau capitol of 49th state, thus 49					
Petr Kalus (RW)—Ostrava, Czech Republic	9	4	1	5	6
#47	2006–2007	Traded to Wild in deal for Manny Fernandez					
Sheldon Kennedy (RW)—Elkhorn, MB	56	8	10	18	30
#33	1996–1997	With Swift Current when bus crashed					
Phil Kessel (RW/C)—Madison, WI	222	66	60	126	56
#81	2006–2009	Dealt to Leafs for consecutive 1st round picks					
Dmitri Khristich (LW)—Kiev, Ukraine	161	58	79	137	90
#12	1997–1999	19-year career in Russia and NHL					
Mike Knuble (RW)—Toronto, ON	307	69	76	145	164
#26	1999–2004	Lost after lock-out during roster purge					
Chuck Kobasew (RW)—Vancouver, BC	158	44	40	84	112
#12	2006–2010	Brad Pitt look-alike was Calgary's first rounder in 2001					
Andrei Kovalenko (RW)—Balakovo, Russia	76	16	21	37	27
#51	2000–2001	20-year pro in Russia and NHL					

BRUINS REGULAR SEASON STATISTICS	GP	G	A	Pts	PIM
David Krejci (C)—Sternberk, Czech Rep.	298	58	156	214	102
#46	2006–2011	Bruins leading goal & point producer in Stanley Cup playoff run					
Mike Krushelnyski (LW/C)—Montreal, QC	162	51	65	116	100
#33, 25	1981–1984	Eight playoff goals as rookie					
Dmitri Kvartalnov (LW)—Voskresensk, USSR	112	42	49	91	26
#10	1992–1994	First Russian with Bruins					
Bobby Lalonde (C)—Montreal, QC	133	14	37	51	59
#19	1979–1981	Nine + NHL years despite 5-foot-5 stature					
Robert Lang (C)—Teplice, Czechoslovakia	3	0	0	0	2
#45	1997–1998	Three Olympic medals with Czechs					
Brian Lawton (LW)—New Brunswick, NJ	8	0	0	0	14
#29	1989–1990	First American to be first overall pick					
Steve Leach (RW)—Cambridge, MA	293	76	83	159	501
#27	1991–1996	Matignon High School; four straight state titles					
Tommy Lehmann (C)—Stockholm, Sweden	35	5	5	10	16
#20	1987–1989	Opted for last seven years in Sweden					
Mikko Lehtonen (RW)—Espoo, Finland	2	0	0	0	0
#68	2008–2010	Skilled, not physical, headed to Swedish Elite League in 2010					
Normand Leveille (LW)—Montreal, QC	75	17	25	42	49
#19	1981–1983	Cerebral hemorrhage ended career					
Ken Linseman (C)—Kingston, ON	389	125	247	372	746
#13	1984–1990	"The Rat" was 1988 playoff scoring leader					
Morris Lukowich (LW)—Speers, SK	36	6	12	18	31
#12	1984–1986	Older brother Ed is a curling legend					
Mikko Makela (LW)—Tampere, Finland	11	1	2	3	0
#42	1994–1995	Runs hockey camps in Alberta					
Eric Manlow (C)—Belleville, ON	11	0	1	1	2
#57	2000–2002	Still kickin' around the AHL in '08					
Cameron Mann (RW)—Thompson, MB	89	14	10	24	40
#10	1997–2001	Failed 1st round pick, won Calder Cup					
Daniel Marois (RW)—Montreal, QC	22	7	3	10	18
#33	1993–1994	Peaked in '89–90 with 76 pts for Toronto					
Tom J. McCarthy (LW)—Toronto, ON	75	32	34	66	37
#19	1986–1988	10th overall pick—Minnesota 1979					
Shawn McEachern (LW)—Waltham	110	26	35	61	56
#14, 17	1995–1996, 2005–2006	Boston University; Stanley Cup in Pittsburgh					
Andrew McKim (C)—St. John, NB	36	1	4	5	4
#45	1992–1994	Three seasons with Berlin Polar Bears					

BRUINS REGULAR SEASON STATISTICS	GP	G	A	Pts	PIM
Peter McNab (C)—Vancouver, BC	595	263	324	587	111
#8	1976–1984	Great bloodlines; father Max a legend					
Rick Middleton (RW)—Toronto, ON	881	402	496	898	124
#16	1976–1988	Selling Nifty-16 Dessert Bars					
Sandy Moger (C)—Hundred Mile House, BC	132	27	23	50	116
#45	1994–1997	NCAA Champ at Lake Superior State					
Doug Morrison (RW)—Vancouver, BC	23	7	3	10	15
#11, 23, 38	1979–1982, 1984–1985	Brother Mark has even fewer GP					
Joe Mullen (RW)—New York, NY	37	8	7	15	0
#11	1995–1996	First American-born 500-goal scorer					
Joe Murphy (RW)—London, ON	26	7	7	14	41
#43	1999–2000	Apparently once told coach "I'm too tired to go"					
Glen Murray (RW)—Halifax, NS	570	206	180	389	408
#44, 21, 27	1991–1995, 2001–2008	Career high 44 G's, 92 PTS in '02–03					
Mats Naslund (LW)—Timra, Sweden	34	8	14	22	4
#26	1994–1995	One Cup during career with Habs					
Peter Nordstrom (LW)—Munkfors, Sweden	2	0	0	0	0
#56	1998–1999	Got homesick and left					
Michael Nylander (C)—Stockholm, Sweden	15	1	11	12	14
#92	2003–2004	One of many not signed post lock-out					
Adam Oates (C)—Weston, ON	368	152	357	509	123
#12	1991–1997	Most career NHL playoff points without a Cup; HHOF candidate					
Chris Oddleifson (C)—Brandon, MB	55	10	11	21	25
#22, 28	1972–1974	Best years were in Vancouver					
Paul O'Neil (C/RW)—Charlestown, MA	1	0	0	0	0
#28	1975–1976	Didn't play right field for the Reds					
Clayton Pachal (C/LW)—Yorkton, SK	11	0	0	0	26
#6, 28	1976–1978	Former 1st round pick					
Brad Palmer (LW)—Duncan, BC	73	6	11	17	18
#21	1982–1983	16th overall pick, Minnesota 1980					
Dave Pasin (RW)—Edmonton, AB	71	18	19	37	50
#37	1985–1986	Slow skater; fast shot					
Barry Pederson (C)—Big River, SK	379	166	251	417	248
#18, 21, 10, 12	1981–1986, 1991–1992	Shipped to Vancouver for Neely					

Pascal Pelletier (RW)—Quebec City, QC   6   0   0   0   0
#42 | 2007–2008 | AHL Player-of-the-Month, Dec '07

Ray Podloski (C)—Edmonton, AB   8   0   1   1   17
#43 | 1988–1989 | Won Memorial Cup with Neely in Portland

Brian Propp (LW)—Lanigan, SK   14   3   9   12   10
#36 | 1989–1990 | Briefly on Neely, Janney line

Jean Ratelle (C)—Lac Ste. Jean, QC   419   155   295   450   84
#10 | 1975–1981 | Class act; poor man's Jean Beliveau

Marty Reasoner (C)—Honeoye Falls, NY   19   2   6   8   8
#36 | 2005–2006 | Star at BC; 16th overall pick in '96

Mark Recchi (RW)—Kamloops, BC   180   42   65   107   71
#28 | 2008–2011 | Retires with 3 Cups (Pittsburgh, Carolina, Boston); HHOF lock

Nathan Robinson (C)—Scarborough, ON   2   0   0   0   0
#51 | 2005–2006 | Black Canadian last in Germany

Randy Robitaille (C)—Ottawa, ON   9   0   2   2   0
#43, 48, 16 | 1997–1999 | MVP of Providence's Calder Cup

Brian Rolston (C/LW)—Flint, MI   338   101   135   236   136
#12 | 1999–2004 | Came from Colorado in Bourque deal

Jean-Yves Roy (RW)—Rosemere, QC   54   10   15   25   22
#43 | 1996–1998 | All-everything at University of Maine

Vladimir Ruzicka (C)—Most, Czechoslovakia   166   66   66   132   105
#38 | 1990–1993 | "Great practice player"

Michael Ryder (RW)—Bonavista, NL   235   63   64   127   87
#73 | 2008–2011 | Played for Coach Julien in Hull, Hamilton, Montreal & Boston

Martin St. Pierre—(C) Embrun, ON   14   2   2   4   4
#47 | 2008–2009 | Paille's teammate in Guelph; first Bruins goal was shorthanded

Sergei Samsonov (LW)—Moscow, Russia   514   164   212   376   103
#14 | 1997–2006 | Rookie of the Year in IHL and NHL

Martin Samuelsson (RW)—Upplands-Vasby, Sweden   14   0   1   1   2
#43 | 2002–2004 | Uppland's best Bruin

Miroslav Satan—(LW) Topolcany, Slovakia   38   9   5   14   12
#81 | 2009–2010 | Won Cup with Pittsburgh in 2009; finished in KHL

Andre Savage (C)—Ottawa, ON   50   8   13   21   10
#54, 28 | 1998–2001 | Michigan Tech'er; now in Germany

Marc Savard (C)—Ottawa, ON   304   74   231   305   275
#71, 91 | 2006–2011 | Concussion in January of 2011 may have ended career

Bob Schmautz (RW)—Saskatoon, SK   354   134   161   295   444
#11, 17 | 1973–1980 | Cherry's beloved lunch-pailer

Tyler Seguin (C/RW)—Brampton, ON   74   11   11   22   18
#19 | 2010–2011 | 2nd overall pick had 3 goals, 3 assists over his first 2 playoff games

Gregg Sheppard (C)—North Battleford, SK   416   155   220   375   130
#19 | 1972–1978 | Led B's playoff scoring in 1974

Dave Silk (RW)—Scituate, MA   64   20   22   42   86
#21 | 1983–1985 | 1980 USA Olympic Gold

Charlie Simmer (LW)—Terrace Bay, ON   198   98   94   192   136
#23 | 1984–1987 | Was on Triple Crown Line in LA

Petri Skriko (LW)—Lappeenranta, Finland   37   6   14   20   15
#18, 29 | 1990–1992 | Four 30-goal seasons as Canuck

Bryan Smolinski (C)—Toledo, OH   136   50   36   86   113
#20 | 1992–1995 | "Smoke" helped eliminate B's in 2008

Kevin Stevens (LW)—Brockton, MA   41   10   13   23   49
#25 | 1995–1996 | Two Cups in Pitt; hat trick vs. B's in '92

Shayne Stevenson (RW)—Newmarket, ON   19   0   1   1   28
#49 | 1990–1992 | B's 1989 pick; 17th overall

Jozef Stumpel (C)—Nitra, Slovakia   424   75   206   281   80
#48, 16, 22 | 1991–1997, 2001–2003 | First Euro to lead B's in scoring

Marco Sturm (LW)—Dingolfing, Germany   302   106   87   193   156
#16 | 2005–2010 | One-third of the Joe Thornton trade; slowed by knee injuries

Tim Sweeney (LW)—Boston, MA   91   19   26   45   34
#51, 41, 42, 16 | 1992–1993, 1995–1997 | Tim, Bob, and Don not related

Petr Tenkrat (RW)—Kladno, Czech Rep.   64   9   5   14   34
#17 | 2006–2007 | First goal with B's in his First B's game

Joe Thornton (C)—London, ON   532   169   285   454   617
#6, 19 | 1997–2005 | First overall pick in 1997

Mike Walton (C)—Kirkland Lake, ON   168   60   57   117   92
#11 | 1971–1973, 1978–1979 | Orr's buddy nicknamed "Shaky"

C.J. Young (RW)—Waban, MA   15   4   5   9   12
#18 | 1992–1993 | Belmont Hill 3-sport star; then Harvard

Alexei Zhamnov (C)—Moscow, Russia   24   1   9   10   30
#10 | 2005–2006 | Broken ankle ended career

Sergei Zholtok (C)—Riga, Latvia   25   2   2   4   2
#11 | 1992–1994 | Died during game in Belarus in 2004

Sergei Zinovjev (C)—Novokuznetsk, Russia   10   0   1   1   2
#54 | 2003–2004 | Achieved stardom in Russia

Scorers

14

ENFORCERS

above:

Darin Kimble played 55 of his 311 NHL games with Boston. Over the years, enforcers have come and gone often, based on their talent level, their ability to fight, and roster chemistry and make-up.

left:

John Kordic of the Canadiens and Jay Miller square off. Miller's enforcing abilities allowed players like Cam Neely to stay on the ice, rather than spend time in the penalty box fighting for themselves. Miller is 13th all-time in Boston career PIMs.

To understand hockey is to understand the role of the enforcer. Hockey is a culture of toughness, and the enforcer role is simply one of the elements. Players get hurt, players block shots, players get beat up, players get crushed, thrown, and stymied, and it's accepted as part of the game. Also accepted is fighting. This is not to say everyone would, should, or is expected to fight, but everyone involved in the game, in whatever on-ice capacity, is aware of the fact that fighting is inherent to the environment.

To have those who don't understand or cannot possibly grasp these concepts overseeing the game itself, and ultimately determining its rules, is completely absurd.

The NHL needs to modify the "instigator rule." Presently (spring 2008), a player earns a two-game suspension and loss of wages following three instigator (fight-starting) penalties. During the 2006–07 season, the NHL general managers voted to extend the limit to five instigators before suspension. The NHL Board of Governors overturned it. The instigator rule, as it stands right now, discourages players from sticking up for teammates who are "attacked," cheap-shotted, or roughed up by opponents who have no reason to fear retribution. If player A can cheap-shot player B, then player C, player B's teammate, should be able to retaliate legally, by acting as an enforcer against player A, without fear of secondary penalty or suspension.

Some are concerned that fighting gives hockey a bad name or a bad image. This is an absurd and dangerous notion. Fighting is a popular part of the game, and an effective way to vent

frustration and carry out traditional retribution, while allowing the players on the ice to effectively police themselves. By not allowing the players to fight when necessary, frustration fouls, high sticks, cross-checks, and dangerous hits from behind become the alternative retribution. This is what truly hurts the game. Meanwhile, the initial acts of "violence"—high sticks and hits from behind—consistently lead to long-term injuries as they go unchecked. Fines and suspensions aren't enough, and it's only because self-policing is discouraged that these incidents reach the fine-and-suspension stage in the first place.

We naturally see fighting in highlight packages on a nightly basis, a custom as familiar to longtime fans as video of dramatic goals. Conversely, it's only the hits from behind and other dangerous stick fouls that make the national nightly news, and reach a non-hockey or not-yet-hockey audience. Again, when players cross the line and someone is injured and hockey gets tarnished, it's not because of fighting, it's because fighting has been unnaturally curbed. These incidents occur simply because the ability of the players to play hockey, to enforce their own code of ethics, and to police the level of violence on the ice themselves has been greatly compromised by the instigator rule. Raising the suspension threshold from three instigator penalties

above:

Chris Nilan, the Montreal Canadiens all-time leader in penalty minutes, and Terry O'Reilly, the record holder for the Bruins, squared off on countless occasions. From left to right, Chris Nilan, Ray Bourque, Mario Tremblay, Chris Chelios, and Terry O'Reilly.

to five would be a start towards solving this problem, although eliminating it altogether would be the smarter alternative. Like the designated hitter rule in baseball's American League, the instigator rule's time should have come and gone.

Fighting is a popular part of the game, and an effective way to vent frustration.

This is not to suggest that widespread brawling is attractive. There are other rules and safeguards in place to prevent line brawls, bench-clearing situations, or from additional players (a third man or even more) from joining altercations. The suspensions and fines for events like these are steep, as they should be. However, to prevent a potential fight or two from occurring in a game, a.k.a. fights done for the right reason (such as to diffuse physical tension and discourage cheap-shot violence), compromises the integrity of the game on the ice.

The hypocrisy of "fighting prevents us from growing the sport" is blatantly transparent. In non-traditional markets where hockey has attempted to expand at all professional levels, the fans (just ask them) find the fights and the physical play as one of the allures of attending the games. No one leaves during a fight. No one runs to the concession stand during a fight. Most everyone is on their feet during a fight.

right:

Brent Hughes played nearly 200 games for the Bruins. Here, he squares off with a young Luke Richardson who, as of 2008, was still active in the League after twenty seasons.

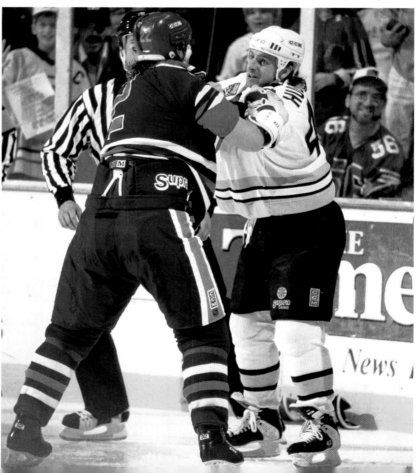

Meanwhile, fighting in hockey is tame compared to the violence and death on race tracks, tame in comparison to the thousands of murders and other acts of brutal violence our children see on TV shows and in the news before they become adults. Should we give the players knives or guns to make it more mainstream? Hockey fighting is honorable: a "mano a mano" duel without weapons. It's an old-fashioned, entertaining, and generally safe way of settling heightened tension, and actually can have the effect of reducing peripheral violence.

Scorers, grinders, and enforcers all understand hockey. This, they have in common. Regardless of their on-ice role, hockey players share an appreciation for the game they all grew up loving. And those very roles can change. Players whose names became synonymous with pugilism didn't necessarily start playing the game with that role in mind. More often than not, fighting and enforcing resulted as the tail end of an evolution.

"A lot of people don't know me. I was more of a Bobby Orr type player," states Jay Miller, earner of 856 Bruins

below:

In an effort to get tougher and harder to play against, the Bruins added free agent Shawn Thornton from Anaheim in 2007-08. En route to 74 season PIMs, Thornton spars with Riley Cote of the Flyers.

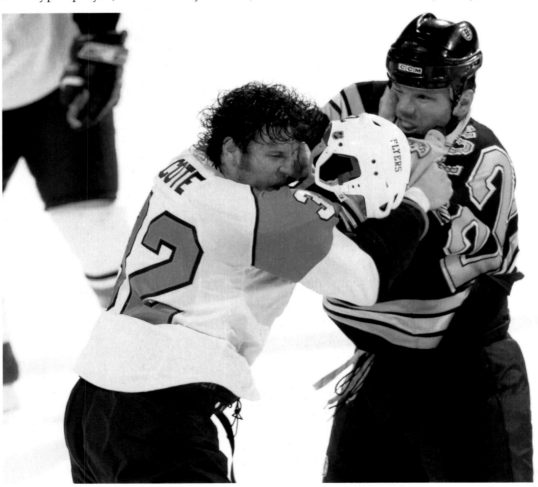

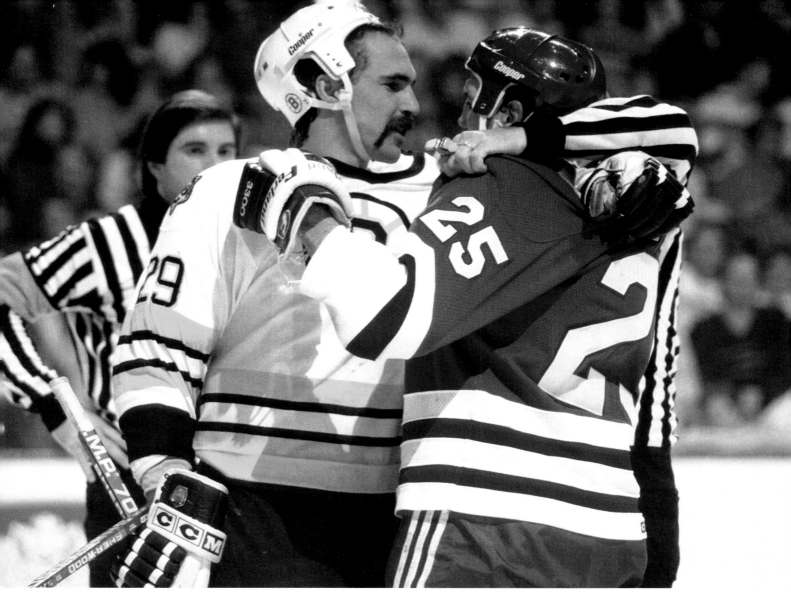

penalty minutes in 216 games. "I'd take the puck at UNH [the University of New Hampshire] and in high school playing left defense, and I would play basically the whole game, and that's what I would do. I would rush the puck and score goals, for the Bay State League in Natick and at UNH. Later, my old coach, Rick Lee, says, 'You ought to do something with your size, instead of fooling around with scoring goals. You can't do it anymore—your speed's gone.'

"I think the scouts knew how I played because I think that's why they drafted me, to create some offense. They didn't draft me to be a tough guy," adds Miller. "I wasn't drafted for that, L.B. [Lyndon Byers] wasn't drafted for that, Bob Probert wasn't; he and others were drafted to be goal scorers and then they molded them into what they needed. That's the same thing that happened to me."

"An enforcer? A disgruntled goal-scorer," P.J. Stock says with a smile. "No, whatever it took to play, to keep me in the

League, whatever I had to do, getting beat up weekly, whatever it was, I'd do it. I found a niche, which was getting beat up, and it paid the bills. I was fortunate my parents were nice enough to bless me with a really thick skull."

Stock, not blessed with size or stature, takes a humble approach to remembering his game. Beat up or beating up, he never backed down from any opponent, even those substantially larger. He'd do whatever necessary, and take whatever abuse might be handed out, to stick up for his team and create an edge.

"The term today is 'energy player,'" Stock adds. "Whatever kept me in there. I was never a fighter growing up, never thought I'd be a fighter. Whatever term you want to use, it kept me in the National Hockey League, and I got to hang out in Boston, New York, Philadelphia, and Montreal for a while."

Stan Jonathan, who won the team's 7th Player Award in 1978, was another Bruin a bit smaller than your average tough guy: a very tough 5-foot-8 inch brawler who always put his teammates first.

"I never did it for myself," Jonathan insists, "I put my teammates first. We all did. That's what I miss the most. We had our hearts in the right place, we were a team, and I'll always be a Boston Bruin.

A Lunch Pail teammate of Jonathan's, John Wensink, nicknamed "Wire," was well known for his haircut and for his tenacious and relentless approach to the game. He literally fought his way into the Bruins lineup starting in 1976–77.

"I'd like to think I could play that regular shift, maybe second or third line," ponders Wensink. "Definitely not first line, but more than just fourth line, but I think I would consider myself an enforcer."

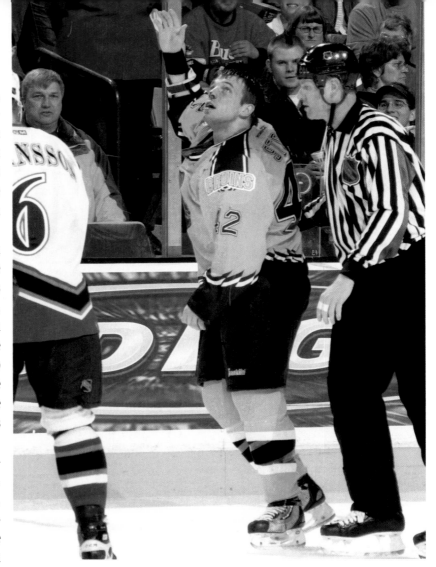

above:

P.J. Stock waving to the crowd at the Garden following a scrap. Undersized as a fighter, Stock garnered great fan support in Boston. Defenseman Calle Johansson of the Capitals looks on.

Wensink's ultimate moment as a Bruins tough guy was caught on tape. After a brawl with the North Stars, he skated over and challenged Minnesota's entire bench. He stopped a few feet away, and with both hands waved them on, signifying "any takers?" There were none.

"Terry [O'Reilly] and I got into it with a couple of their guys, Jensen was one I think, and then I made my little trip," remembers Wensink. "I hadn't seen the whole thing—all I'd ever seen was the little clip where I stopped in front of the bench—[until] about two years ago [when] a buddy of O'Reilly's in Phoenix, who invited the Bruins alumni out there for a few days, had the whole thing, from the fights, through the stop, until I skated out of the Zamboni doors in the old Garden. That was a weak moment, whatever amount of time that took, the nine seconds or the three seconds. Grapes, he keeps that out in front of people [by showing it on TV], and I think that will be around a long time."

below:

Stan Jonathan pounds a turtling (later coach of the Bruins) Robbie Ftorek of the Quebec Nordiques in 1979-80. Bulldog, fire plug, whatever the preferred term for an undersized fighter, Jonathan fit it. A fiery fan favorite with no quit from 1975 to 1982.

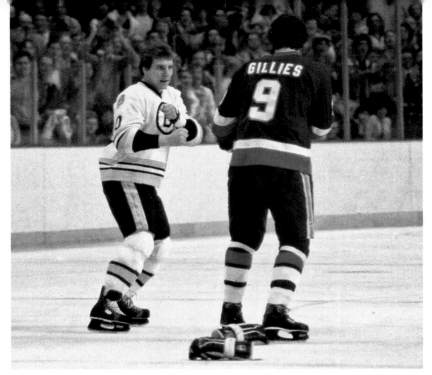

Then soon-to-be Bruins left wing Al Secord had a different perspective on Wensink's famous moment.

"I guess my first impression [of the Bruins at that time] was when I saw a video of John Wensink challenging the entire Minnesota bench. Do you remember that?" Secord asks. "I think they had a five-man brawl and then Wensink came over to the bench, and he gave them the finger wave and nobody would come over. Then, I think it was the following spring, I was drafted by Boston. You know, Stan Jonathan, Wayne Cashman, and Terry O'Reilly, and I'm thinking, 'This is gonna be one of my toughest training camps of all time. I'm gonna have to fight everybody.' Especially with Don Cherry having and wanting such a tough team. I thought it was going to be nuts and I was going to have to earn my way.

"Actually, when I got to camp in Fitchburg, Massachusetts, the toughest part was rookie camp," Secord clarifies. "We had a couple of exhibition games against the Islanders and the Flyers and we had bench-clearing brawls. We went up to Portland, Maine, on a bus. I had three fights, finally got thrown out after the third one. I had a couple more against the Flyers and I was exhausted after two days. I had a couple goals and five or six fights and I guess Don Cherry was quite impressed.

"When I got to the main camp I was expecting to fight Jonathan, Wensink, Cashman, and O'Reilly, but when I got there, it was the quietest training camp I had been to in the last five years," Secord continues. "I had been to juniors, and those were just crazy, and then to rookie camp and then to the main camp. The only thing I remember was Milbury and Cashman hitting each other like cavemen with their sticks right over the head. It was a stick fight. Cashman hit him over the head—I remember Milbury had the Jofa helmet, and Cashman was hitting the Jofa and then it would slide down to his shoulder, and Cashman didn't wear a helmet, so Milbury

above:

Al "Rocky" Secord drops the mitts with a man considered by many to be one of the toughest fighters of his era, Clark Gillies of the Islanders. The perfect example of a player having to prove his toughness early in his career, Secord left Boston and became a strong goal scorer in Chicago.

Wensink came over to the bench, and he gave them the finger wave and nobody would come over.

is swinging back, hitting him over the head and bouncing it off his shoulder. The other guys jumped in and stopped it. That was my introduction to the Bruins training camp."

Secord didn't need to fight the veterans to impress Don Cherry. The effort he showed in rookie camp was enough to earn him a spot on the club.

"I remember, after the second rookie game against the Islanders, Cherry had watched my last fight when I finally got thrown out, and he came in the dressing room to specifically talk to me about the fight. I belonged on the team, or I had a real good shot because I was the kind of guy he was looking for," Secord remembers. "He came in saying, 'Next time do this' or 'Do that,' and that was my first introduction to Don Cherry."

A second home during the hockey season for pugilists is the penalty box, which just happens to be Steve Babineau's second home as well. It's a great spot from which to get shots.

"I changed penalty boxes quite a bit from game to game, just to mix things up, change my angles, and depending on if I was looking for shots of a specific player," explains Babs. "I couldn't change during a game because the strobes in the ceiling were hard-wired to a little control box, which I would set up at the beginning of the night in one of the boxes.

"[Gord] Kluzak is killing Ray Neufeld of Hartford during a fight right in front of the penalty box," Babs adds. "He whipped him, just whaled on him. And since it was near the end of the period, the guys were escorted off the ice to their dressing rooms. As Gordie starts away, he skates right in front of me and I yell out, 'Way to go, Gordie!' Instantly I get a backhanded glove punch right in my chest. I forgot I was sitting in the visitor's penalty box, and more importantly, that Whalers enforcer Torrie Robertson was sitting in there with me. 'You're in the wrong box, buddy,' Robertson says. 'Oops, sorry,' I answered," recalls Babineau.

"I shut up and started taking pictures."

An incident that made the Kluzak-Neufeld fight unforgettable for Babs.

Enforcers can remember individual fights with great detail. It's a habit they learn while in the business, because remembering fights means remembering an opponent's tendencies and habits, and to adjust means a chance to win the next time out.

They also remember fights for pure entertainment purposes.

"Wayne Van Dorp, I one-punched him and I got a standing-O," Lyndon Byers recalls proudly. "It was the third period of a Quebec Nordiques game and he was mouthing off. I had fought him in the first period and knuckled him lefty, then in the second period he went to run me and I sticked him in the face, and I caught him for four stitches. So he was royally pissed off at me at the end of the second. It was perfect. Mike Milbury was coach, so 'Dooner' put me out, second shift of the third period, and Van Dorp came out all wound up. I looked at [referee] Paul Stewart and I said, 'Do I have to fight this dummy again? I kill him every time.' We were in a TV time-out, and 'Stewy' looked at Van Dorp and said, 'Do you want to fight 'em again?' and Van Dorp said, 'Yeah, I want to kill 'em,' and Stewy said alright. The linesman dropped the puck right in the middle of a TV time-out and I one-punched him and knocked him out on his butt. The Garden went berserko. It was nuts."

"I think I had a fight with Stephen Peat once," remembers Stock. "No one got hurt. It was a lot of fun, it got a lot of press, and the guys joked about it. It was fun, fun going to the rink after that, couple T-shirts floating around. It was a Saturday or Sunday afternoon. The guys liked it [for its duration and intensity]. We were winning the game. Just a moment that worked out well. It's tough to pick that one moment; there was a bunch of them."

above:

A rare photo of a somewhat calm Chris "Knuckles" Nilan, of course taken while he sat in the penalty box. The proudest NHL moment of the Northeastern product's career: with Boston against Hartford on March 31, 1991, he picked up a record ten different penalties (42 PIMs) in one game.

"Back when I was in the minors we used to have Dave Brown, myself, John Kordic, and Chris Nilan," recalls Jay Miller. "We were all fighting in the same little division and we'd all learn from each other, and then all of a sudden we all get called up and we're fighting each other again, just in a bigger show. I'd have to say those guys taught me more—you really learned it from experience—they taught me through going through it and gaining experience. Back then if you lost you figured out a way to win. Fortunately, we'd have a chance to fight that person the next night, and maybe eight times a year, and you had a chance to defend your honor and make sure it didn't happen again.

"When I fought Dave Brown I fought him lefty; he couldn't fight rightie," Miller points out. "Your opposite hand, he could never figure it out. By the time he figured it out it was too late. Rick Tocchet fought with both hands. That was scary. Which one do you grab? I learned to do both, more from my early boxing days. Dave Brown, my first fight ever at the Garden, an afternoon game, is obviously always one that I'll remember, but they sent me back down after.

below:

Jim McKenzie of the Hartford Whalers and Cam Neely discuss matters from their respective penalty boxes at the old Garden. Goal scorer Neely, who crosses all player talent categories, would enforce for himself whenever necessary.

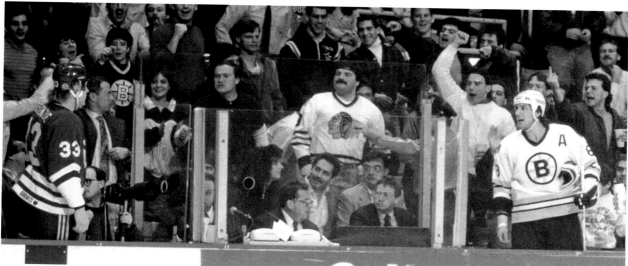

"I would think the Chris Nilan fight was the biggest one, the back-to-back after he butt-ended Rick Middleton," Miller continues. "That would have to be the big one but I had numerous really good ones with the fans. John Kordic, having two Boston kids going at it in the Garden, how much better can you get? They hyped it up more than goal scorers. You look at the old annals of the League, the *Globe* and the *Herald*, they didn't care as much about the goal scorers. They looked at Montreal playing Boston and they interviewed Nilan and myself before they interviewed Ray Bourque and Claude Lemieux. I think that's why we went as far as we did in 1988. I think myself and L.B. really stuck up for our guys and really gave it to them, and I think our guys were more confident. That really helped, it created room. Just think if you could create room now; with a kid like Crosby with some room, he's gonna kill ya."

Fighting, and fighting at the right time and for the right reason, provides a true indication of a team's chemistry and togetherness.

"We'd actually fight in practice. I remember fights in practice throughout the year," says Secord, who came up with the Bruins in 1978–79. "It was like a family, brothers having fights, but that was part of it; but if someone else picked on one of us during a hockey game, that just wasn't going to happen. We stuck up for each other."

"All you have to do is think of John Bucyk, Bobby Orr, Derek Sanderson, Wayne Cashman, Ray Bourque, Cam Neely," adds Byers. "Then to play on successful teams; honestly, that's what I think about—teammates and former guys. Andy Moog, Ray, Cam, Terry O'Reilly, John Wensick: guys that would bleed to death for you. It's that simple. I knew that anybody I played with and wore the Black and Gold, they would bleed for me man, and that's a pretty awesome thing."

"I had been going to the Bruins games all my life, sitting there watching all of the Bruins games," points out Miller. "It was very important to me because that was the Bobby Orr era. I was 12 when they won the Stanley Cup, and I'm sitting there watching the game. Ten years later, I was putting on the same uniform as him. The exciting part about that was, knowing that when I was 12, dreaming about it and it's not even close, people would laugh at you. 'I want to be a Bruin,' I'd say. When I got to college I still didn't know I could play for the Bruins, believe it or not. Coming from Natick and watching all of these Canadians around me playing at UNH, getting drafted, and playing in the League.

below:

John "Wire" Wensink battled everywhere. Not sure if a fight resulted from this encounter with Canadiens Hall-of-Fame defenseman Larry Robinson, working the slot in front of goalie Ken Dryden.

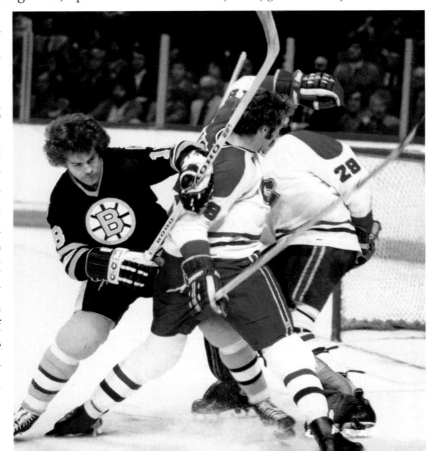

above:

This Terry O'Reilly-Steve Jensen fight erupted out of a face-off on December 1, 1977. That's Nick Beverley (#26) to the left with Peter McNab. North Star Alex Pirus on the right would soon be pummeled by John Wensink, who after the fight challenged the entire Minnesota bench and received no takers.

Then I get drafted and I'm thinking there's still no way, but three years later I've got a B's uniform on my back. It was kind of a whirlwind situation where all of a sudden I was there. I always dreamed about it but never thought it was going to happen. Like Bob Sweeney, or Bob Carpenter, or any of the Bruins that grew up around here, you'd be growing up dreaming of it and people would say, 'Yeah, you're good but you're not that good.' That's what it was all about, and then having all of your friends and family watching you."

The dream of playing the game he loved, for the team he loved—it could have been a scorer talking, a playmaker, a grinder, or an enforcer. Dreams come true via hard work regardless of position and status. Just ask Terry O'Reilly, the all-time leader in penalty minutes for the Bruins, who broke into the League in 1972 with very little fanfare, and limited talent.

"Well, it was, at the time, the game was a very physical game," states O'Reilly. "There were very few rules restricting third man in, bench-clearing brawls...the fines were very, I would say, lenient. Suspensions were unheard-of for a fight, so it was a very physical game. If you look at the names of the teams, you know, the Broad Street Bullies, the Big Bad Bruins. For me, the NHL had just expanded, the WHA [World Hockey Association] had just come into being, so the level of professional hockey was somewhat distributed and watered

down. It gave me a little extra room to get in there and it was a very physical brand of hockey, and since my skating was weak I could specialize in the other parts of it to buy myself some time. That's basically what I did: I showed a willingness to hit and scrap and all that, while I worked on my skating."

O'Reilly's overall time in Boston practically coincides with that of photographer Steve Babineau. The two arrived at about the same time, and they have skated together and shared common interests. One of those interests is dogs, more specifically, Dachshunds.

"Yep, we've talked about them quite a bit along the way," says O'Reilly. "He's had three or four, we [my family and I] have four now. We both love our Dachshund dogs."

Al Secord is another former Bruin tough guy who's familiar with the life and times of Babineau.

"He was a good guy," Secord states. "I'm really impressed and happy for him that he's had such a long, successful career. I remember he used to skate with us every once in a while, and he was always around. He was part of the fabric."

Babineau would provide Secord with shots of him playing pretty much whenever Secord wanted them, which wasn't often. Players usually think about such collectibles, or about rounding up personal treasures or memories, well after their time has come and gone.

"My kids were sitting around with me and wanting to know, wanting to see some pictures, and we have a couple of grandbabies and they said they wanted to have some of the old stuff, and I said [they] could have it when I'm gone," says Wensink. "They said they wanted stuff like that now and I instantly thought of Steve Babineau. I wasn't sure what I had, but I knew Steve would have it. He's definitely the guy. When I was playing the game, I never thought of collecting stuff, but when its all over, 20, 30 years later you're going, 'Boy, I wish I would have had some stuff.' It's mostly for the grandkids."

Pride, camaraderie, and memories: for the enforcers, maybe even more so than for the grinders, goalies, and playmakers,

above:

2007-08 Bruins rookie Milan Lucic tallied 89 PIMs for the season, here fighting Barret Jackman of the Blues. Lucic is a new version of an old Bruin, qualified as a scorer, a grinder, and an enforcer.

below:

Mike Milbury is second all-time on the Bruins career penalty minutes list with 1,552.

it's all about defending and honoring the name on the front of the jersey.

"I truly believe that the guys who came to the rink didn't need anything else other than the fact that they were gonna put that jersey on, to get motivated," states Byers. "That was it. It was pretty simple. Once the boys back in the day laid the groundwork, it was pretty obvious and it was pretty solid."

below:

Like Milbury and many other Bruins defenseman before him, the present captain, Zdeno Chara, although better served on the ice than in the penalty box, will do whatever necessary to defend the spoked-B.

"[Boston] was really the last pit stop for me in the National Hockey League and it was my favorite, my best, and my most cherished one," points out Stock. "I played with some great players, one who went on to become the MVP of the NHL. Some great leaders, a great team, and it was fun to be a part of it."

"Boston laid a real good groundwork," states Secord, who spent the bulk of his 12 NHL seasons with the Blackhawks. "I would say I had more success in Chicago, but I actually enjoyed more, my years in Boston. It was such a great, tight group of guys. We had a reunion a few years ago in Phoenix and it was the first time since the late '70s or early '80s that we'd all been together in one spot. We had such a nice time out there: we had a little golfing and had a couple of events. We played a charity hockey game. And it was just amazing that after all of those years, we got together—everyone is very fond of one another—and we didn't miss a beat. It was like we were picking up the conversation from yesterday. We all joined in and continued the camaraderie. We had so much in common. We were so close. We were like a bunch of overgrown kids, a band of brothers."

above:

A scrap with the Islanders. Left to right: Goalie Chico Resch, Garry Howatt, Bruin Wayne Cashman, Brad Park, Islanders Wayne Merrick and Bob Bourne. Behind Cashman are goalies Gerry Cheevers of the B's, and Billy Smith of the Isles.

Enforcers whose careers included or began after 1973-74, the season in which Steve Babineau took his first professional photo at a Bruins game. Defensemen included on this enforcer list were taken off the defensemen list.

BRUINS REGULAR SEASON STATISTICS	GP	G	A	Pts	PIM
Darren Banks (LW)—Toronto, ON	20	2	2	4	73
#20, 56 | 1992–1994 | Sixteen different minor league teams					
Ken Baumgartner (LW)—Flin Flon, MB	151	1	4	5	318
#22 | 1997–1999 | While playing, business degree at Hofstra					
Ken Belanger (LW)—Sault Ste. Marie, ON	122	5	8	13	317
#16 | 1999–2001 | Reluctant enforcer—hated fighting					
Dennis Bonvie (RW)—Antigonish, NS	23	1	2	3	84
#76, 22 | 2001–2002 | AHL career PIM leader					
Wade Brookbank (D/LW)—Lanigan, SK	7	1	0	1	15
#28 | 2006–2007 | Younger brother Sheldon in NHL					
Lyndon Byers (RW)—Nipawin, SK	261	24	42	66	959
#8, 12, 33, 34 | 1983–1992 | Scored last goal of 1990 Final					
Dean Chynoweth (D)—Calgary, AB	94	2	8	10	259
#47, 28 | 1995–1998 | WHL coach and executive					
Brian Curran (D)—Toronto, ON	115	3	7	10	407
#34 | 1983–1986 | Won Memorial Cup with Neely in Portland					

BRUINS REGULAR SEASON STATISTICS	GP	G	A	Pts	PIM
Doug Doull (LW)—Glace Bay, NS	35	0	1	1	132
#56 | 2003–2004 | Once suspended for charging Nedved					
Aaron Downey (RW)—Shelburne, ON	1	0	0	0	0
#45 | 1999–2000 | Survived horrific stick cut to leg artery					
Glen Featherstone (D)—Toronto, ON	99	7	13	20	274
#6 | 1991–1994 | Won IHL title with Chicago Wolves in 2000					
Bill Huard (LW)—Welland, ON	2	0	0	0	0
#61 | 1992–1993 | Member of first-ever Providence Bruins team					
Brent Hughes (LW)—New Westminster, BC	191	25	22	47	511
#42, 18 | 1991–1995 | Finished with Austin Icebats					
Jamie Huscroft (D)—Creston, BC	70	0	7	7	247
#28 | 1993–1995 | Seven teams; finished with Cap's					
Stan Jonathan (LW)—Ohsweken, ON	392	91	107	198	738
#17 | 1975–1983 | Bloodied Bouchard, Game 4, '78 Final					
Darin Kimble (RW)—Lucky Lake, SK	55	7	3	10	177
#29 | 1992–1993 | Seven goals with B's was career/season high					

BRUINS REGULAR SEASON STATISTICS	GP	G	A	Pts	PIM
Dan LaCouture (LW)—Hyannis, MA #28 | 2005–2006 | Suspended by Ducks; headed to Europe	55	2	2	4	53
Dan Lacroix (LW)—Montreal, QC #40 | 1994–1995 | Islanders' assistant coach	23	1	0	1	38
Guillaume Lefebvre (LW)—Amos, QC #92 | 2009–2010 | 4 teams in the "Q", 4 teams in the "A", and 3 in the big show	1	0	0	0	0
Dean Malkoc (D)—Vancouver, BC #29, 44 | 1996–1998 | Memorial Cup runner-up with Kamloops	73	1	0	1	156
Troy Mallette (LW)—Sudbury, ON #29 | 1996–1997 | Injuries finished him in Tampa in '97	68	6	8	14	155
Nevin Markwart (LW)—Toronto, ON #17 | 1983–1988, 1989–1992 | Big heart; tireless sparkplug	299	39	67	106	769
Alan May (RW)—Swan Hills, AB #40 | 1987–1988 | Has blog at alanmayshockeytruth.com	3	0	0	0	15
Sandy McCarthy (RW)—Toronto, ON #10 | 2003–2004 | Juniors with Manny Fernandez in Laval	37	3	1	4	28
Marty McSorley (D)—Hamilton, ON #29 | 1999–2000 | Brashear stick incident ended career	27	2	3	5	62
Jay Miller (LW)—Wellesley, MA #29 | 1985–1989 | With Byers, an intimidating one-two punch	216	13	20	33	858
Carl Mokosak (LW)—Fort Saskatchewan, AB #45 | 1988–1989 | Had 46-goal, 363 PIM Junior season	7	0	0	0	31
Brantt Myhres (LW)—Edmonton, AB #55 | 2002–2003 | Career ended by a Georges Laraque left	1	0	0	0	31
Andrei Nazarov (LW)—Chelyabinsk, Russia #62 | 2000–2002 | Tenth overall pick in 1992—SJ	110	1	6	7	364
Chris Nilan (RW)—Boston, MA #30 | 1990–1992 | As Hab, notorious for Middleton high stick	80	11	14	25	463
Jeff Odgers (RW)—Spy Hill, SK #36 | 1996–1997 | Radio commentator in Atlanta	80	7	8	15	197

BRUINS REGULAR SEASON STATISTICS	GP	G	A	Pts	PIM
Krzysztof Oliwa (LW)—Tychy, Poland #33 | 2002–2003 | "Polish Hammer" won a Cup in NJ	33	0	0	0	110
Colton Orr (RW)—Winnipeg, MB #75 | 2003–2005 | Dominated fights as rookie, but waived	21	0	0	0	27
Willie Plett (RW)—Paraguay, South America #25 | 1987–1988 | 1977 Calder Trophy winner	65	2	3	5	170
Marc Potvin (RW)—Ottawa, ON #29 | 1994–1996 | Minor league coach; took his own life in '06	33	0	1	1	16
Jeremy Reich (LW)—Craik, SK #53 | 2006–2008 | Good grit and grind in 2008 playoff round	90	2	3	5	141
Andre Roy (LW)—Port Chester, NY #49 | 1995–1997 | Calder in Providence; Stanley in Tampa	13	0	2	2	12
Kevin Sawyer (LW)—Christina Lake, BC #14, 19 | 1995–1997 | Head injury ended career in '03	4	0	0	0	5

BRUINS REGULAR SEASON STATISTICS	GP	G	A	Pts	PIM
Al Secord (LW)—Sudbury, ON #20 | 1978–1981 | Had 54-goal season with Blackhawks in '82–'83	166	39	26	65	337
Bruce Shoebottom (D)—Windsor, ON #40, 45 | 1987–1991 | Appreciative fans threw shoes on ice	35	1	4	5	53
Louis Sleigher (RW)—Nouvelle, QC #25 | 1984–1986 | Not true heavy; finished career with B's	83	16	21	37	65
Al Stewart (LW)—Fort St. John, BC #31 | 1991–1992 | Three seasons as Maine Mariner	4	0	0	0	17
P.J. Stock (C)—Montreal, QC #42 | 2001–2004 | His "ass-kicker" T-shirts became popular	130	1	12	13	282
Shawn Thornton (LW)—Oshawa, ON #22 | 2007–2011 | Also won Cup with Anaheim in 2007	290	21	27	48	460
John Wensink (LW)—Cornwall, ON #18 | 1976–1980 | "Wire" challenged the North Stars' bench	248	57	55	102	429

CHAPTER

15

GRINDERS

above:

Derek "Turk" Sanderson was another Bruin who left after Boston's second Cup and headed for the money of the WHA, where he played only eight games for the Philadelphia Blazers. He returned to the Bruins in February of 1973 and wore #17, his old #16 since taken by Fred O'Donnell. This is a shot from his second game back.

left:

Don Marcotte and Gregg Sheppard, taken at Madison Square Garden in New York. Marcotte earned renown as a penalty killer and as a shadow, a left winger who covered the opponent's most volatile scorer. Sheppard was a third line center with some scoring punch, whose career bridged the end of the Big Bad Bruins through to the start of Cherry's Lunch Pail Gang.

Those Bruins forwards who are not "scorers" or "enforcers" are "grinders," because a gritty, grinding style of play is the fundamental characteristic of what it means to be a Bruin. It's what these fans and the organization look for and want. We could have called these other forwards "skaters," or simply "forwards," but "grinders" seemed the appropriate way to go. One will notice from the compilation below, that those who didn't have much desire to grind or battle, will have very few numbers in the "games played" category.

Meanwhile, a beautiful thing about the Bruins over the last 35 years is that so many of the great players fit into so many physical categories. Cam Neely may be the ultimate example. He's a grinder, a scorer, and an enforcer. To different degrees in each of the categories, Terry O'Reilly would be another example of a guy who had all three labels covered.

Steve Babineau saw Taz's career from start to finish.

"If a guy was between Terry and the puck, he wasn't going around them," Babineau points out, "he was going through him. Going into the corner, he didn't have the stickhandling of, say, a Neely, but he had the 'feet' handling capabilities like no other. Even when his stick was in an awkward position, he'd still come out of the corner with the puck in his skates and he'd make a play. I used to watch him work on his footwork at practice. He'd literally bring the puck out with his feet."

The typical solid grinder fights on occasion, scores on occasion, but mostly shift disturbs, digs, mucks in the corner, and works hard everywhere. Some listed as grinders do one or

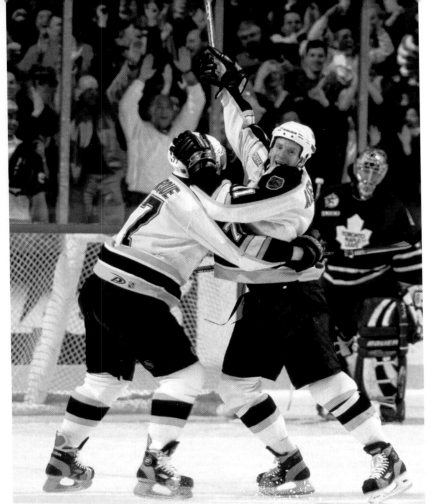

left:

P.J. Axelsson celebrating a goal with Ray Bourque against Toronto goalie Curtis Joseph. Axelsson through 2007-08 was the most recent, longest tenured Bruin, having started his career in the Hub in 1997. A smart two-way forward, "Axey" is a penalty killing phenom.

two of these things well, while some do them all well. Most would make pretty good penalty killers.

Swede P.J. Axelsson, a Bruin since 1997, will go down as one of Boston's best ever penalty killers.

"You play for the sign on your jersey," Axelsson states. "You play for the organization, you play for the guys in the room. The longer you are in one place, you like the sign [emblem] a lot more."

It's just what you'd expect to hear from a talented grinder, and what you'd hope to hear from a Bruin.

While Axelsson tallies a point in about every three of

> I was a pretty good goal scorer, but if I wasn't going to score all the time, I had to come back and help, so I was more a good two-way player.

his games, Don Marcotte scored about every other game, in a career that began four decades ago and encompassed 15 years, from the late '60s to the early '80s. Each will go down as one of the most effective two-way players in team history.

"I came up with the Bruins. I was signed when I was 16 years old," Marcotte remembers. "I was a pretty good goal scorer, but if I wasn't going to score all the time, I had to come back and help, so I was more a good two-way player. That's

what kept me in the League all of those years—I could score a bit, but I'd help the defense, kill penalties, and play against all of the stars from the other teams, which was good.

"I played with mostly all the new kids coming up," Marcotte continues. "My first year when I came up I played with [Derek] Sanderson and [Ed] Westfall, and then [Gregg] Sheppard came in and I played with him for a year—that was probably my best year ever—then I lost him right away and I played with Andre Savard who came up the next year after that. All the new kids coming up...I ended up playing with them because I was a good two-way player, so I could cover up for them."

Norwood, Massachusetts, native Tom Songin began his 43-game NHL/Bruins career in 1978. A productive offensive player at Boston College, and literally a point-a-game man at the American Hockey League level, Songin's role changed in Boston. The last step to the NHL is the steepest, and on endless occasions, based on talent, role, ice time, and opportunity, players will find their AHL and NHL numbers differing dramatically. Scorers become grinders hoping to score.

"My first goal was on assists from Wayne Cashman and Jean Ratelle," recalls Songin. "That was after I went out

to the Pacific Hockey League to play. There was the Long Beach Sharks [then Rockets], San Diego Mariners, Phoenix Roadrunners, and San Francisco Shamrocks. I made it, and I had good numbers. At the end of the season I got a call; Johnny Carlton, a Bruins scout, invited me to camp. I played in all of the exhibition games that year, but was sent down as the last cut, and spent the season in Rochester."

Songin received a call-up and spent the last 17 games with Boston.

"It was a privilege, a big honor, and I was very happy and lucky," Songin adds. "My family was happy. It was a thrill and a half. I don't know what to say. It's a little odd because it really wasn't a dream come true; when I was a kid I thought I'd be a baseball player."

Bob Sweeney entered Boston College almost a decade after Songin. He too was a prolific scorer there, and a one-time Beanpot MVP. His NHL career represented balance, with points, penalty minutes, and perseverance. He played for 10 seasons, with his first six in Boston.

"Any kid growing up in the Boston area, if you had a chance to play for your hometown team, that was your dream come true," states Sweeney. "A few of us, including myself, had that opportunity. Bobby Carpenter was a teammate, Johnny Carter, Andy Brickley. Mike Milbury was our coach. It was a unique situation during my era. We had four or five guys from the Boston area and it was a successful era for the Bruins. It was a special time for us. We never got to the finish line so to speak, to capture the Cup, but we had a good run for about six years there and we're proud of that.

Those four players, Axelsson, Marcotte, Songin, and Sweeney, represent a good portion of the four different decades Steve Babineau covered the Boston Bruins.

For reference and memories, the players listed below all did a lot of mucking, grinding, and battling for the Bruins, without distinctively thrusting themselves into the scorer or enforcer categories.

left:

Bob "Swoop" Sweeney was a college scorer and former Beanpot MVP at Boston College whose role changed after turning professional. The tall forward became a battling grinder with Boston, here being held by Jamie Macoun of the Calgary Flames.

below:

Wayne Cashman, one of the great cornermen in hockey history, a grinder who could work the walls, attempts to score on Gary "The Cobra" Simmons of the California Seals during the 1975-76 season. A former captain, "Cash" played more than a thousand games for Boston.

Grinders

1. Peter Douris   2. Robert "Butch" Goring   3. Landon Wilson   4. Rob Dimaio   5. Dave Poulin

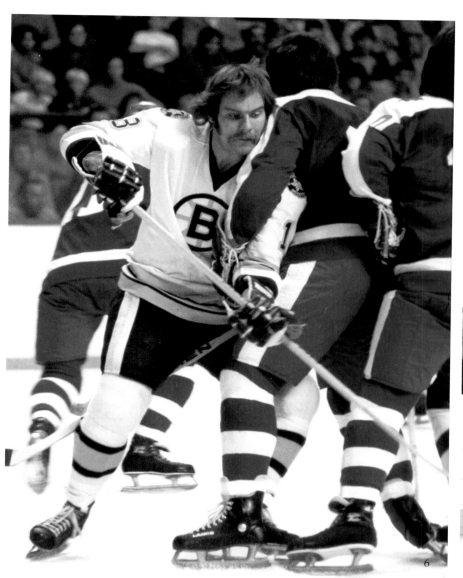

6

7

8

9

10

6. *Hank Nowak* 7. *Andre Savard* 8. *Martin Lapointe* 9. *Luc Dufour* 10. *Dave Forbes*

The Crowder brothers played tenacious hockey for the Bruins during the eighties, with Keith's (right) career spanning the entire decade. Older brother Bruce, who played 390 less games than his sibling in Boston, went on to coach Northeastern University.

Forwards whose careers included or began after 1973–74, the season in which Steve Babineau took his first professional photo at a Bruins game.

BRUINS REGULAR SEASON STATISTICS	GP	G	A	Pts	PIM
Earl Anderson (RW)—Roseau, MN	64	12	16	28	10
#16, 27, 28 | 1975–1977 | Traded for Walt McKechnie in '75					
Scott Arniel (LW)—Kingston, ON	29	5	3	8	20
#29 | 1991–1992 | Coaches the Manitoba Moose in the AHL					
Brent Ashton (LW)—Saskatoon, SK	87	19	24	43	58
#18 | 1991–1993 | Nine different NHL teams in 14 seasons					
Per-Johan Axelsson (LW)—Kungalv, Swe	797	103	184	287	276
#57, 11 | 1997–2009 | Won Olympic Gold with Team Sweden in 2006					
Dave Barr (RW)—Toronto, ON	12	1	1	2	7
#17, 27, 32 | 1981–1983 | Great junior player in Lethbridge					
Steve Begin (C)—Trois-Rivieres, QC	77	5	9	14	53
#27 | 2009–2010 | Member of rival Canadiens for 4 seasons					
Byron Bitz (RW)—Saskatoon, SK	80	8	8	16	49
#61 | 2008–2010 | Traded with Craig Weller & 2nd rounder to FLA in Seidenberg deal					
Randy Burridge (LW)—Fort Erie, ON	359	108	115	223	275
#37, 12 | 1985–1991 | Twice won Bruins 7th Player Award					
Gregory Campbell (LW)—London, ON	80	13	16	29	93
#11 | 2010–2011 | Came with Horton from Panthers; son of NHL exec Colin Campbell					
Wayne Cashman (LW)—Kingston, ON	1027	277	516	793	1041
#12 | 1964–1965, 1967–1983 | Bruins Captain; best corner-man ever					
Carl Corazzini (C)—Framingham, MA	12	2	0	2	0
#52 | 2003–2004 | Speed to burn his best attribute					
Lou Crawford (LW)—Belleville, ON	26	2	1	3	29
#37, 39 | 1989–1990, 1991–1992 | Coach Marc Crawford's brother					
Bruce Crowder (RW)—Essex, ON	217	43	44	87	133
#32 | 1981–1984 | Outscored younger brother in '82 playoffs					

BRUINS REGULAR SEASON STATISTICS	GP	G	A	Pts	PIM
Keith Crowder (RW)—Windsor, ON	607	219	258	477	1261
#18 | 1980–1989 | Rode shotgun with Linseman and Simmer					
Rob Dimaio (RW)—Calgary, AB	272	35	62	97	301
#19 | 1996–2000 | "The Pocket Tocket" played bigger than size					
Brian Dobbin (RW)—Petrolia, ON	7	1	0	1	22
#51 | 1991–1992 | Star with London Knights of OHL					
Clark Donatelli (LW)—Providence, RI	10	0	1	1	22
#50 | 1991–1992 | 62 pts in 43 GP for BU in '85–86					
Dave Donnelly (C)—Edmonton, AB	62	9	12	21	65
#29 | 1983–1986 | Part of Bellows/Kluzak draft day deal					
Shean Donovan (RW)—Timmins, ON	76	6	11	17	56
#22 | 2006–2007 | Speed to burn; not a finisher					
Peter Douris (RW)—Toronto, ON	148	24	25	49	38
#16 | 1989–1993 | Member of Boston's last Cup Final team					
P.C. Drouin (LW)—St. Lambert, QC	3	0	0	0	0
#40 | 1996–1997 | Cup of coffee during B's worst season					
Luc Dufour (LW)—Chicoutimi, QC	114	20	15	35	154
#29 | 1982–1984 | 35th overall pick in 1981					

BRUINS REGULAR SEASON STATISTICS	GP	G	A	Pts	PIM
Mikko Eloranta (LW)—Turku, Finland	118	18	23	41	76
#22 | 1999–2002 | Striking resemblance to PJ Axelsson					
John Emmons (C)—San Jose, CA	22	0	2	2	16
#23 | 2001–2002 | Very rare Bruin from California					
Peter Ferraro (RW)—Port Jefferson, NY	51	6	9	15	44
#42 | 1998–2000 | He and brother Chris played at University of Maine					
Tom Fitzgerald (RW)—Billerica, MA	71	4	6	10	40
#12 | 2005–2006 | Player Development Director for Pittsburgh					
Dave Forbes (LW)—Montreal, QC	284	53	52	105	220
#14 | 1973–1977 | Career marred by Boucha stick incident					
Doug Gibson (C)—Peterborough, ON	52	7	18	25	0
#22, 27 | 1973–1974, 1975–1976 | Finished career in Austria					
Mike Gillis (LW)—Sudbury, ON	125	17	24	41	104
#14, 22, 34, 33 | 1980–1984 | Nicknamed Dobie after TV show					
Matt Glennon (LW)—Hull, MA	3	0	0	0	2
#13, 39 | 1991–1992 | Starred at Archbishop Williams High School					
Robert "Butch" Goring (C)—St. Boniface, MB	39	13	21	34	6
#22 | 1984–1985 | Came after Cups with NYI					
Bob Gould (C/RW)—Petrolia, ON	77	8	17	25	92
#18 | 1989–1990 | Checking center on last Cup Final team					
Rod Graham (LW)—London, ON	14	2	1	3	7
#28 | 1974–1975 | Later coached Kingston of the OHL					
Travis Green (C)—Castlegar, BC	146	21	17	38	146
#39 | 2003–2006 | Face-off specialist; best known as Leaf					
Michal Grosek (LW)—Vyskov, Czech Rep.	96	5	20	25	104
#22 | 2002–2004 | European winger idolized Neely					
Bob Gryp (LW)—Chatham, ON	1	0	0	0	0
#28 | 1973–1974 | Scored 38 goals with '72–73 Boston Braves					
Paul Guay (RW)—Providence, RI	5	0	2	2	0
#37, 45 | 1988–1989 | Starred at Mount St. Charles Academy					
Ben Guite (C)—Montreal, QC	1	0	0	0	0
#50 | 2005–2006 | Dad Pierre played in WHA					

BRUINS REGULAR SEASON STATISTICS	GP	G	A	Pts	PIM
Matti Hagman (C)—Helsinki, Finland	90	15	18	33	2
#28 | 1976–1978 | First Finn born and trained to make NHL					
Taylor Hall (LW)—Regina, SK	7	0	0	0	4
#23 | 1987–1988 | Average 2 pts a game final year of junior in Regina					
Jay Henderson (LW)—Edmonton, AB	33	1	3	4	37
#38, 51 | 1998–2001 | Last player taken in '97 draft					
Matt Herr (C)—Hackensack, NJ	3	0	0	0	0
#63 | 2002–2003 | Big scorer at Hotchkiss Academy in CT					
Kenneth D. Hodge (C/RW)—Windsor, ON	112	36	40	76	30
#10 | 1990–1992 | Could be listed as scorer; Ken's son					
Jeff Hoggan (LW)—Hope, BC	46	0	2	2	33
#32 | 2006–2008 | College hockey with Nebraska-Omaha Mavericks					
Benoit Hogue (LW)—Repentigny, QC	17	4	4	8	9
#33 | 2001–2002 | Eight teams; won a Cup with Dallas					
Ron Hoover (C)—Oakville, ON	17	4	0	4	31
#39, 44 | 1989–1991 | Drafted by Whalers out of Western Michigan					
Ryan Hughes (C)—Montreal, QC	3	0	0	0	0
#47 | 1995–1996 | 22nd overall pick for Quebec in 1990					
Joe Hulbig (LW)—Norwood, MA	31	2	2	4	12
#48 | 1999–2001 | Suffered head injury vs. Ottawa in Nov. 2000					
Dave Hynes (LW)—Cambridge, MA	22	4	0	4	2
#27 | 1973–1975 | Two time 50-point scorer at Harvard					
Brad Isbister (LW)—Edmonton, AB	55	6	17	23	46
#21 | 2005–2006 | Izzy or isn't he; failed to replace Knuble					
Greg Johnston (RW)—Barrie, ON	183	26	28	54	119
#29, 39 | 1983–1990 | Eight straight seasons split NHL/minors					
Martins Karsums (RW)—Riga, Latvia	6	0	1	1	6
#44 | 2008–2009 | Sent to Tampa Bay in the deal for Mark Recchi					
Steve Kasper (C)—Montreal, QC	564	135	220	355	450
#11 | 1980–1989 | Fine career overshadowed by coaching					
Jarmo Kekalainen (LW)—Tampere, Finland	27	4	3	7	14
#29 | 1989–1991 | Became big shot hockey exec					
Chris Kelly (C)—Toronto, ON	24	2	3	5	6
#23 | 2010–2011 | Deadline pick-up had 5 goals and 13 points in postseason					
Fred Knipscheer (C)—Fort Wayne, IN	27	6	3	9	16
#43, 48 | 1993–1995 | Series-winning goal vs. Habs in '94					

238

BRUINS REGULAR SEASON STATISTICS	GP	G	A	Pts	PIM
Doug Kostynski (C)—Castlegar, BC	15	3	1	4	4
#25, 34 | 1983–1985 | Finished career in Finland					
Antti Laaksonen (LW)—Tammela, Finland	38	7	5	12	4
#57 | 1998–2000 | Won Calder Cup with Providence					
Steve Langdon (LW)—Toronto, ON	7	0	1	1	2
#26 | 1974–1976, 1977–1978 | Called up to play four playoff games in '76					

	GP	G	A	Pts	PIM
Josh Langfeld (LW)—Fridley, MN	18	0	1	1	10
#23 | 2005–2006 | National champion for Michigan; GWG vs. BC in '98					
Martin Lapointe (LW)—Ville St. Pierre, QC	205	40	43	83	255
#20 | 2001–2004 | Five-million-dollar-a-year free agent					
Drew Larman (C)—Canton, MI	4	0	0	0	0
#43 | 2009–2010 | Spent the following season with Everblades of ECHL					
Guy Larose (C)—Hull, QC (4 playoff games)	0	0	0	0	0
#41 | 1994–1995 | Son of Montreal multi-Cup winner Claude Larose					
Jeff Lazaro (LW)—Waltham, MA	76	8	19	27	98
#14 | 1990–1992 | Wasn't black, but endured racial slurs					
Pat Leahy (RW)—Boston, MA	49	4	4	8	19
#55, 83 | 2003–2006 | Specialized in shot blocking; broke hand					
Richie Leduc (C)—Perrot, QC	33	4	4	8	14
#18 | 1972–1974 | Five playoff games, 9 PIM, in 1974					
Moe Lemay (LW)—Saskatoon, SK	14	0	0		23
#36, 37 | 1987–1989 | Helped beat Habs in 1988 playoffs					
Milan Lucic (LW)—Vancouver, BC	278	64	87	151	390
#17 | 2007–2011 | Bruiser won Memorial Cup with Vancouver Giants in '07					
Craig MacDonald (C)—Antigonish, NS	18	0	3	3	8
#33 | 2003–2004 | Harvard man; NHL journeyman					
Craig MacTavish (C)—London,ON	217	44	66	110	74
#32, 27, 14 | 1979–1984 | Last NHLer to go without a helmet					
Brad Marchand (RW)—Halifax, NS	97	21	21	42	71
#63 | 2009–2011 | Huge part of Cup win, scored 11 postseason goals and a plus-12					

BRUINS REGULAR SEASON STATISTICS	GP	G	A	Pts	PIM
Don Marcotte (LW)—Asbestos, QC	868	230	254	484	317
#21, 29 | 1965–1966, 1968–1982 | Guy Lafleur's shadow; lunch-pailer					
Marquis Mathieu (C)—Hartford, CT	16	0	2	2	14
#61 | 1998–2001 | Pest center for Providence Calder Cup					
Trent McCleary (RW)—Swift Current, SK	59	3	5	8	33
#25 | 1996–1997 | Edgy and inexpensive acquisition					
Marty McInnis (RW)—Hingham, MA	96	11	13	24	46
#10 | 2001–2003 | Former BC star; 13-year NHL career					
Walt McKechnie (C)—London, ON	53	3	3	6	8
#18 | 1974–1975 | Played Sarnia Junior B with Phil Esposito					
Scott McLellan (RW)—Toronto, ON	2	0	0	0	0
#33 | 1982–1983 | Career ended after two years in minors					
Glen Metropolit (C)—Toronto, ON	82	11	22	33	36
#13 | 2007–2008 | Made team on camp try-out; made an impact					
Mike Millar (RW)—St. Catharines, ON	15	1	4	5	0
#42 | 1989–1990 | Later played 10 seasons in Germany					
Bob Miller (C)—Medford, MA	263	55	82	137	13
#14, 32 | 1977–1981 | UNH and 1976 U.S. Olympic Team					
Jon Morris (C)—Lowell, MA	4	0	0	0	0
#29 | 1993–1994 | Went from Bruins to Italy					
Mark Mowers (C)—Decatur,GA	78	5	12	17	26
#18 | 2006–2007 | Gymnast wife trained with Bela Karolyi					
Ray Neufeld (RW)—St. Boniface, MB	15	1	3	4	28
#19 | 1988–1990 | Whaler during team's first NHL season					
Eric Nickulas (RW)—Hyannis, MA	45	7	10	17	24
#72, 21, 47 | 1998–2001, 2005–2006 | Tabor Academy and UNH					
Kirk Nielsen (RW)—Grand Rapids, MN	6	0	0	0	0
#60 | 1997–1998 | Four years at Harvard; two with P-Bruins					
Kraig Nienhuis (LW)—Sarnia, ON	87	20	16	36	39
#38 | 1985–1988 | Won national championship with RPI in '85					
Jim Nill (RW)—Hanna, AB	76	4	11	15	143
#8 | 1983–1985 | Distinguished assistant GM with Red Wings					
Petteri Nokelainen (RW)—Imatra, Finland	90	7	6	13	29
#56 | 2007–2009 | 16th overall pick of New York Islanders in 2004					
Hank Nowak (LW)—Oshawa, ON	111	18	15	33	81
#18 | 1974–1977 | Boston last NHL stop; playoff goal in '75					
Fred O'Donnell (RW)—Kingston, ON	115	15	11	26	98
#16 | 1972–1974 | Went to Canucks for Bobby Schmautz					
Billy O'Dwyer (C)—Boston, MA	102	13	21		93
#10 | 1987–1990 | A "Southie," Don Bosko High School, Boston College					
Samuel Pahlsson (C)—Ornskoldsvik, Sweden	17	1	1	2	6
#27 | 2000–2001 | Won a Cup with Anaheim					
Daniel Paille (LW)—Welland, ON	117	16	16	32	32
#20 | 2009–2011 | Played on two OHL championship teams in Guelph					
Grigori Panteleev (LW)—Gastello, USSR	50	8	6	14	12
#13 | 1992–1995 | Played 2006 Olympics with Latvia					

BRUINS REGULAR SEASON STATISTICS	GP	G	A	Pts	PIM
Davis Payne (LW)—Port Albernie, BC #44, 17 | 1995–1997 | Long-time minor league head coach	22	0	1	1	14
Scott Pellerin (C/LW)—Shediac, NB #33 | 2001–2002 | Scored MN Wild's first ever exhibition goal	35	1	5	6	6
Rich Peverley (LW)—Guelph, ON #49 | 2010–2011 | Two game-winning goals and 12 points in run to Cup	23	4	3	7	2
Dave Poulin (C)—Timmins, ON #19 | 1989–1993 | Hero vs. Whalers in Game 4 of 1990 playoffs	165	34	68	102	117
Wayne Primeau (C)—Scarborough, ON #20 | 2005–2007 | One-third of the trade for Joe Thornton	101	13	16	29	115
Sean Pronger (C)—Dryden, ON #46 | 1999–2000 | Older brother of Chris	11	0	1	1	13
Joel Prpic (C)—Sudbury, ON #39 | 1997–1998, 1999–2000 | 6-foot-7; played at St. Lawrence	15	0	3	3	2
Jake Rathwell (RW)—Temiscamingue, QC #16 | 1974–1975 | Was once a Buckaroo and a Sword	1	0	0	0	0
Dave Reid (LW)—Toronto, ON #34, 31, 36, 17 | 1983–1988, 1991–1996 | NHL Network commentator	387	89	92	181	115
Doug Roberts (RW)—Detroit, MI #28 | 1971–1974 | Name not on Cup, but on team for '72 win	55	5	8	13	9
Kent Ruhnke (RW)—Toronto, ON #29 | 1975–1976 | Signed to a five-game tryout agreement	2	0	1	1	0
Derek Sanderson (C)—Niagara Falls, ON #23, 27, 17, 16 | 1965–1974 | The legendary Turk	389	135	159	294	686
Craig Sarner (RW)—St. Paul, MN #29 | 1974–1975 | On 1972 USA silver medal Olympic team	7	0	0	0	0
Andre Savard (C)—Temiscamingue, QC #11 | 1973–1976 | Sixth overall pick in 1973 draft	228	52	62	114	144
Dave Scatchard (C)—Hinton, AB #38 | 2005–2006 | Was Joe Thornton's first fight; both rookies	16	4	6	10	28
Peter Schaefer (LW)—Regina, SK #72 | 2007–2008 | One of the weirdest stick blades in hockey	63	9	17	26	18
Sean Shanahan (C/RW)—Toronto, ON #7 | 1977–1978 | One of two to wear number 7 between Espo and Ray	6	0	0	0	7
Barry Smith (C)—Surrey, BC #28 | 1975–1976 | 1975 Memorial Cup MVP for New Westminster	19	1	0	1	2
Vladimir Sobotka (C)—Trebic, Czech Rep. #60 | 2007–2010 | Traded to St. Louis; first goal for Blues was against Bruins	134	6	16	22	64
Tom Songin (RW)—Norwood, MA #19, 28 | 1978–1981 | On Fullerton Wall, Northwood School	43	5	5	10	22
Yan Stastny (C)—Quebec City, QC #43 | 2005–2007 | Son of Peter, brother of Paul	38	1	5	6	29
Mike Stevens (LW)—Kitchener, ON #36 | 1987–1988 | Brother Scott a Hall-of-Fame inductee	7	0	1	1	9
Cam Stewart (LW)—Kitchener, ON #26, 16 | 1993–1997 | Panthers to Wild in expansion draft	83	3	7	10	72

BRUINS REGULAR SEASON STATISTICS	GP	G	A	Pts	PIM
Mike Sullivan (C)—Marshfield, MA #42 | 1997–1998 | Head coached Bruins to 2004 Division title	77	5	13	18	34
Ron Sutter (C)—Viking, AB #10 | 1995–1996 | A twin; one of six brothers to play in NHL	18	5	7	12	24
Bob Sweeney (C/RW)—Concord, MA #42, 20 | 1986–1992 | Bruins Foundation charity director	382	81	112	193	504
Chris Taylor (C)—Stratford, ON #50, 38 | 1998–1999 | 16 pro seasons; still going in Germany	37	3	5	8	12
Tim Taylor (C)—Stratford, ON #26 | 1997–1999 | Hip replacement ended career in Tampa	128	24	18	42	112
Dave Thomlinson (LW)—Edmonton, AB #41 | 1991–1992 | 43rd overall pick by Toronto in '85	12	0	1	1	17
Nate Thompson (C)—Anchorage, AK #51 | 2006–2007 | Providence 'C' was 2003 6th rounder	4	0	0	0	0
Rick Tocchet (RW)—Scarborough, ON #22 | 1996–1997 | '97, went to DC in blockbuster	67	32	22	54	131
Graeme Townshend (RW)—Kingston, Jamaica #48 | 1989–1991 | Coached Greensboro in ECHL	22	2	5	7	19
Tony Tuzzolino (C)—Buffalo, NY #46 | 2001–2002 | Michigan State grad; plays in Italy	2	0	0	0	0
Kris Vernarsky (C)—Detroit, MI #76 | 2002–2004 | Last played near hometown in Port Huron	17	1	0	0	2
Jim Vesey (C/RW)—Boston, MA #54 | 1991–1992 | Attended Christopher Columbus High School	4	0	0	0	0
Ben Walter (C)—Beaconsfield, QC #72, 56 | 2005–2007 | Dad Ryan played 15 years in NHL	10	0	0	0	4
Wes Walz (C)—Calgary, AB #37, 13 | 1989–1991 | 11 seasons in NHL, four in Swiss League	73	9	12	21	44
Dixon Ward (RW)—Leduc, AB #29 | 2000–2001 | Almost a goal a game at University of North Dakota	63	5	13	18	65
Blake Wheeler (RW)—Robbinsdale, MN #26 | 2008–2011 | Big forward; part of deal to Atlanta at deadline for Rich Peverley	221	50	60	110	131
Trent Whitfield (C)—Alameda, SK #42 | 2009–2010 | Played for Mike Babcock on strong Spokane teams in late '90s	16	0	1	1	7
Landon Wilson (RW)—St. Louis, MO #27 | 1996–2000 | Bruins traded 1st round pick for him	130	12	21	33	91
Chris Winnes (RW)—Ridgefield, CT #40 | 1990–1993 | Northwood School and UNH	29	1	4	5	6
Stephane Yelle (C) Ottawa, ON #18 | 2008–2009 | Two Cups with the Avalanche; retired in 2010	77	7	11	18	6
Rob Zamuner (LW)—Oakville, ON #17 | 2001–2004 | Surprise pick; '98 Olympic Team Canada	178	26	24	50	58
Jeff Zehr (LW)—Woodstock, ON #54 | 1999–2000 | Chris Simon gave him "body bag" threat	4	0	0	0	2

Grinders

A WINTER CLASSIC

above:

The ice crew is already at work at sunrise in the background of this set-up shot by photographer Steve Babineau in left field at Fenway Park on December 30, 2009.

left:

Fenway Park, January 1, 2010, from the top of the corner pavilion reserved seats in left field. Bruins fans celebrate Mark Recchi's tying goal late in the third period.

It may be unfair to say that the NHL's marquis mid-season event peaked in its third year at Fenway Park, but at the same time it's hard to imagine a more magical convergence of history, atmosphere, and sport.

Buffalo in 2008 was unique. Chicago's Wrigley Field in 2009 was memorable. Boston in 2010 took it to an unsurpassable level.

"This was an unbelievable scenario," stated Bruins Head Coach Claude Julien after his team's 2–1 Winter Classic victory, "not just the game but even looking around. This is my second one [Heritage Classic with Montreal in Edmonton in 2003], but there's no doubt there was something special about this park that kept you in awe."

"To come here as a kid when I was seven or eight to watch baseball, and to have worked for the Red Sox, and then to be working for the Bruins for decades and to see hockey at Fenway, it's really difficult to describe," Steve Babineau reflected. "The photography angles and conditions were obviously unusual, and the whole scene was amazing."

Throughout the lead-up to the Classic, Babineau's photography captured this reverence with surreal images of a hockey rink on not-just-any ball field combined with photos of the participants; each person reflecting the joy, the wonder, and the anticipation.

Turning North America's oldest major league ball park into the home of the Boston Bruins Hockey Club began three weeks before the New Year.

"We have a really great nucleus of people that have come together the past three years, we've been working really well

together," said NHL ice guru Dan Craig 22 days before the game, "and each time we do this we gain more confidence on how this is to be done, and to get the quality of ice that we require for an NHL regular season game."

Make no mistake, bad ice would mean bad everything. Without Craig and his crew painstakingly taking care of the essentials, there was no point to the rest of the proceedings. Ice conditions need to be almost perfect for an outdoor game of hockey to be played at its highest level.

"As a sports person I get chills, just to think that we're able to come in here and have such a great event," Craig added.

Mother Nature provided the proper chills as well. New England cooperated for the most part; the weather hovered at or below freezing during much of the preparation. The only glitch came on December 27th and 28th with rain squalls adding an extra half-inch of ice.

above:

The Fenway Hawk oversees the early rink development proceedings from above the first baseline on December 13th.

below:

The very first spray of water over the metal plate base flooring from the NHL's "Ice Man" Dan Craig and his crew on December 16th. From left, Craig, Don Moffatt, John Owen, Francois Martindale, Rob Block, and Mike Craig.

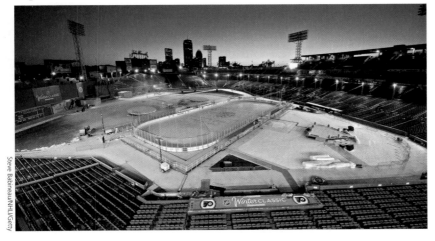

left:

After an evening of light snowfall, Fenway Park awaits the Winter Classic; photo taken at sunrise on December 30th.

right:

Heading to the first skate, left to right: Bruins Alternate Governor Charlie Jacobs, Bobby Orr, Gary Doak, Milt Schmidt, Derek Sanderson, Ken Hodge, Cam Neely.

"We were going to put down logos, but Mother Nature decided she wanted us to wait a little bit longer," Craig said smiling, "the weather is unpredictable. We'll take our shot when we can, get our markings down, our logos down…we'll have everything down and be ready for what's next."

What came next was the first "public" skate, for a group of citizens who were anything but typical. It was a group that included names like Neely, Orr, and Schmidt. The first skate provided the media and the NHL staff a taste of the hockey magic that would soon follow.

"This is certainly the Cadillac of pond hockey if you want to know the truth," laughed Bruins great Ken Hodge. "This is not what it was like back home back in the fifties, but it's great. The atmosphere, look at it around here, festive atmosphere, it's gonna be a great crowd, great weather, it's gonna be fantastic for the game."

The day following the alumni skate, December 31st, the current editions of the Bruins and Flyers practiced on the outdoor rink for the first time.

As if scripted from a children's story book, just as the Boston boys began to emerge from the dugout, a heavy snow began falling. It was a real, life-size, Fenway Park, hockey rink snow globe.

"We got here today and it was just cloudy, and then it started to snow, and we looked at each other and we were like, 'Is this snow real?'" Bruins center Marc Savard said. "It seemed surreal. We had fun with it and it was a great moment for all of us, something we won't forget."

And just like life on a northern pond, the Bruins were forced to man the shovels, clearing away the accumulated snow in order to continue practice.

"Walking out there when it was snowing was an amazing feeling," stated 42-year-old kid Mark Recchi, "that first time walking out, it was really cool."

below:

Team photo in toques on practice day, December 31st, 2009, taken by Brian Babineau on film with an early 1900's Brownie box camera.

above:

Toque-less team photo.

"The ice is just unbelievable," stated impressed Flyers forward Simon Gagne. "It's hard, it's maybe some of the best ice I've skated on in a long time. If it snows a lot it may be tough to control the puck, but the quality of the ice is top notch for now."

Everything was falling into place. New England, a haven for pond hockey for more than a century, was poised to host the ultimate outdoor game in the ultimate venue.

"What a build up," recalls Babs, "what a wild couple of weeks. It all started for me when the Fenway hawk, a hawk that lived there and used to swoop down during Red Sox games, flew down, startled the heck out of me and landed about ten feet away. They were working on the rink and here's this huge bird that came down and was standing on the railing thinking 'what the hell is going on here?' That was the beginning for me, from that, right through to an absolutely surreal Bruins game at Fenway."

The Bruins came in fresh off a 4–0 win two nights before at their regular home rink, the TD Garden, against the Atlanta Thrashers. The Flyers came in on a four-game winning streak behind their new goalie, Michael Leighton. Philadelphia had outscored their opponents 17 to 6 over the hot stretch.

To begin the game-day festivities it was only fitting that the ultimate representatives of the Black-and-Gold and Orange-and-Black rivalry, Bobby Orr and Bobby Clarke, met at center ice to drop the opening pucks for the 2010 Winter Classic.

below:

Ceremonial captains Bobby Orr and Bobby Clarke meet at center ice before dropping the first pucks.

right:

Game on! The national anthem concludes and a stealth bomber flies over Fenway Park, January 1, 2010.

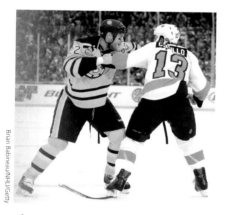

above:

Shawn Thornton and the Flyers' Daniel Carcillo square off in the first fight in Winter Classic history.

The Flyers' defensive prowess held up during the early stages of the game, as did that of the Bruins: no score after one. The biggest early save came from Tim Thomas, who, with his D-men sprawling aside, robbed Flyers center Jeff Carter on an in-close backhander.

The major highlight of the first period came at the 12:01 mark when Bruins enforcer Shawn Thornton and Flyers agitator Daniel Carcillo engaged in the first fight in Winter Classic history. It lasted 14 seconds, and the crowd went nuts as the two headed to the penalty box.

"That's why I love playing here," said Thornton later.

The Classic remained scoreless until the 4:42 mark of the second period when Flyer rookie Danny Syvret scored his first career NHL goal while Thomas was preoccupied with cross checking Hartnell in front.

"I just sort of caressed it, was sort of fading away from the net, I just threw it at the net," said Syvret. "I didn't expect it to beat the goalie, but obviously he was trying to clear in front, and that's what happens when we get traffic in front, and luckily it went in. I'll never forget it."

Thomas more than made up for his overzealous behavior, shutting down the Flyers the rest of the way. His efforts included stopping Claude Giroux and Arron Asham on breakaways in the second period. He would turn aside 24 of the 25 total shots he faced.

At the other end, it was up to the Bruins scorers to give most of the 38,112 fans in attendance something to cheer about. They took their sweet time, mainly because of the stalwart play of netminder Leighton. Among his 24 saves, he snared a challenging slapshot from Bruins defenseman Derek Morris, which was labeled for the top shelf late in the first, and turned aside a slot opportunity midway through the second.

After two periods, the "villains" from Philadelphia led 1–0 and had outshot the Bruins 18–15.

Despite the low-scoring affair, the atmosphere in the ball park was electric. There was cheering, laughing, chatter, and singing coming from all directions. The crowd stood for most of the first period, settled in, and then began to rise section by section again in the third. In the final stanza, their anxious enthusiasm was almost immediately rewarded.

Marco Sturm came close to tying the score two minutes in. After that gasp, Bruins fans would again be forced to hold their collective breath until the B's eventually cashed in on a late power play opportunity.

With Flyers defenseman Kimmo Timonen off for tripping, Boston finally got on the board at the 17:42 mark. Fenway Park erupted as Mark Recchi tipped home a Derek Morris centering pass, with a second assist to David Krejci.

"You could feel the energy when we tied it up," said winning goalie Thomas. "At that point I was very grateful to tie the game, because the [Flyers] goal was basically mine. I lost my cool and wasn't following the puck, so when we scored the tying goal it was very exciting."

"We really wanted to accomplish something here and have a big win," said Recchi while reflecting on his tying goal. "Derek made a heck of a play, but our whole power play, guys battled for loose pucks. We were able to create that opening. Mo' made a heck of a pass to me, I was in my spot, and was fortunate to bank it in."

"I didn't look around," recalled Bergeron, "but I could hear the crowd, it was unbelievable. We told ourselves, 'We have to score, we have to hear that crowd go nuts,' and they did. It was awesome and it got us going to overtime after that goal."

below:

Bruins bench with coaches in fedoras; left to right, Geoff Ward, Claude Julien, Doug Houda, Craig Ramsay, physical therapist Scott Waugh; players, Marco Sturm, Mark Recchi, Daniel Paille, Patrice Bergeron, David Krejci, Blake Wheeler (standing), Byron Bitz (half of face), Shawn Thornton, Johnny Boychuk.

above:

Fenway Park from ice level; left to right, linesman Brian Murphy, Simon Gagne, Johnny Boychuk, Tim Thomas, Patrice Bergeron, Mike Richards, Mark Recchi, Daniel Paille, Claude Giroux, Oskars Bartulis.

below:

Mark Recchi and Chris Pronger battle for a loose puck.

After the final two minutes of regulation ticked off the clock, the crowd clamored and cheered continuously while waiting for the start of the five minute four-on-four.

Early in the wide open extra session, the Flyers had two great scoring chances but came up empty. Moments later, on the ensuing rush off a sloppy line change, Patrice Bergeron spun off a check at the left point in the Flyers' zone, waited along the left wing boards for Sturm to rush to the net, and found him. Bergeron centered, Sturm steered the puck in, and the Bruins were winners.

"It took us a long time, I think we only had two chances in the first two periods and that wasn't good enough," Sturm told NBC Sports, "we wanted to show something here in our town and we were finally rewarded and we're happy about it. It was a great feeling, I'm still shaking, and I hope I get to do something like that again."

"We were focused on the game, but in those moments when they were shoveling snow, or fixing the glass, or fixing the ice, you realize that it is special," recalled Bruins Captain Zdeno Chara. "It doesn't matter how much you hear about it or read about it, it's totally different and just a special day today and yesterday. It's going to be in our memories for the rest of our lives."

"You want to play well and win games for your fans but this was extra special," said Morris, "they've done a great job of supporting us all year and they came out and were amazing. It was a perfect situation."

Entering 2012, the Bruins are the only home team to win a Winter Classic.

"It was fun to be a part of, that's for sure," said Philadelphia defenseman Chris Pronger. "We saw how the crowd was getting into it during warm-ups and during the course of the game; it was a lot of fun to be a part of it."

"The experience is once-in-a-lifetime," said Philly Head Coach Peter Laviolette, a Franklin, Massachusetts, native. "It's not just being a cliché. Fenway Park. Bruins. Flyers. Forty-thousand people on a perfect day. You couldn't ask for anything better for the game of hockey. It was a great day of hockey."

above:

At 1:57 of overtime, Marco Sturm of the Bruins, in behind Flyers defenseman Braydon Coburn, tips the puck past goalie Michael Leighton to win the Winter Classic.

left:

From ice level, Sturm reacts to the game winner. The Bruins won 2–1.

The next day, January 2nd, more than 33,000 hockey fans returned to Fenway to take in the Legends Classic game, featuring NHL greats and Hollywood stars and big wigs. The game was played to raise money for three charitable foundations. The black team, coached by Bruins great Derek Sanderson, featured former Bruins scoring star Rick Middleton, Hall-of-Famer Pat LaFontaine, and actor Kiefer Sutherland.

"I've never been to Fenway before," declared Sutherland, "so to be able to go out there and look back at this wall, with the pennant from 1903, it's pretty awesome."

Gold was coached by comedian Lenny Clarke and included the likes of Hall-of-Fame defenseman Brad Park, actor Tim

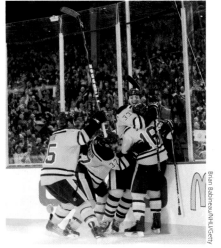

above:

The celebration begins; left to right, Johnny Boychuk, Patrice Bergeron, Zdeno Chara, Marco Sturm.

Brad Park, Milan Lucic, Cleon Daskalakis, and Terry O'Reilly at the first skate.

Red Sox catcher Jason Varitek skating with Bobby Orr.

Comedian Lenny Clarke, honorary coach and Cambridge native, with actor-comedian Denis Leary, Worcester native, at the Legends Game.

Actor Kiefer Sutherland and Bruins head coach Claude Julien share a laugh on the bench at the Legends Game.

Bruins principal Charlie Jacobs with Milt Schmidt, former Bruins equipment manager Dan Canney in the background, Tom Werner, part of Red Sox ownership.

Rob Simpson and Heidi Androl, the original hosts of NHL.com's All-Access Pregame Show, prepare to tape the December 31, 2009, practice day edition.

Cam Neely of Team Gold follows Rick Middleton of Team Black in Legends Game at Fenway, January 2, 2010.

Robbins, actor and Worcester native Denis Leary, and Bruins president and legend Cam Neely. Gold won the game 9–5, but the big number: more than $200,000 raised for each of the charities.

"The Bruins Foundation gives away a lot of money to various children's charities each year," said Neely. "I heard this is the largest-attended fundraising event the city has ever had."

It was an entertaining conclusion to what could best be described as a week-long festival of hockey, as complete a celebration of the sport as one might ever see in Boston, short of the Bruins winning the Stanley Cup.

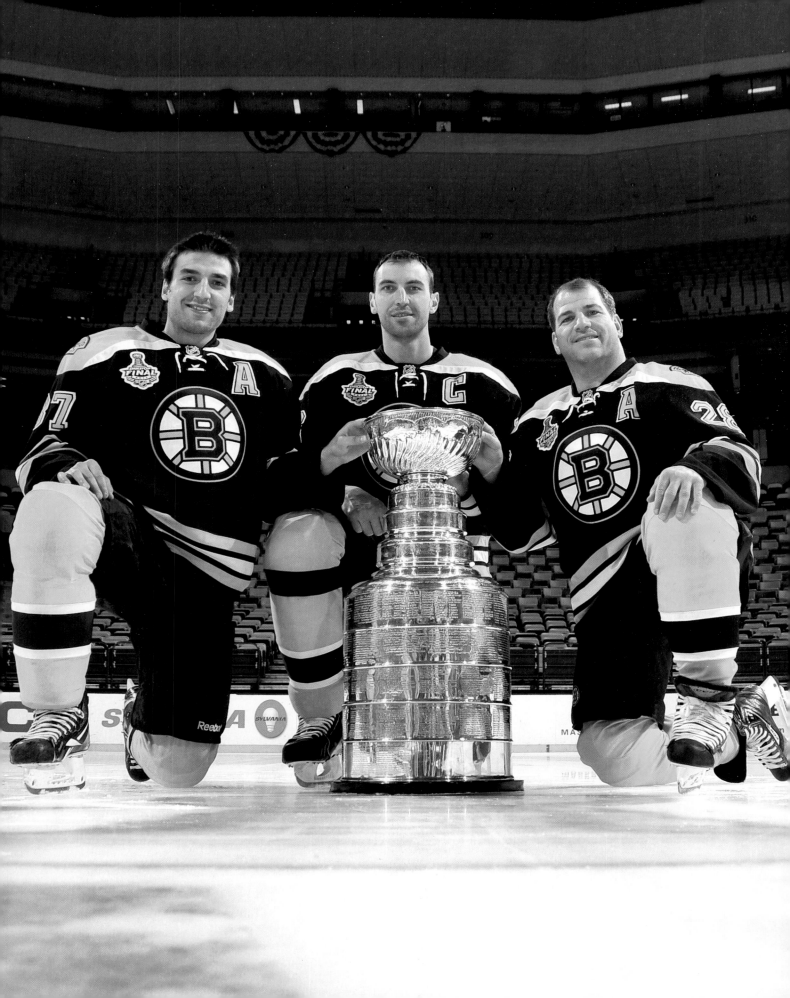

above:

At age 37, Tim Thomas became the oldest player ever to win the Conn Smythe Trophy as postseason MVP. With a 1.98 goals against average and a .940 save percentage, Thomas became the fifteenth goalie and only the second American (after Brian Leetch) to win the award.

left:

The Bruins captains with Lord Stanley's chalice: Patrice Bergeron, Zdeno Chara, and Mark Recchi.

The pain of their second round elimination at the hands of the Philadelphia Flyers in the spring of 2010 festered in the minds of the Bruins core during the off-season that followed. The blown 3–0 series lead simply added a layer of embarrassment. The Bruins were a talented team on the verge of contending for a title. They had balance, they had toughness, and they had goaltending. Boston was missing just a couple of pieces to the personnel puzzle and maybe a little extra motivation to push them over the top. Following the loss to the Flyers, they had all the inspiration they needed. They simply had to wait.

"It stung and it stung hard, and not just for the players but for our fan base," remembered Head Coach Claude Julien. "You learn lessons through adversity and disappointment, and there's no bigger example of it. We were missing key guys, but we failed to win one more game out of four, and it stuck with us."

The 2010–11 campaign opened with a trip to Europe. The Bruins played down to their competition in Belfast, Northern Ireland, beating an all-star team from Britain's Elite Ice Hockey League 5–1 in an exhibition, in a game purposefully closer than the score.

After two days of flying, settling in, and practicing in Prague, Czech Republic, the Bruins bussed back and forth to the northern city of Liberec on October 5th, and dominated a festive tune-up against the White Tigers of the Czech Extraliga 7–1.

Boston then had four days to think about the start of the season.

Brian Babineau/NHLI/Getty

"We have some unfinished business from last year," stated Captain Zdeno Chara, "for sure we want to do better, and we have all the tools in place. Guys are really motivated, and we can do it, we just have to play hard the whole season, be consistent, and stay healthy. You have to have a little bit of luck, but for sure the energy is there and we're all looking forward to the start of the season."

Like the Penguins in 2008 (Stockholm) and the Blackhawks in 2009 (Helsinki), the Bruins planned on being the third consecutive team to open the season at the NHL Premiere Games in Europe and go on to win the Stanley Cup.

Four evenings later, after plenty of time to bond, hobnob, and see Prague's many sights, the B's opened their regular season with the first of back-to-back games against the Phoenix Coyotes.

Game one went to Coach Dave Tippett's Western Conference club 5–2, but the match marked the debut of new Bruin Nathan Horton. Acquired along with grinder Gregory Campbell from Florida in the off-season, Horton gave a preview of his sniper skills, scoring both Boston goals in the 3rd period.

"It's great to be with this club," Horton said, "an Original Six club. We're excited to get this season going and we'll be ready to bounce back tomorrow."

In game two of the set, Horton, the third overall pick in the 2003 draft, ripped home another goal and added an assist in the Bruins' 3–0 victory.

"It's the best feeling to be a Boston Bruin," Horton declared.

Another new Bruin also left his mark in the second game of the season. Rookie forward Tyler Seguin, selected 2nd overall by Boston in that summer's NHL Draft, notched his first career goal on a breakaway.

"I didn't imagine my first NHL game in Europe, let alone my first NHL goal," Seguin said. The tally displayed a microcosm of his skill set: high speed, hands, and finish.

above:

The Bruins opened the 2010–2011 regular season in Prague, Czech Republic, against the Phoenix Coyotes.

below:

Rookie Tyler Seguin, the 2nd overall pick in the 2010 NHL Draft, scores his first NHL goal in Prague on Sunday October 10, 2010, at 9:14 of the third period. He outraced Coyotes defenseman Dave Schlemko and beat goalie Ilya Bryzgalov to seal the Bruins 3–0 win.

Brian Babineau/NHLI/Getty

Steve Babineau/NHL/Getty

right:

NHL referee Kevin Pollock watches as Nathan Horton lands a right against Ottawa Senator Zack Smith. After being acquired from Florida in the summer of 2010, Horton, the former third overall pick in the 2003 NHL Draft, truly began to live up to his potential.

Steve Babineau/NHL/Getty

above:

Gregory Campbell (#11) was acquired by the Bruins along with Nathan Horton from the Florida Panthers on June 22, 2010, for Dennis Wideman and two draft picks. Rookie Brad Marchand was the Bruins third round pick in the 2006 NHL Draft. Both proved to be key additions in Boston's Cup-winning season.

below:

Along with fellow rookie defenseman Johnny Boychuk, Adam McQuaid was a pleasant surprise for the Bruins fans.

Steve Babineau/NHL/Getty

Another development of symbolic and practical importance emerged during the first two games. The previous season's number-one goalie, Tuukka Rask, took the loss in the first game before former Bruins number-one Tim Thomas picked up the shutout victory in game two. As the season unfolded, following off-season hip surgery and a new workout regimen, Timmy would quickly re-acquire his old position as headliner. Thomas would earn eight wins and a no-decision in his first nine starts.

Horton and Campbell's continuous enthusiasm and appreciation for their new surroundings seemed to bolster the team chemistry. Given their previous experience, in a non-playoff, completely non-traditional market, they sent out an almost subliminal "you don't know how great you've got it" message.

"Gregory Campbell had always been that worker we needed him to be," said Julien, "but here he really seemed to relish that role, because of the appreciation of the fans and his teammates for what he was doing."

The grinder averaged 13-and-a-half minutes a night, won almost 52 percent of his face-offs, fought 11 times, and chipped in 13 goals and 16 assists on the season. Horton, meanwhile, emerged as the player many expected him to be when he was drafted by Florida eight years earlier.

"We saw a guy improve in the area that had been his biggest question mark, and that was consistency," stated Julien. "In the second half he really took off. He was engaged, he was involved physically in all areas, we saw him fight, he scored goals, he worked hard every night, and I think that's the thing a lot of people had basically questioned about his game."

With the new faces well acclimated and healthy skaters in Dennis Seidenberg, David Krejci, Marco Sturm, and eventually

Marc Savard, players who had missed all or part of the playoff series against the Flyers in spring 2010, the Bruins started to click.

After a middling November, they dominated in the month of December, and finished the 2010 portion of the schedule with a record of 20–11–5.

The new year brought monumental injuries and acquisitions. Exactly three weeks after the Penguins' Sidney Crosby suffered a concussion in the Winter Classic against Washington on January 1st, another head injury occurred. This time to Bruins first line center and power play specialist Marc Savard, on a hit by

above:

Timmy being Timmy. Tim Thomas had the highest save percentage in NHL regular season history (since the inception of the statistic) with a mark of .938.

below:

Bruins center Marc Savard announced the end of his season due to post-concussion syndrome on February 7, 2011.

above:

It takes all four lines playing well to win the Stanley Cup. General Manager Peter Chiarelli added some depth with center Chris Kelly, in exchange for a 2011 second round draft pick. The two-way center and penalty killer added 5 goals and 13 points in the postseason.

right:

Chiarelli also acquired center Rich Peverley and a draft pick from Atlanta for defenseman Mark Stuart and forward Blake Wheeler. Peverley had 12 playoff points including two game-winning goals, one of which came in Game 4 of the final.

former teammate Matt Hunwick in Colorado. The irony was thick. Young defenseman Hunwick had been traded to the Avalanche in late November for a prospect to clear cap space for Savard's return from injury reserve following a concussion suffered the previous season. "Savvy" came back, played 25 games, and was again knocked from the lineup on the Hunwick hit, likely for the rest of the season, and possibly for his career.

On February 7th, Savard announced he was done for at least the rest of this season and the playoffs.

A cruel blessing in disguise ensued: The loss meant Bruins General Manager Peter Chiarelli would be seeking depth at the center position leading up to the trade deadline. He found it in two players who turned out to be key playoff performers. Rich Peverley arrived from Atlanta with AHL defenseman Boris Valabik for winger Blake Wheeler and defenseman Mark Stuart, and Chris Kelly was acquired from Ottawa for a second round draft pick.

Kelly played strong two-way hockey, became a vocal leader in the dressing room and on the bench, and chipped in timely scoring. Peverley ended up being one of his wingers on a playoff line with Michael Ryder.

"Having been a center most of his career, and being asked to play wing, both wings in fact," Julien said in reference to Peverley, "that was huge. His speed, his talent in tight around the net, he was a real committed player. No matter where you put him he did the job, and the perfect example is [in the Stanley Cup final] replacing Horton when he went out and filling that gap. We didn't feel that pain or loss as much as we thought we would."

The last piece of the puzzle, and the worst kept secret in hockey, was the Bruins' desire to obtain a puck-moving defenseman before the deadline, more specifically, impending free agent Tomas Kaberle of the Toronto Maple Leafs. On February 18th, Chiarelli pulled the trigger, sending a first and second round pick

and former first rounder Joe Colborne to the Leafs, for a man expected to almost single handedly resuscitate a dying power play.

With Kaberle on board the man advantage went just 7 for 67, but for the season the Bruins ended up scoring the fifth most goals in the NHL, with 13 double-digit goal scorers, the most in the League. At the other end they gave up the second fewest and, with 103 points, ended up the third playoff seed in the Eastern Conference. The B's officially wrapped up the Northeast Division crown with a 3–2 victory over the Atlanta Thrashers on April 2nd.

For their efforts, the B's earned a first round match-up against their ancient nemesis, the Montreal Canadiens. The Habs finished just seven points behind Boston and, given the rivalry, the talent match-ups, and the hazardous nature of first round series—vis-à-vis higher seeds under pressure often getting bumped—this would be no easy task.

Challenge would be an understatement. In the 33rd postseason meeting between the two clubs, the most in NHL history, the Bruins would be survivalists.

Montreal won Games 1 and 2 in Boston, 2–0 and 3–1, to take early control of the series. To make matters worse, B's captain Zdeno Chara, a Norris Trophy candidate and a dominating player in his 13th NHL season, missed the second game with an unknown illness. In the Beantown media mania and panic, some were absurd enough to suggest that the team's leader could have played but didn't.

"It was horrible," Chara said. "I tried. I couldn't move, I was really sick. I still don't really know what it was but it was unbelievable."

Chara had played while ill in Game 1. He returned to the lineup in Montreal in Game 3, and the B's returned to the win column 4–2.

In Game 4 in Montreal, the Bruins fell behind by two goals eight minutes into the second period. With the series on the line, down in games and goals, Boston answered back at the Bell Centre, the most hostile of environments. Defenseman Andrew Ference scored on a slapper at the midway point of the game, and Patrice Bergeron tied it heading into the third.

Steve Babineau/Boston Bruins

above:

The Bruins played to 100 percent capacity at the TD Garden during the 2010–11 regular season and playoffs. This shot is from Game 5 of the first-round series against Montreal.

below:

At 9:03 of the second overtime of Game 5, Nathan Horton shovels home a rebound off an Andrew Ference point shot to win the game for Boston. David Krejci looks on as Canadiens James Wisniewski, Roman Hamrlik, and goalie Carey Price fail to recover. After losing the first two games of the series, the win gave Boston a 3–2 series lead.

Steve Babineau/Boston Bruins

above:

Tim Thomas pokes the puck away from Canadien Brian Gionta as Scott Gomez (#11) and Chris Kelly do battle in the third period of Game 7 of the Eastern Conference quarterfinal. Defenseman Johnny Boychuk looks on.

A minute and a half into that period, Montreal again took the lead on a goal by defenseman P.K. Subban.

That's when the Bruins' depth took over.

Playoff hockey is all about balance and effort from four lines. Often times the biggest goals come from the most unlikely sources. With just more than six minutes remaining in regulation, center Chris Kelly tied the game on assists from Ryder and Peverley. Then just 1:59 into overtime, former Canadien Ryder won it for Boston, with assists from both his hard working linemates. The series was tied at two.

"That line had three goals...in overtime that was a great play by the three of them," said Patrice Bergeron.

"When we got down 3–1 we knew we just had to get back to what brought us success all season," said Ryder, "we called a time-out, got our bearings...it just shows in playoff time you can never quit and it's a good character win for our team."

The Bruins never led in regulation but won the game. It was an obvious turning point in the series. Boston was getting offensive contributions from a variety of sources, and Tim Thomas, although a bit leaky and deep in his crease at times, made huge saves, including stopping Michael Cammalleri on a breakaway midway through the third period.

It was the perfect transition into Game 5 in Boston, which would turn into a goaltending extravaganza featuring Thomas and Carey Price. Price faced 51 shots, Thomas 45, and both made incredible saves in a game that went to double overtime.

"That was pretty impressive," Montreal defenseman Hal Gill, a Concord native and former Bruin for eight seasons, told reporters. "Both of them played lights out. That's good playoff hockey. It is fun to be a part of those games. Unfortunately it didn't go our way."

The Bruins won it on Nathan Horton's goal at the 9:03 mark of the second extra session.

While the Bruins faithful thought their club had finally turned the corner never to look back, the series was hardly over. Montreal won Game 6 on home ice 2–1, forcing the deciding match back in Boston.

No surprise to anyone, the finale of this amazing series

below:

The Bruins celebrate Nathan Horton's goal at 5:43 of overtime to win Game 7 of their opening round series against Montreal, April 27, 2011.

also went to overtime. Again Horton was the hero, winning a nail-biter the Bruins never trailed, at 5:43 of period number four.

"That's the tightest series I've ever been a part of," said Thomas after, "and watching so many series on TV, one of the closest statistically I've ever heard of…it was back and forth and both teams showed a ton of character and a ton of heart."

Three days later the Bruins would have an opportunity to right a wrong that had haunted them for 12 months: a chance for payback against the Philadelphia Flyers in round two.

Aside from a 3–2 overtime win in Game 2, it wasn't much of a series. The Bruins dominated in a sweep, the other scores being 7–3, 5–1, and 5–1 with two empty netters. The 2010 playoff loss may never be forgotten, but it was behind them.

"I saw our team getting better and better as the playoffs moved on," said Coach Julien, "and going over those hurdles made us a better team. When we jumped those two major hurdles in Montreal and Philly, we felt pretty good."

Through the first two rounds, the Bruins had exorcized past demons, while the Eastern Conference final would feature more of an unknown challenge, the resurgent Tampa Bay Lightning. First year General Manager Steve Yzerman and first year Coach Guy Boucher had quickly turned the franchise around. A non-playoff team for three years, the Bolts found themselves one round from the Stanley Cup final.

above:

Milan Lucic scores a power play goal at 12:02 of the first period in Game 4 of the Eastern Conference semi-final against Philadelphia. The Bruins won the game 5–1 and swept the series 4–0 on Friday, May 6.

below:

Bruins rookie forward Brad Marchand barrels down the wing against the Flyers. After a solid 21-goal, 41-point regular season, Marchand was a one-man wrecking crew and Boston's third-leading scorer in the playoffs.

Steve Babineau

above:

With Patrice Bergeron missing the first two games of the Eastern Conference final due to injury, the Bruins shuffled the line-up. Rookie forward Tyler Seguin stepped in to tally a goal and an assist in his first playoff game and two goals and an assist in his second.

below:

The 2010–11 season began in David Krejci's home country of the Czech Republic. It ended with Krejci being the Bruins leading playoff scorer with 12 goals, 23 points, and a team high four game-winning goals.

Steve Babineau/Boston Bruins

right:

Seguin's second goal of the game against Dwayne Roloson at 6:30 of the second period of Game 2 gave the Bruins a 4–2 lead. Boston held on to win 6–5 and even the series at 1–1.

"Their transition game was outstanding," points out Julien, "they frustrated a lot of teams by sitting back in the neutral zone and waiting for teams to turn the puck over, but they had a much better team than people gave them credit for, a good goaltender, and up front some great scoring potential."

Tampa proved that scouting report accurate in Game 1, winning in Boston 5–2, with five different goal scorers and 32 saves from Dwayne Roloson. Two nights later, the Bruins would even the series in a 6–5 barn burner.

Of note to start the series, Chris Kelly moved up from the third line to center rookie Brad Marchand and Mark Recchi in place of Patrice Bergeron. "Bergie" missed the first two games of the series after taking a shoulder-to-head hit from Claude Giroux during the third period of Game 4 against the Flyers. The absence of Bergeron also made room for the insertion of rookie Tyler Seguin into the playoff lineup for the first time. He made the most of it; tallying a goal and an assist in his first appearance, and adding two more goals and an assist in his second. The Bruins had discovered another offensive weapon, which meant for now B's tough guy and catalyst Shawn Thornton was the odd man out.

Despite Bergeron's concussion history, the Bruins' post-season leading scorer at the time returned for Game 3.

In Tampa the two teams would continue to swap victories, again with the road team winning first. Game 4 featured the Bruins' biggest meltdown of the playoffs and proved the resiliency of the Lightning. Down 3–0 in the game, Mike Smith replaced Roloson in net, and Tampa stormed back to pull out a 5–3 win.

Lord Stanley

Steve Babineau/NHLI/Getty

"Somehow, we started getting stretched out again [through the neutral zone]," Julien said postgame, "they started getting speed, they started getting momentum, and after they scored a couple goals, we almost looked like we were paralyzed out there."

Tied at two, the series returned to Boston where the B's took command with a 3–1 victory. The third period featured the save of the series, Thomas diving back with his stick on the goal line to stop Steve Downie's bid to tie the game off a rebound. Meanwhile, the B's goal scorers were a reflection of the regular and post seasons with key acquisitions coming up big at important times. Nathan Horton scored his seventh of the playoffs, rookie phenom Brad Marchand scored his sixth, the game winner, and Rich Peverley closed it out with an empty netter, his second goal and eighth point of the playoffs.

In Game 6, led by the irreplaceable Marty St. Louis and his two goals, the Bolts held on for a 6–5 victory. David Krejci took over as the Bruins postseason scoring leader with a hat trick, but it wasn't enough in a losing effort.

above:

Tim Thomas, with some help from Patrice Bergeron, turns away a great Brett Clark scoring chance at 6:33 of the second period in Game 5 of the Eastern Conference final. Lightning forward Steven Stamkos, who fed a pass, watches on the right. Thomas made 33 saves as the Bruins won 3–1 to take a 3–2 series lead.

left:

Nathan Horton scored the lone goal of Game 7 against the Lightning at 12:27 of the third period, tipping in a centering feed from David Krejci. Left to right, Milan Lucic, Krejci, Eric Brewer, Steven Stamkos, Dwayne Roloson, Mattias Ohlund, Horton.

Chapter 17

Steve Babineau/Boston Bruins

Steve Babineau/Boston Bruins

above:

Group hug?! Patrice Bergeron, Zdeno Chara, and quickly off the bench, back-up goalie Tuukka Rask, are the first to mob Tim Thomas after the Game-7 victory against Tampa Bay on Friday, May 27, 2011.

below:

The Bruins surround NHL Deputy Commissioner Bill Daly and the Prince of Wales Trophy after winning the Eastern Conference final against the Tampa Bay Lightning.

"We battled hard," said Krejci, "we just have to take the positives and carry them through to the next game."

The final game of the series would be the last one played in the Eastern Conference in the month of May. The winner of Game 7 would have four days off before the start of the Stanley Cup final on June 1st.

It was "oldies but goodies" night in Boston, featuring 37-year-old Thomas and 41-year-old Roloson starting in net. The two dominated, once again proving why some, including Boston University Head Coach Jack Parker, have playfully suggested that hockey should be renamed "goalie." In the end Thomas came out on top 1–0. The game was penalty-free and featured Horton's third game-winning and second series-winning goal of the playoffs.

"Once I saw how well Dwayne Roloson was playing it started to dawn on me that [needing a shutout to win] might be the case, but I tried not to focus on it and I took it one shot at a time," Thomas told CBC Sports. "Who would have ever guessed with all the goals we've given up in this series that we'd win the final game 1–0."

Fans, teammates, and opponents who had watched Thomas all season would have guessed it; he was the clear cut favorite as playoff MVP heading into the Cup final.

Steve Babineau/Boston Bruins

Bring on the Western Conference Champion Vancouver Canucks.

Maybe the most amazing thing about Boston winning the Stanley Cup is the fact that they found a way to bounce back from the types of losses they suffered in Games 1 and 2 on the road.

They lost the first match 1–0 when Raffi Torres scored with 19 seconds remaining in regulation. They lost the second game 3–2 when Alex Burrows scored 11 seconds into overtime.

The Bruins seemed undaunted.

When the scene switched to Boston, so did some of the personnel. Feisty fan favorite Shawn Thornton was inserted back in the line-up at the expense of Seguin. With number 22 leading the way, the Bruins' traditional hard-hitting approach took over early in Game 3. But it was a Vancouver hit that may have changed the series.

Five minutes into the game, Canucks defenseman Aaron Rome stepped up with a late shoulder hit to the head of Horton, who flew back, hit his head on the ice, and lay motionless just inside the Canucks' blueline. Horton was carted off on a stretcher and taken to Mass General Hospital. Fortunately, the report came down that he was moving all of his extremities. Needless to say, the Bruins used the hit as motivation.

"It was intense, it was emotional," said Chara, "we actually had a few guys speaking up throughout the final, but

above:

The Bruins starting line-up listening to the national anthems before Game 1 in Vancouver; left to right, Johnny Boychuk, Brad Marchand, Mark Recchi, Patrice Bergeron, and Zdeno Chara.

left:

Alex Burrows, chased by Zdeno Chara, on his way to the game-winning wraparound goal against Tim Thomas just 11 seconds into sudden death overtime to win Game 2 for Vancouver 3–2.

below:

Bruins defenseman Andrew Ference pins Canuck Mason Raymond along the boards during Game 5 of the Stanley Cup final in Vancouver. The Canucks took a 3–2 series lead with a 1–0 victory.

above:

Boston College product Cory Schneider, who replaced Roberto Luongo in the Vancouver net early in the third period of Game 4, watches as Brad Marchand crushes and upends Daniel Sedin. Marchand scored a backbreaking goal at 13:29 of the second period to give Boston a 3–0 lead, just two-and-a-half minutes after Michael Ryder had tallied. The Bruins won 4–0 to even the series at two victories apiece.

above:

Bruins goalie Tim Thomas hurdles fallen Canuck Ryan Kesler during Game 6. The Bruins pounded out a 5–2 victory, this time chasing netminder Luongo from the contest just eight-and-a-half minutes into the first period.

in that game we made sure everyone stayed focused because Games 3 and 4 were so huge for us."

The Bruins went on to win the game 8–1.

Horton was done for the series with a concussion, while Rome was suspended the rest of the series for the hit.

In Game 4, the Bruins dominated again, winning 4–0 with huge early saves from Thomas, two goals from Peverley, one from Ryder, and one from dominant rookie Brad Marchand, easily one of the most effective and most important all-around players in the series.

"We're gonna put these last two games behind us," said Canucks Head Coach Alain Vigneault, "we play real well at home, and we're going to go feed off the energy from our fans and give it our best shot."

Steve Babineau/NHLI/Getty

left:

Before each playoff home game a Bruins legend would serve as honorary captain and launch the passing of an enormous banner through the crowd at the TD Garden. For Game 6 it was none other than 93-year-old former Bruins captain, head coach, and general manager Milt Schmidt who won his first Cup in 1939 at the age of 21. Schmidt remembers 1939 better than most of us remember 2001.

below:

Brad Marchand gives the Bruins a 2–0 lead and celebrates the goal in Game 7 of the Stanley Cup final in Vancouver.

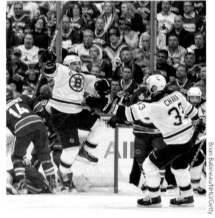

Brian Babineau/NHLI/Getty

Steve Babineau/Boston Bruins

Lacking thus far for Vancouver were the high scoring Sedin twins, who through four games had combined for just two points. Also, starting goaltender Roberto Luongo seemed a bit unsure of himself, after being yanked in Game 4 when he gave up his 12th road goal of the series.

Back in British Columbia, however, Vigneault received what he had envisioned from his team and their fans in Game 5. He also saw a bounceback from Luongo, who shut out the Bruins 1–0.

"I know what to do to get ready and have my A-game," Luongo said with a shrug, "so I thought we all played well and stepped up our level of play, and took it to a new level to win this game."

Luongo's apparent secret formula at home: a game day stroll along a seawall to clear his head.

"Yeah, I did that again today," Luongo admitted, "I put my hoodie on and my headphones...I put my head down and I focus on the journey and everything I need to do to be ready for the game. I don't know if they have any seawalls in Boston but I'm going to look for one."

No such luck. Game 6 in Boston was more of the same for the netminder and the Canucks in the unfriendly confines of the TD Garden.

above:

Patrice Bergeron's second goal of Game 7 came shorthanded at the 17:35 mark of the second period, and pretty much put the game out of reach.

top:

Bruins executives made their way to the bench to celebrate the Stanley Cup victory with the hockey staff.

bottom:

While on the ice: Gregory Campbell leaps on to Dennis Seidenberg, Zdeno Chara on left, part of Tomas Kaberle on right (#12), with Patrice Bergeron and Tyler Seguin ready to join.

right:

The two longest tenured Bruins celebrate. Patrice Bergeron was drafted in the 2nd round in 2003 and played 73 games that very next season as an 18-year-old. Tim Thomas first joined the organization in 2002–03, when he played 43 games in Providence and 4 with Boston. He's been a regular with the big club since 2005.

Luongo allowed three quick first-period goals and was pulled after just eight-and-a-half minutes. Back-up Cory Schneider gave up a goal a minute later, and the Bruins were off to the races with a 4–0 lead. The four goals in 4:14 established a Cup final record for the fastest four goals by one team.

Marchand, Milan Lucic, Ference, Ryder, and Krejci all scored in Boston's 5–2 victory.

The Bruins franchise would play in its first ever Stanley Cup final Game 7.

"It's tremendous for the city and the organization," Mark Recchi said after Game 6. "Not too many people counted on us being at this point right now, so it's a great feeling, we battled hard tonight, we came to play, and it's coming down to one game and this is what we dream of."

above:

The 2011 Stanley Cup Champion Boston Bruins, June 15, 2011.

Three questions intertwined heading into Game 7. Would the "homer" series phenomenon, with the host team winning each game, be broken? With their latest win and Luongo getting yanked early, did the Bruins plant a big enough seed of doubt in the minds of the Canucks, even with the series returning to Vancouver? And were the Bruins' momentum and team confidence now insurmountable?

The answer to all of these questions was "yes!"

Patrice Bergeron scored the all-important first goal, the only one the Bruins would need, at 14:37 of the first period. He added a shorthanded goal in the second. Before and after that tally, Marchand would also score twice, capping off a Cup final that saw the rookie ring up five goals and two

right:

Captain Zdeno Chara hoists the Cup following his fifth season in Boston, reaching his stated goal of winning it all by the end of his first free agent contract. In Prague prior to the Cup season, he signed a seven-year contract extension to commence in October of 2011.

top:

Bergeron and Thomas after the Cup hand-off.

bottom:

After his fourth pro season, Milan Lucic, the Bruins 2nd round pick in 2006, has a Stanley Cup to go with the Memorial Cup he won with, ironically, his hometown Vancouver Giants of the Western Hockey League in 2007.

assists. The only player more valuable: goaltender Tim Thomas, who allowed just eight goals in seven games, and became the oldest player ever to win the Conn Smythe Trophy as playoff MVP.

Twenty-five playoff games: sixteen victories.

New England waited 39 years between Cups. The people of this historic hockey region poured into the streets to show their appreciation and prove their intrinsic love for the game. The Bruins victory parade was the largest of any kind for any championship in Boston's history.

"We have amazing fans in Boston and New England," team President Cam Neely said after the win, "the support they've given us the last few years, they've been there, they've been waiting for this, it's a pretty special moment for everyone involved and anyone who's a Bruins fan."

Chapter 17

Brian Babineau/NHLI/Getty

Adam McQuaid and
Brad Marchand

Steve Babineau/Boston Bruins

Shawn Thornton and "The Sheriff"
Shane Hnidy

Steve Babineau/Boston Bruins

Gregory Campbell

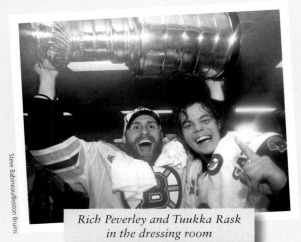

Steve Babineau/Boston Bruins

Rich Peverley and Tuukka Rask
in the dressing room

Brian Babineau/NHLI/Getty

Team President and
Hockey Hall-of-Famer
Cam Neely

Brian Babineau/NHLI/Getty

Head Coach Claude Julien

Steve Babineau/NHLI/Getty

The whole organization
celebrates together.

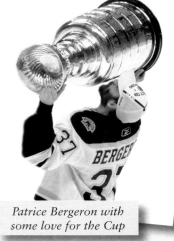

Steve Babineau/NHLI/Getty

Patrice Bergeron with
some love for the Cup

Brian Babineau/Boston Bruins

Michael Ryder, Chris Kelly, Tyler Seguin

Steve Babineau/Boston Bruins

Daniel Paille, Dennis Seidenberg, Andrew Ference, Tyler Seguin. The leather bomber jacket, awarded by teammates to the Bruin's most valuable player after each playoff victory, is wrapped around the Cup.

Lord Stanley

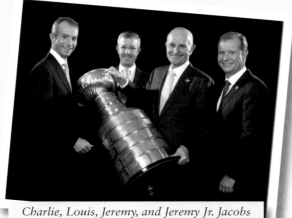

Steve Babineau/Boston Bruins

Charlie, Louis, Jeremy, and Jeremy Jr. Jacobs

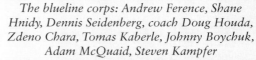

Steve Babineau/Boston Bruins

The blueline corps: Andrew Ference, Shane Hnidy, Dennis Seidenberg, coach Doug Houda, Zdeno Chara, Tomas Kaberle, Johnny Boychuk, Adam McQuaid, Steven Kampfer

Steve Babineau/Boston Bruins

Steve Babineau/Boston Bruins

David Krejci

Bruins hockey staff; standing left to right, Derek Repucci, John White-side, Scott Waugh, Matt Falconer, James "Beets" Johnson; kneeling, Don Del Negro, Keith Robinson

Steve Babineau/Boston Bruins

The coaching staff, left to right; Bob Essensa (goalie coach), Doug Jarvis, Claude Julien, Doug Houda, Geoff Ward

It's hard to believe that 38 years have gone by since I shot my first game back in the 1973–74 season. I have photographed the action at close to 1,900 total games, and have driven many miles around our great Northeast region and across Canadian provinces. I've seen so many players come through the Bruins organization (400 or so). I have so many memories of the Garden, NHL players, and friends I have met along the way. And what's great for me with this book is that I have captured all this through my camera, which will allow me to keep those memories forever. I really have bled Black and Gold for 38 years, just like all the die-hard Bruins fans. However, my closeness with the organization and its players makes me feel like I've bled a little more than most.

Starting out as a young fan working freelance as a photographer for *The Hockey News* for three years, which at the time paid very little but got me into games for nothing, I was living the dream of every Bruins fan. Plus, I had the best seat in the house. However, I quickly found out that my passion as a Bruins fan changed and would be recognized when Bruins management took notice of my work. It started to look like I really knew what I was doing.

I got married in June of 1973 just before I started covering games for the first time. I really feel my wife, Anita, just thought at the time I had figured out a

The first hockey magazine Babineau ever bought, March 1964.

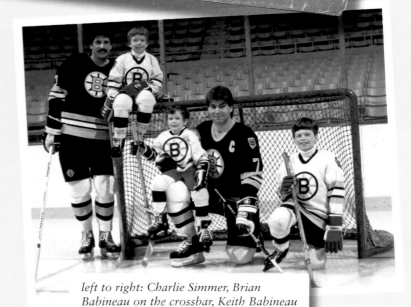

left to right: Charlie Simmer, Brian Babineau on the crossbar, Keith Babineau on Bourque's knee, Ray Bourque, Chris Babineau. "My three sons"—1985.

Ray Bourque, Steve Babineau, and Cam Neely after a team photo. (Nice moustache)

Ed Fowler

way to go to games without paying for a ticket. Thank God I married a Canadian girl; I think I had a little more rope to pursue this career. After all, she had attended all those Boston Braves and New England Whalers games when I had season tickets during the '72–'73 season.

After we got married and I started to convert our apartment bathroom into a darkroom three days a week to supply material to *The Hockey News, Hockey Digest*, and various local publications,

> *Thank God I married a Canadian girl; I think I had a little more rope to pursue this career.*

Bobby Orr and Chris Babineau prior to Orr's Hall-of-Fame induction in Toronto.

my rope was getting shorter. Fortunately, not much later, I found myself in 1977 as team color photographer for a storied Original Six franchise. Plus, I was now shooting mostly color film, which I could not develop at the apartment, so my rope got extended even further. Meanwhile, other opportunities opened up with national publications, the Topps card company, and various other clients. When that money started to arrive, it understandably made Anita happy!

During the first 20-year span of my photography business, I also held a full-time job with Dennison and G.C.C. Technologies, working as a distribution, manufacturing, and inventory control manager. The experience I gained working in these companies, I feel, helped me later when I established my own business, in how to deal with scheduling, budgets, relationships, and other responsibilities. I was able to manage my regular job and shoot 50 to 60 hockey games a year, to be away from home so much, to have four kids, and to be successful with the photography because of Anita's understanding and her appreciation of my passion for the game.

In 1964, when I was 13 years old, I asked my mother for 50 cents to buy a copy of *Hockey Illustrated*. Little did I realize that that book would set me on a path into sports photography. Up until then there was very little written about hockey in *Sports Illustrated* or

Brian Babineau took this picture of dad Steve setting up Sergei Samsonov, Ray Bourque, and Joe Thornton for a shot at center ice.

In 1964, when I was 13 years old, I asked my mother for 50 cents to buy a copy of Hockey Illustrated. Little did I realize that that book would set me on a path into sports photography.

Sport Magazine, yet here was a magazine dedicated to the game of hockey, loaded with black-and-white pictures. It was the issue with a color action cover of Chicago Blackhawk goalie Glenn Hall and defenseman Elmer "Moose" Vasko skating into the camera, and it changed it all for me. How that photographer (Harold Barkley) stopped the action and made a great color image was something that I had never seen before. I bought every issue of that magazine from then on and had to convince my mother to let me buy three copies of each issue a few years later. That's when they put full-color pinups in the centerfold section, and I wanted to put the pictures on my bedroom wall while keeping one issue intact. Barkley, a photographer in Toronto, dominated with

Brian Babineau at age one, posed wearing a Bruins t-shirt in front of the team photo. Little did he know he'd be taking the team picture seventeen years later.

Chris and Brian Babineau with Terry O'Reilly on the bench at the old Garden.

Don Cherry holding one-year-old Chris Babineau at Steve Babineau's apartment during a meeting to review photography.

his color work on all the great players: Howe, Mahovlich, Delvecchio, Ullman, Mikita, Sawchuk, Beliveau, Richard, etc. The only disappointing thing was they never ran Bruins players; maybe Bucyk once. My bedroom was plastered with these pinups. Barkley's work definitely had an impact on my direction in life. I consider him a pioneer in hockey photography, being one of the first to use strobe photography in game situations. Just recently, I also found out that he was more of a glamor, all-around photographer, and also that he was disabled. I wish I had met him. It was a thrill for me years later when my work started to appear in the same magazine. I wonder if my son Brian looks at my work the same way I look at Barkley's.

Good luck happens to all of us sometime in life and having my first camera stolen by someone who broke into our house in 1972 turned out to be a blessing in disguise. The insurance claim allowed me to buy a better camera with adaptable lenses. This allowed me to get closer to the action from wherever I was sitting, oftentimes in obstructed-view seats in those early days.

A chance phone call to *Hockey News* editor Charlie Halpin asking him why they didn't have any pictures of the W.H.A. players, and his response—"Kid, we just don't have any"—opened the door. He asked me if I'd like to shoot for him until he could get me a season credential. My first thoughts were that my mom was going to kill me for making this phone call to Montreal, and what was I going to do with my Whalers season tickets that I bought for me and Anita (if I wasn't shooting)! I'm grateful to Charlie for taking that call and giving me the break that I needed to shoot professional hockey, even if it was the other league at the time. I was shooting on a credential for the biggest hockey publisher in the world and it was just a matter of time before I was shooting the "big show" and the Bruins for *The Hockey News*. A year later that experience began.

I shot for the Bruins for two seasons and supplied all of their color photography for brochures, posters, yearbooks, and programs, using available light photography, which I had figured out how to use to get good results. That's when I figured I had to step up to the next level and get a new camera that worked with strobe lighting that could be mounted in the catwalk at the Garden. I had the camera covered finance-wise, but the strobes were a minimum $6,000 investment. I sat down one night with Paul Mooney, president of the Bruins and the Garden, and explained the advantage of the high-quality images produced using these strobes. It would enhance their yearbook, press guide, program covers, and merchandise posters and prints. Taking better pictures using this equipment would mean more revenue for the team. So I asked Mr. Mooney to buy the strobes and in return I would give the team three years' worth of yearbook pictures and any updated blowups needed for the Boards and Blades Club. I figured this was a no-brainer for the building and the team. His response was, "Kid, you buy the strobes, I'll have them installed for you and let you use the electricity for nothing."

I figured that my career had reached a roadblock. I explained my dilemma to my parents, and despite the fact they had no clue what I was talking about, they loaned me the $6,000 for the strobes. That decision, along with a new

Babs and P.J. Stock. Brian took this from a ladder on the ice.

Babs and Phil Esposito displaying the limited-edition print of his jersey retirement night when Ray Bourque handed over number 7.

274

Scrapbook

Brian, Terry O'Reilly, and Babs the first year the Fleet Center opened. O'Reilly was playing in the NHL alumni All-Star game the next day.

Keith and Brian in 1988 at the Garden, and twenty years later in the same pose at the TD Banknorth Garden: Keith an assistant equipment manager and Brian a team photographer.

camera, opened up doors with new clients within just one season. I recouped my investment by signing contracts to supply images of NHL players to various licensees of the League. I thank Mr. Mooney for putting the ball in my court on decision making, and for giving me the freedom with the team and building to use my strobes with no restrictions.

It didn't dawn on me until I was hired by Tehabi Books as a photo editor for a book that was being written by Clark Booth, *The Boston Bruins: Celebrating 75 Years*, that I had captured one-third of the history of this storied franchise with my work. It really hit home that all the time and effort that I had put in meant something. I researched Booth's story lines, scrambled through all of my pictures, and also did research at the Hockey Hall of Fame and Boston Public Library to find additional photography, which in some cases did not exist. It then sunk in that while my work covered the Bruins, it was far more than that. The library of images I had compiled on the game over 35 years was a significant body of work. It made me feel as though all of the effort was justified on a lot of levels.

I was so lucky to be accepted by all the players, coaches, and staff of the organization. It made my job easier to have their confidence and support on ideas. I think they knew I was going to accomplish the end result in the most efficient way. To have so many players simply call me Babs from decade to decade made me feel like I was part of the team. Veteran players telling rookies and new Bruins to go see Babs for pictures became a tradition passed from Cheevers to Cashman to O'Reilly to Park to Bourque to Thornton to Murray to Chara.

A fringe benefit to my hockey-shooting career has been a little taste of the rock-and-roll world. I've always loved Neil Young's music, ever since first seeing him way back in 1970 at what is now the Wang Center. I ended up going to see him a number of times (concert details a little hazy), and I started taking photos of his concerts. The man is a legend, and his music, his change in styles, has opened my ears to rock, folk, country, blues, or whatever he was playing. I also related to Neil because of other similarities—being a tall drink of water, I myself 6-foot-3; I was thin, about 155 pounds soaking wet back in the day; I sang in the church choir; and people say I look just like him. I've since gone on to respond that I'm his stunt double.

In 1988 I asked Bill Brett, sports photographer with the *Boston Globe*, if he could pull some strings and get me a pass to shoot Neil at Great Woods in Mansfield, Massachusetts. He was then playing blues with a new band and performing for two nights. Mission accomplished: I got to shoot both shows. The kicker was that I met Neil prior to the second show at his hotel with 10-year-old Brian in tow. I introduced myself as the Bruins photographer and he quickly responded as if I knew his dad, Scott. His late father was a Hall of Fame sports writer in Canada. The connection was made. I've since amassed an archive of more than 10,000 images of Neil in concert, and I've provided him photos for a number of purposes, including his Bridge School charity, for which our photo and poster efforts have helped raise more than $150,000.

Many hockey players love Neil, especially the older ones and the Canadian ones, so I've swapped quite a few concert

Babs, daughter Jamie Babineau and Neil Young on the steps of his studio in Mountainview, California, 1992.

Brian Babineau

Bruin Adam Oates and his former teammate in St. Louis, Blues scorer Brett Hull. This in-game photo "opportunity" was requested before the game by Oates.

Babs talks hockey with Neil Young's father Scott, prior to a charity concert in Mountainview. The late Scott Young was a Hockey Hall-of-Fame honored sports writer.

Brian Babineau

Neil Young. Steve Babineau has provided countless concert photos for the rock star's music paraphernalia and for his Bridge School charity.

photos for cool hockey stuff. Al Iafrate gave me an All-Star jersey once, Joe Juneau hit me up for some recordings and photos, and Juneau and others have made donations to The Bridge School.

The best was Adam Oates. He approached me a few days before Christmas one year, asking me if I could get him one of Neil's guitars signed for his buddy Brett Hull. My first response was, "Are you crazy? Neil's not going to give up a guitar like you give up hockey sticks." I went home that night and wondered how I could find a compromise. I took a chance and called Neil's ranch in California and spoke to his wife, Peggi. She said giving up a guitar was indeed unlikely, but explained that one of his favorites was a D45 Martin acoustic. So I asked her if I was able to find a similar

guitar and send it to the ranch, would Neil sign it for Brett Hull? Absolutely! So I went guitar hunting to a classic guitar store in Cambridge, [MA] and to my amazement they had a beat-up D45 Martin guitar that still sounded great. "Oatsie" sent me a check for the guitar, I couriered the guitar to California, Neil signed it, and Oatsie gave it to "Hullie" for Christmas. That was a pretty damn good gift if you ask me, and I'm glad I could help out with something so cool.

Rob Simpson is a Neil fan as well; I found that out even before he agreed to write (and edit) this book for me with his publisher. But it was eight months or so after our writing agreement that Neil came rolling into town, late in 2007. Every night of the concert tour seemed to conflict with Bruins games, which Rob helped commentate on television. One night, though, he was able to run (literally) over after a home game and catch most of the show at the Orpheum. Post-concert, after a patient wait, Rob was able to meet Neil and talk hockey with him for five or 10 minutes. Despite Rob's love for the man's music, it was 18 years between Neil shows for Simpson (his first was in Melbourne, Australia, in 1989). I'm very happy I was able to hook him up.

"Simmer" and I crossed paths many times running around the Garden while

⟩⟩BRIAN: MY DAD IS A GANGSTA! ⟩⟩KEITH: PLEASE ARREST THIS MAN!

The Hockey News

September 30, 2003 Vol. 57 No. 4

BOSTON BRUINS

The
Untouchable
One

**Boston-area paparazzi
loses mind, dons fedora**

A mocked up cover of The Hockey News, *with Babs as a gangster, September 30, 2003, [designed by Jamie Hodgson]. This shot was taken after an "Untouchables" shoot with Joe Thornton, who turned out to be not-so-untouchable.*

To have so many players simply call me Babs from decade to decade made me feel like I was part of the team.

he was reporting for NESN, and we saw a lot of each other during the 2010 NHL Winter Classic. I was getting shots and he was the ice-level reporter for the national radio broadcast. What a spectacle at Fenway Park, which over the years had actually become kind of my third home. Although I'm associated mostly with the Bruins, I developed a strong relationship with the Red Sox and the ball park starting in 1976. That's when I began working as a freelance photographer for Century Publishing and the magazine *Baseball Digest*. Just three years later, this led to an opportunity to work for the Fleer trading card company, which began making baseball cards in 1979. For the next fourteen years I took action and posed shots

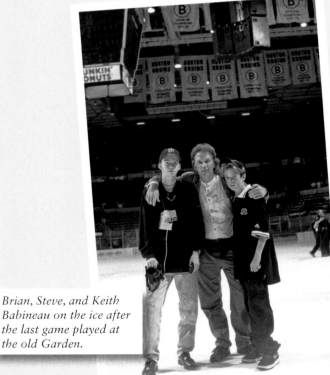

Brian, Steve, and Keith Babineau on the ice after the last game played at the old Garden.

Lauren Roache

Brian, Jamie, and Babs worked together behind the scenes at practically every Bruins game the last few seasons.

at ball parks all around the east coast. Some of my more monumental baseball card photos include rookie cards for Cal Ripken Jr., Roger Clemens, Don Mattingly, and Kirby Puckett among others. In 2003 the Red Sox officially added me and my son Brian to their five-man photography staff. The timing was great as the Sox won their first World Series in 86 years the very next season. The club was generous enough to reward both of us with diamond watches in 2004 and then with diamond championship rings after their title in 2007. This became maybe the biggest year of my career as Brian and I also earned NBA title rings shooting for the Boston Celtics, and I sold my entire NHL archive of more than 250,000 images to the National Hockey League.

Capturing baseball images was a great way to spend my hockey off-season, getting to know Fenway, getting to know some great people in the game of baseball, and adding to my sports photography legacy. Then in 2010 my sporting worlds merged. The Winter Classic on New Years Day at Fenway Park will rank with my most unforgettable memories. I'll never forget being able to wander around the field, although it was snow covered, in the same spots my childhood heroes Ted Williams, Chuck Schilling, and Carl Yastremski had wandered. I was in a roaming mode during the third period of the Classic, capturing the essence of the ball park, the crowd, and the event. As is often the case

Brian Babineau

Ray Bourque, Milt Schmidt, and Bobby Orr standing behind Steve Babineau at the 2007 alumni golf tournament.

with photography, luck played a big part in my day. I just happened to be perched high above the Red Sox first base dugout, shooting towards the Green Monster and the goal the Bruins were attacking. When Mark Recchi finally tied the game late in the period, and Marco Sturm won it in overtime, I was in a great spot to record history with a terrific backdrop.

The only thing missing in my four decades of work was a Stanley Cup championship. This dream would come true for all of us Bruins fans in 2011. The emotion of being in Vancouver for Game 7 with my son Brian chokes me up as I think about it. This sums up the entire championship experience: I was at center ice just inside an entry-way, about fifteen rows back from the ice, while Brian was working in the corner on the opposite side of the ice to my right. We could see each other the whole time. I remember looking up at the clock with two minutes left in the game; Brian looked up at me, smiled, and held up a clenched fist. I started to cry. Needless to say it was a joyous, monumental event for him and me, for the Bruins, and for the city and our fans. I thought of all the players who had worked so hard over the years and never won, guys like Terry O'Reilly and Rick Middleton, and I was very happy for (team President) Cam Neely.

As you'll often find with hockey people, and often times learn from hockey people: it's family first. The same goes for me. The fact that I have been lucky enough to have two of my sons, Brian and Keith, attend games and work over the last 18 years with me has been very special. Keith was eight years old when he started filling water bottles on the

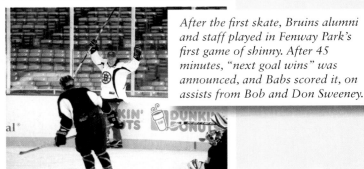

After the first skate, Bruins alumni and staff played in Fenway Park's first game of shinny. After 45 minutes, "next goal wins" was announced, and Babs scored it, on assists from Bob and Don Sweeney.

Mike Ivins/Red Sox

Steve Babineau/The Hockey News

Your author, who handled live ice-level reporting for the national radio broadcast of the Winter Classic, mock interviewing Bruins Director of Player Personnel Scott Bradley. To the left is our field producer and to the right is Scott Fitzgerald from the Bruins scouting staff.

Rusty Daschund

The family core of Sports Action Images: Jamie, Steve, and Brian Babineau.

Lou Capozzola

Babs's son Keith Babineau, a long-time locker room attendant at the TD Garden, Babs, and Brian in Vancouver after Game 7.

Our beloved photographer sips from Lord Stanley's Cup with an assist from mullet-laden defenseman Adam McQuaid.

Brian Babineau

Glace Bay, Nova Scotia, native Anita Babineau with the person she's put up with all of these years, Babs.

Brian Babineau

Jamie Babineau, the Stanley Cup and Patrice Bergeron.

Steve Babineau

players' bench, then moving to visiting team locker room attendant for most of the next 17 years. For one year, when he was 25, he was able to work the home locker room on an interim basis as assistant equipment manager. It was quite a thrill taking the 2007–08 team photo knowing he was in the picture.

Brian was 15 years old when he took his first picture, and for 19 years he's been assisting me in expanding our responsibilities as team photographers for the Boston Bruins, Boston Celtics, Boston Red Sox, Manchester Monarchs, and the Boston Garden. Brian went to school to bring the ever-changing technology in today's photography, such as digital images and photo editing, to the table, enabling us to expand our photography capabilities beyond being game action shooters. His computer graphics work and ideas have brought some creative promotional concepts to the table for the Bruins and the Garden. I'm sure that in the early stages of his photography I taught him a few things, but he has taught the old man a lot more in the new age of photography. I would have been overwhelmed had I tried to handle it all myself. Brian will carry the torch with the Bruins hopefully for another 38 years and keep the Babs name rolling for a few more decades.

My dad always told me to leave something behind. Four great kids—Chris, Brian, Keith, and Jamie—this book, and a few hundred thousand or so photographs on the game of hockey…I think he's smiling!

Scrapbook

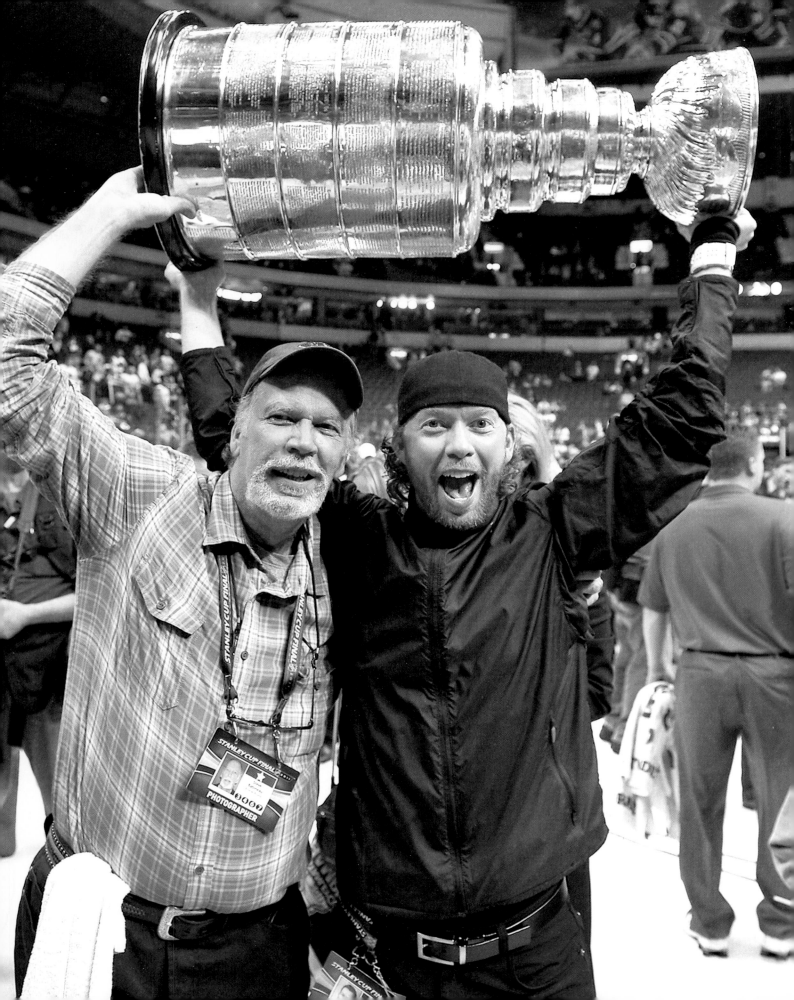

INDEX

Note: Page numbers referring to individuals and events in photos and photo captions are referenced in italics. Italicized page references featuring "n" indicate that the individual or event is referred to in the caption but does not appear in the accompanying photo.

A

Adams family, *48n*
Adduono, Rick, 206
Aitken, Jonathan, 190
Albelin, Tommy, *113*
Alberts, Andrew, *188*, 190
Allen, Bobby, 190
Allison, Jason, *204*, 206
Anderson, Earl, 236
Andreychuk, Dave, 108, 206
Androl, Heidi, *249*
Armstrong, Bob, *33–35*
Arniel, Jamie, 206
Arniel, Scott, 236
Art Ross Trophy, 54, 63
Asham, Arron, 245
Ashton, Brent, 236
Atlanta Thrashers, 244
Auld, Alex, 174
Awrey, Don, *73*
Axelsson, P.J. "Axey," 153, 230, *230*, 233, 236

B

Babineau, Anita, 10, 108, 270–271, 272, *281*
Babineau, Brian, 14, 15, *15*, 103, *119n*, *270*, *272*, *272n*, *273*, *274n*, 275, *278*, 279, *279*, 280, 281
Babineau, Chris, *270*, 271, *273*, *249*, 281
Babineau, Jamie, *276*, *279*, *279*, 281

Babineau, Keith, *270*, *275*, *278*, *280*, 281
Babineau, Steve "Babs," *1*, 1–15, *2*, *7*, *11*, *15*, *36*, 224, *224*, *271*, *272–273*, *274*, *275*, *276*, *277*, *278*, *279*
   and 2010 NHL Winter Classic, 241, 244, 278, 279–280
   and 2011 Stanley Cup, 280
   on Bobby Orr, 6–7, 47, 53–54, 55–58, *62n*
   on Cam Neely, 112, 118–119, 126
   career, 7–13, 14–15, 26–27, *164n*
   childhood, 1–3
   on coaches, 154–155
   on defensemen, 177–178, *177n*
   on Don Cherry, 129–130
   first press credentials, 12, *12n*
   as freelance baseball photographer, 278–280, 281
   on the Garden, 23, 31
   on Gerry Cheevers, 160, *160n*
   hockey career, 4–6
   on John Bucyk, 46, 47–48
   on Pat Burns, 153
   in penalty box, 219–220
   on Phil Esposito, 68
   as photographer of Bruins games, 241, 270, 281
   pickup hockey at the Garden, 85–86
   on Ray Bourque, 95, 99, 100–103, 104–105, 108
   sale of photo archive, 15, 279
   scrapbook, 270–279
   strobes, 31, *169n*, 244
   on Terry O'Reilly, 229–230
Bailey, Scott, 174
Bales, Mike, 174
Banks, Darren, 226
Barahona, Ralph, 206

Barkley, Harold, 272–273
Baron, Marco, *173*, 174
Barr, Dave, 236
Bartkowski, Matt, 190
Bartulis, Oskars, *247*
Bates, Shawn, 206
Bathgate, Andy, 8
Bauer, 14
Bauer, Bobby, 20
Baumgartner, Ken, 226, *226*
Beaupre, Don, *121*
Beauregard, Stephane, *27*
Beddoes, Clayton, 206
Beers, Bob, 97, 182, 183, *188*, 190
Begin, Steve, 236
Belanger, Ken, 226
Belanger, Yves, 174
Bellows, Brian, *181*
Bennett, Bill, *143*, 206
Beraldo, Paul, 206
Berard, Bryan, 190
Bergeron, Patrice, 206, *206*, *246*, *246*, *247*, *247*, 248, *250*, 256, 257, 259, *259n*, *260*, *261*, *262*, *264*, *265*, *266*, *267*, *268*
Berman, Len, 67
Berthiaume, Daniel, *173*, 174
Bester, Allan, *80*
Beverley, Nick, *5*, 190, *223*
Big Bad Bruins, 33, 130
Bitz, Byron, 236, *246*
Billington, Craig, *173*, 174
Blair, Wren, 51
Blatny, Zdenek, 206
Blue, John, 174, *174*
"Blue" (Don Cherry's dog), *134*
blueliners, 177–193
Blum, John, 190
Boards and Blades Club, 13, 274

Bobby Orr Museum, 60
Bochenski, Brandon, 206
Bodger, Doug, *114*
Bodnarchuk, Andrew, 190
Bonvie, Dennis, 226
Booth, Clark, 275
Bossy, Mike, 113
Boston Braves, 9–10, *11*, 12
Boston Bruins, 281
　and 2010 NHL Winter Classic, 241,
　　243, *244*, 245–249
　and 2010–11 Stanley Cup campaign,
　　251, 252, 253–261, *257*, *261*
　Bull Gang, *36*
　captains, 46, *89*, 99, *106*, *186–187*
　coaches, 145–157, *271*
　defensemen, 177–193
　enforcers, 211–227
　in Europe, 251, 252, *252*, 253
　executives, *36*, 48, *267*
　fundraising of, 249
　goaltenders, 159–175, *257*, *261*
　grinders, 229–236, 255
　Honored Numbers, *33–35*
　jerseys, *9*, *11*
　ownership families, *48n*
　pizza, *37*
　scorers, 195–209
　Seventh Player Award, *129n*, 166, 216
　Stanley Cup wins, 19–20, 54–58,
　　57, 69, 70, 81, *265*, *266*,
　　267, *267*, 268, *268*
Boston Bruins: Celebrating 75 Years
　(Booth), 275
Boston Celtics, 281
Boston Garden, *16–17*, *17*, 17–37, *19*,
　　20, *29*, *32–33*, *256*, *262*, 264, 274
　arena, 23–24
　atmosphere of, 17–19
　bandbox, 17
　concourse, 24–25
　demolition, 33
　dogs, 25–26
　four-sided clock, 20
　Gallery Gods, 29–30
　history of, 17
　interior, rooms in, 21–23
　Last Hurrah, 33, *140*
　last official Bruins game, *23*
　mice and rats, 25–26
　"obstructed view," *19*
　penalty box, *29*
　press box, 27–29
　small ice surface, 115
　Stanley Cup wins, 19–20, *20*
Boston Globe, 17, 51, 55, 134, 276
Boston Record American, 54, 67
Boston Red Sox, 278–279, 281
Bouchard, Dan, *72*
Bouchard, Pierre, 42, *81*

Boucher, Guy, 258
Bourque, Chris, *102*, 103, *109*
Bourque, Christiane, 102, *109*
Bourque, Melissa, *109*
Bourque, Ray, *1*, *4*, *9n*, 14, 22–23, *24*,
　　27, *31*, *36*, *37*, *47*, *75*, *93*, *94–95*,
　　95, 95–109, *96*, *97*, *98*, *99*, *100*,
　　101, *102*, *103*, *104*, *105*, *106*, *107*,
　　108, *109*, *116*, 120, *126*, 148, 163,
　　177, *179*, *184*, 184–185, 186, *188*,
　　199, 200, *204*, *212*, 222, *230*, *270*,
　　271, *272*, *274n*, *279*
　All-Star Game MVP, *102*, 102–103
　awards, *96*, *100*, 102–103
　on Brad Park, 178
　on the Bruins, 97–98
　captain, 99, *106*, *198n*
　and Esposito's jersey, 74, *74*
　jersey retirement, *109*
　at Last Hurrah, 33
　records and statistics, 42, 95, *95*, 109
　Stanley Cup playoffs, 105–108
　on Terry O'Reilly, 92
Bourque, Ryan, *109*
Boutilier, Paul, 190
BOW line, 46
Bower, Johnny, *160*
Bowness, Rick, 157, *157*
Boxmeer, John Van, *69*
Boychuk, Johnny, 190, *246*, *247*, *248*,
　　257, *262*, 269
Boyes, Brad, 206
Boynton, Nick, *127*, 190
brawls, 43–44, 70–72, 81–85, 211–214
Brennan, Rich, 190
Brett, Bill, 246
Brewer, Eric, *260*
Brickley, Andy, 24, *25*, 83, 87, 89–90,
　　198–200, *205*, 206, 233
Bridge School, 247
Brimsek, Frank "Mr. Zero," 20, 159, 160
Broderick, Ken, *173*, 174
Brookbank, Wade, 226
Brooks, Ross, 174, *174*
Broten, Neal, *24*
Brown, Dave, 221
Brown, Sean, 190
Brown family, *48n*
Bryzgalov, Ilya, *252*
Buckley, Jerry, 12
Bucyk, Anne, 48
Bucyk, John "the Chief," 1, *14*, *33–35*,
　　38–39, *39*, 39–49, *40*, *41*, *42*, *43*,
　　44, 44–45, *46*, *47*, 48, *49*, *57*, *63*,
　　69, *71*, *93*, 120, 222
　awards, 42, 48
　as captain, 46
　"Chief Night" number one, *49*
　"Chief Night" number two, *39*, *47*, *47*
　on craziest guy, 142

　Detroit, years in, 43
　on Don Cherry, 134
　on fights and brawls, 43–44
　hip check, 44, 195
　Hockey Hall of Fame, induction
　　into, 48
　jersey retirement, 47, *49*
　at Last Hurrah, 33
　on the old Garden, 18
　on Phil Esposito, 67–68, 79
　post-retirement, 39–40
　records and statistics, *40n*, 42–43,
　　42n, 44, *44n*, 48, *49*
　retirement, 47
Bull Gang, *36*
Burke, Sean, *117*
Burns, Pat, 153, *153*, 157
Burridge, Randy, *22–23*, *31*, 236, *236*
Burrows, Alex, 262, *262*
Burrows, Dave, *44*
Byce, John, 206
Byers, Lyndon, *31*, 86, 113–114, 123,
　　215, *219*, 220, 222, 225, 226

C

Calder Trophy, 52, *108*, *166n*
Campbell, Clarence, 140
Campbell, Colin, 44
Campbell, Gregory, 236, 252, 253,
　　253, 265, 268
Campbell, Wade, *97*
Cancer Center, Tufts-New England
　Medical Center, 123
Canney, Dan, 21, *132*, 249
Carcillo, Daniel, 245, *245*
Carey, Jim, *163n*, 164, *165*, 174
Caron, Jordan, 206
Carlton, Johnny, 233
Carpenter, Bobby, *31*, 202, *205*, 206,
　　223, 233
Carriere, Larry, *201*
Carroll, Andy, *37*
Carson, bill, 19
Carter, Anson, *204*, 206
Carter, Jeff, 245
Carter, John, *31*, *205*, 206, 233
Casey, Jon, 174, *174*
Cashman, Wayne, 12, 30–31, 40, *44*,
　　49, 56, 67–68, 81, 91, 97, 130,
　　131, *137*, 142, *142*, *201*, 218–219,
　　222, 231, *233*, 236
Celebrity Marketing, 163
Chara, Zdeno, *186–187*, 190, *225*,
　　247, 248, 250, 252, 256, 261, 262,
　　262, 265, 267, *271*
Cheevers, Gerry, *14*, 40, 52, 57, 62,
　　66, 71, 72, *72*, 97, 136–137, 138,
　　143, *143*, 147, *147*, 154, 155,
　　157, *159*, 159–161, *160*, 162,
　　162–163, 163, 164, 174, 198

Chelios, Chris, *212*
Cherry, Don "Grapes," *5, 57, 69,* 89,
        92, 93, 129, 129–143, *130, 131,*
        132, 134, 136, 138–139, 140, 141,
        143, 147, 156, *182n,* 219, *243*
    on Bobby Orr, 60
    "Coach's Corner," 60, 139–140
    controversy, 140–141
    1979 Stanley Cup playoffs, 136–137
    statistics, *131n,* 135, 136, 157
Cherry, Rose, 129
Chervyakov, Denis, 190
Cheveldae, Tim, 174
Chiarelli, Peter, 80, 148, 255, *255n*
Chistov, Stanislav, 206
Christian, Dave, *31,* 206
Chynoweth, Dean, 226
Cimetta, Robert, 207
Clancy, King, 29–30
Clapper, Dit, 20
Clapper, Dit, daughter of, *33–35*
Clark, Brett, *260*
Clark, Gordie, 149, 207
Clarke, Bobby, 195, *244*
Clarke, Lenny, *248, 249*
Cloutier, Jacques, *25*
coaches, 145–157. *See also* Cherry,
        Don "Grapes"
Coburn, Braydon, *248*
Coffey, Paul, 58, *118,* 190, *190*
Colborne, Joe, 256
Collins, Kevin, *116*
Colorado Avalanche, 108, 255
Compuware, 72
Conn Smythe Trophy, 54, 57, 70, *251*
Corazzini, Carl, 236
Cormier, Ernie, 56–57
Cornforth, Mark, 190
Cote, Alain, 190
Cote, Riley, *214*
Courtnall, Geoff, 207
Cowley, Bill, 21
Craig, Dan, *242, 242,* 243
Craig, Jim, 164, *165,* 174
Crawford, Lou, 236
Creighton, Fred, 156, *156,* 157
Crosby, Sidney, 254
Crowder, Bruce, 236, *236*
Crowder, Keith, *97,* 236, *236*
Crozier, Roger, 8
Cunniff, John, 89, 90, 149, *149*
Curran, Brian, 226
Cusick, Fred, *36*
Czerkawski, Mariusz, *204,* 207

D

Dachshunds, 224
Dafoe, Byron "Lord Byron," 161, *171,*
        174
Dallman, Kevin, 190

D'Amico, Johnny, 136
Daskalakis, Cleon, 163–164, 170–171,
        172, 174, *249*
defensemen, 54, 177–193. *See also*
        Bourque, Ray; Orr, Bobby
DelGuidice, Matt, 164, 174
DelNegro, Don, *104*
Delvecchio, Alex, 8
DeMarco, Albert T., 190
Dempsey, Nathan, 191
Dennison and G.C.C. Technologies,
        271–272
Derlago, Bill, 207
Desjardins, Eric, *115*
Detroit Red Wings, 43
Dimaio, Rob, *234, 236*
Doak, Gary, 48, 53, 130–131, *138,*
        143, 147, 183, *183, 188,* 191, *243*
Dobbin, Brian, 236
Donatelli, Clark, 236
Donato, Ted, *204,* 207
Donnelly, Dave, 236
Donovan, Shean, 236
Douglas, Jordy, *176–177*
Doull, Doug, 226
Douris, Peter, *234,* 236
Downey, Aaron, 226
Downie, Steve, 260
Drouin, P.C., 236
Dryden, Ken, *30–31, 73,* 137, *222*
Dufour, Luc, *235,* 236
Dumart, Woody, 20, 40
Dumb and Dumber, 114
Dunbar, Dale, 191
Dupont, Kevin Paul, 17, 28, 99

E

EA SPORTS, 14
Eagleson, Alan, 65
Easton, 14
Edestrand, Daryl, *162,* 191
Edmonton Oilers, 121, 152
Ehrhoff, Christian, *263*
Elik, Todd, 207
Ellett, Dave, 191
Ellis, Ron, *91*
Eloranta, Mikko, 236–237
Emma, David, 207
Emmons, John, 237
enforcers, 211–227
Eriksson, Anders, *13*
Esposito, Phil, *3, 12, 14, 33–35, 53,*
        59, 64–65, 65–75, *66, 67, 68, 69,*
        70, 71, 72, 73, 74, 135, *274*
    awards, 74
    on coaches, 146, 155
    Hockey Hall of Fame, induction
        into, 74
    jersey retirement, 74, *75*
    memoirs, 65

on new power play rules, 68–69
in New York, 70–72
post-retirement, 72–73
records and stats, *65n,* 67–68, *68n,*
        69, 72, 75
retirement, 72
Stanley Cup playoffs, 69–70
Tampa Bay, 72–73
"The Trade," 52, 66–67
Esposito, Tony, *3,* 69, *89*
Euro Connection, *190*
Ewing, Patrick, 3

F

Featherstone, Glen, 226
Fedyk, Brent, *27*
Fenway hawk, *242, 244*
Fenway Park
    and 2010 NHL Winter Classic, *240,*
        242, 243, 247, 248
    conversion into hockey rink,
        240–244
    and Legends Classic game, 248, *249*
Ference, Andrew, 191, 256, *256n, 263,*
        265
Fergus, Tom, *101, 204,* 207
Fernandez, Manny, 174
Ferraro, Peter, 237
fighting, 43–44, 70–72, 81–85, 211–214,
        245, *245,* 252–253, 260–261.
        See also enforcers
Finley, Brian, 174
Fiset, Stephane, *124*
Fitzgerald, Tom, 92, 237, *237*
Fitzpatrick, Mark, *112*
Fleet Center, *1,* 33, 102. *See also* TD
        Banknorth Garden
Flett, Bill, *162*
Floating Hospital for Children, 123
Flockhart, Ron, 207
"Foghorn," 29–30
Forbes, Dave, *235,* 237
Forbes, Mike, 191
Forristall, John "Frosty," 161
Foster, Dwight "Dewey," *132, 138,*
        143, 207
Foster, Norm, 175
Fox, Michael J., *127*
Ftorek, Robbie, *149,* 157, *217*
Fuhr, Grant, 168

G

Gadsby, Bill, 8
Gagne, Simon, 244, *247*
Gainey, Bob, *170*
Gallery Gods, 29–30
Galley, Garry, *31, 177, 189,* 191, 199
"garbage goals," *67n*
Gare, Danny, 133
Gelinas, Martin, 107

Gibson, Doug, 237
Gilbert, Gilles, 26, 136, 137, 143, 161, 162, 175
Gill, Hal, 191, 191, 255
Gillies, Clark, 81, 83, 218
Gillis, Mike, 237
Gionta, Brian, 259
Girard, Jonathan, 191
Giroux, Claude, 245, 247, 259
Glennie, Brian, 46
Glennon, Matt, 237
goal scorers, 195–209
goaltenders, 159–175
Gomez, Scott, 255
Gonchar, Sergei, 191
Goren, Lee, 207
Goring, Robert "Butch," 56, 147, 148–149, 148, 157, 200, 234, 237
Gould, Bobby, 31, 237
Gradin, Thomas, 112, 207, 207
Graham, Rod, 237
Grahame, John, 173, 175
Grahame, Ron, 175, 175
Granik, Gail, 141
Graves, Adam, 107
Green, Travis, 237
Greenberg, Nate, 8, 12–13, 14–15, 19, 27–29, 28, 30, 59–60, 63, 65, 67, 70, 98, 134, 140, 141
Grenier, Martin, 108
Greschner, Ron, 66
Gretzky, Wayne, 14, 58, 61n, 67, 168, 231
grinders, 229–236
Grisdale, John, 201
Grosek, Michal, 237
Gruden, John, 191
Gryp, Bob, 237
Guay, Paul, 237
Guerin, Bill, 100, 205, 207
Guidolin, Armand "Bep," 135, 155, 155–156, 157
Guite, Ben, 237

H

Hackett, Jeff, 175
Hadfield, Vic, 52
Hagman, Matti, 237
Hajt, Bill, 133
Hall, Glenn, 272
Hall, Taylor, 237
Hall of Fame. See Hockey Hall of Fame
Halpin, Charlie, 11–12, 273–274
Halward, Doug, 191
Hamill, Zach, 207
Hammond, Ken, 191
Hamrlik, Roman, 256
Harkins, Brett, 207
Harrigan, Paul, 1, 11
Hart Trophy, 54, 74

Harvey, Fred "Buster," 60
Hasek, Dominik, 161
Hawgood, Greg, 31, 113, 191
Healey, Eric, 207
Heinze, Steve, 204, 207
Henderson, Jay, 237
Henderson, Peter, 127
Henning, Lorne, 40
Herr, Matt, 237
Hervey, Matt, 191
Hextall, Bryan, 60
Hilbert, Andy, 207
Hill, Mel "Sudden Death," 20
Hill, Sean, 121
Hillier, Randy, 188, 191
Hitchman, Lionel, 10
Hitchman, Lionel, daughter of, 33–35
Hnidy, Shane "The Sheriff," 268, 269
Hockey Hall of Fame
    Bobby Orr, 62
    Brad Park, 178
    Cam Neely, 111n, 116, 123–126
    Harry Sinden, 145n
    John Bucyk, 48
    Phil Esposito, 74
Hockey Illustrated, 12, 272
Hockey News, 11, 11–12, 26, 273–274, 278
Hodge, Ken R., 21, 25–26, 33–35, 52, 67–68, 69, 132, 145, 200–201, 201, 207, 243, 243
Hodge, Kenneth D. (Ken Jr.), 120, 201–202, 237, 237
Hodgson, Jamie, 278n
Hoffmeyer, Bob, 79
Hoggan, Jeff, 237
Hogue, Benoit, 237
Holland, Heidi, 23, 25, 26, 28, 154
Holmgren, Paul, 81
Honored Numbers, 33–35
Hoover, Ron, 237
Horton, Nathan, 207, 250, 251, 251, 253, 254, 255, 256, 260, 260, 261
Horvath, Bronco, 39, 47
Houda, Doug, 246, 267
Housley, Phil, 181
Houston, Ken, 43
Howatt, Garry, 81
Howe, Gordie, 8, 12, 43, 67, 115
Howe, Marty, 191
Hrechkosy, Dave, 53
Huard, Bill, 226
Hughes, Brent, 213, 226
Hughes, Ryan, 237
Hulbig, Joe, 237
Hull, Brett, 276, 277
Huml, Ivan, 207
Hunwick, Matt, 191, 255
Huscroft, Jamie, 226

Hynes, Dave, 237
Hynes, Gord, 27, 191

I

Iafrate, Al, 191, 191, 277
instigator rule, 211, 212–213
Irvine, Ted, 26
Isbister, Brad, 237
Itech, 14

J

Jack Adams Award, 153n
Jackman, Barret, 224
Jackman, Richard, 191
Jacob family, 48n, 269
Jacobs, Charlie, 48, 243, 249, 269
Janney, Craig, 31, 112, 115, 207, 207
Jensen, Steve, 217, 223
jersey retirement
    Bobby Orr, 63
    Cam Neely, 123, 127
    John Bucyk, 47, 49
    Phil Esposito, 74, 75, 77
    Ray Bourque, 109
    Terry O'Reilly, 10, 91, 92, 93
Jillson, Jeff, 127, 191
Johansson, Calle, 216
Johnson, Tom, 13, 47, 135, 155, 155n
Johnston, Eddie, 2, 160, 164
Johnston, Greg, 237
Jonathan, Stan "Little Chief," 49, 71, 84, 129, 130, 131, 132, 138–139, 139, 143, 216, 217, 218, 226, 226
Joseph, Curtis, 230
Joyce, Bobby, 207
Julien, Claude, 79, 154, 157, 157, 241, 246, 249, 251, 253, 255, 258, 259, 268, 269
Juneau, Joe, 200, 204, 207, 277
Jurcina, Milan, 191

K

Kaberle, Tomas, 191, 255–256, 265, 269
Kalus, Petr, 207
Kampfer, Steven, 191, 279
Karmanos, Peter, 72
Karsums, Martins, 237
Kasatonov, Alexei, 97, 190, 191
Kasper, Steve, 152, 152–153, 154, 157, 231, 237
Keans, Doug, 170, 170, 175
Keenan, Mike "Iron Mike," 154, 154–155, 157
Kekalainen, Jarmo, 237
Kelleher, Chris, 191
Kelly, Chris, 237, 255, 255, 257, 257, 259, 269
Kelly, Dick, 4
Kennedy, Sheldon, 207
Kesler, Ryan, 263

Kessel, Phil, *205, 206,* 207
Khristich, Dmitri, 207
Kimble, Darin, *211,* 226
Klima, Petr, 106
Kluzak, Gord, 115, 164, *181, 188, 189,* 191, 219
Knipscheer, Fred, 237
Knuble, Mike, 207
Kobasew, Chuck, 207
Koharski, Don, 168
Kolarik, Pavel, 191
Korah, Jerry, *78*
Kordic, John, *211–212,* 221
Kostynski, Doug, 238
Kovalenko, Andrei, 207
Kraut Line, 20
Krejci, David, 208, 246, *246,* 253–254, *256, 259,* 260, *260,* 265, *269*
Krushelnyski, Mike, *205,* 208
Kultanen, Jarno, 192
Kurtenbach, Orland, 1–2
Kutlak, Zdenek, 192
Kvartalnov, Dmitri, *204,* 208

L

Laaksonen, Antti, 238
Lacher, Blaine, *24, 172,* 175
LaCouture, Dan, 227
Lacroix, Dan, 227
Lady Byng Memorial Trophy, 42
Lafleur, Guy, 41, *103, 137*
LaFontaine, Pat, 251
Lalonde, Bobby, 208
Lambert, Yvon, 137, *183*
Lane, Gord, 81
Lang, Robert, 208
Langdon, Steve, 238
Langfeld, Josh, 238
Laperriere, Jacques, *104*
Lapointe, Guy, *30–31, 81,* 192
Lapointe, Martin, *235,* 238
Larman, Drew, 238
Larose, Guy, 238
Larson, Reed, *186,* 192
Lashoff, Matt, 192
Last Hurrah, 33, *140*
Laviolette, Peter, 248
Lavoie, Dominic, 192
Lawton, Brian, 208
Lazaro, Jeff, 238
Leach, Jay, 192
Leach, Steve, *27,* 208, *208*
Leahy, Pat, 238
Leary, Denis, 249, *249*
Leduc, Richie, 238
Ledyard, Grant, 192
Lee, Rick, 215
Leetch, Brian, *188,* 192
Lefebvre, Guillaume, 227
Legends Classic game, 248, *249*

Lehmann, Tommy, 208
Lehtonen, Mikko, 208
Leighton, Michael, 244, 246, *248*
Lemaire, Jacques, *18*
Lemay, Moe, 238
Lemelin, Reggie, *31,* 152, 161, 167–171, *168, 169,* 175
Lemieux, Claude, 221
Lemieux, Mario, 14, 103, *103*
Lester B. Pearson award, 74
Lester Patrick Award, 48
Leveille, Normand, *8, 33, 205,* 208
Lewis, Dave, *155,* 157
Lindsay, Ted, 24, 43
Linseman, Ken "the Rat," 195–196, *196,* 200, 208
Louisville Slugger, 14
Lowe, Kevin, *119*
Lucic, Milan, *224,* 238, *249, 258, 260,* 265, *267*
Lukowich, Morris, 208
Lumley, Harry "Apple Cheeks," 159
Lunch Pail Gang, 33, 130, 134, 143, *143,* 161, *182n. See also* Cherry, Don
Luongo, Roberto, *263,* 264, 265, 266
Lupul, Gary, 114
Lussier, Ray, 54, 55

M

MacDonald, Craig, 238
Maciver, Norm, *127*
Macoun, Jamie, *232–233*
MacTavish, Craig, 238
Magnuson, Keith, *3,* 89
Makela, Mikko, 208
Maley, David, *113*
Malkoc, Dean, 227
Mallette, Troy, 227
Maluta, Ray, 192
Manchester Monarchs, 281
Manery, Randy, *84*
Manlow, Eric, 208
Mann, Cameron, 208
Maple Leafs, 20, 70
Mara, Paul, 192
Marchand, Brad, 238, *253, 258,* 259, 260, *262,* 263, *263, 264,* 265, *266–267, 268*
Marcotte, Don, 17, 21, *47,* 48, *57, 60,* 61, *132,* 137, *228–229,* 230–231, 233, 238
Markwart, Nevin, 227
Marois, Daniel, 208
Marotte, Gilles, 7, 52
Marshall, Bert, *67*
Marshall, Rick, 4, 7
Martin, Pit, 52
Masterton Trophy, 118
Mathieu, Marquis, 238
May, Alan, 227

McCarthy, Sandy, *227*
McCarthy, Tom J., 208
McCleary, Trent, 238
McCrimmon, Brad, *189,* 192
McDonald, John, 175
McEachern, Shawn, *204,* 208
McEwen, Mike, *87*
McGill, Bob, *80*
McGillis, Dan, 192
McInnis, Marty, 238
McKechnie, Walt, 238
McKenney, Don, *33–35*
McKenzie, Jim, *221*
McKenzie, John "Pie," 4, *4, 47,* 48, 66, 160
McKim, Andrew, 208
McLaren, Kyle, *13,* 192, *192*
McLean, Ron, 60
McLellan, Scott, 238
McNab, Peter, *30–31,* 77, 85, *85,* 98, 131, *136,* 137, *137, 138, 143, 161,* 208, *208,* 223
McQuaid, Adam, 192, *253, 268, 269*
McSorley, Marty, 227
Medford Youth Hockey coaches, 48
Melnyk, Larry, 192
Metropolit, Glen, 238
Middleton, Rick "Nifty," 62, 63, 78, 90, 91, *98, 106n,* 112, 115, 118, 131, *132,* 132–133, 136, *136, 138–139, 143,* 196–199, *197, 198,* 200–201, *205,* 208, 221–222, 248, *249,* 280
Mikita, Stan, 140
Milbury, Mike "Dooner," *36,* 77, 78, 85, *85,* 106, 114, 130, 131, *132, 135,* 138, *138–139,* 142, *143,* 146, *146,* 149, 152, 154, 157, 169, 182, *182,* 183, 184, *188,* 192, *205,* 218–219, 220, *224, 225,* 233
Millar, Mike, 238
Millen, Greg, *197*
Miller, Bobby, *132, 138–139, 143,* 238, *238*
Miller, Jay, 26, 86, *211–212,* 214–215, *215,* 221–222, 227
Mission, 14
Moffat, Mike, 175
Moger, Sandy, 208
Mohns, Doug, *12, 33–35,* 47
Mokosak, Carl, 227
Monahan, D. Leo, 67
Montador, Steve, 192
Montreal Canadiens, 19, 20, 41, 57, 81, 115, 136–138, 151–152, 256, 257, 258
Moog, Andy, *9n, 31,* 106, *158–159,* 161, *163n, 168,* 169–170, 175, *184,* 222
Mooney, Paul, 13, *37, 274,* 275
Moran, Ian, 192
Morris, Derek, 192, 246, 248

Morris, Jon, 238
Morrison, Doug, 208
Morrisonn, Shaone, *127*, 192
Mowers, Mark, 238
Mullen, Joe, *116*, 208
Murdoch, Bob, *56, 139*
Murdoch, Don, *135*
Murphy, Brian, *247*
Murphy, Gord, 192
Murphy, Joe, 107, 208
Murray, Glen, *127, 199, 206*, 208
Murzyn, Dana, *120*
Myhres, Brantt, 227
Myre, Phil, *12*
Myrvold, Anders, 192

N

Naples, Roger, 29
Naslund, Mats, 208
Nazarov, Andrei, 227
Neely, Ava, *127*
Neely, Cam "Bam Bam," *9n, 10, 14, 23, 31, 47, 110–111, 111, 111–127, 112, 113, 114, 115, 116, 117, 118, 119, 120, 121, 122–123, 123, 124, 125, 126, 127*, 148, 152–153, 195, 199, 203, *203n, 212n, 221*, 222, 229, *243*, 249, *249, 267, 268, 271*, 280
    awards, 118, *125*
    on Boston Bruins, 119–120
    vs. Canadiens, 1988, 115
    on cheap shots, 116–117
    collage poster, 119, *119*
    Hockey Hall of Fame, induction
        into, *111n*, 116, 123–126
    injuries, 116, 117, 118, 119, *119n*, 121
    jersey retirement, 123, *127*
    nicknames, 114
    on Phil Esposito, 79
    post-retirement, 123, 126, 179
    records and statistics, 113–114, 115, 117, 121, *123n, 127*
    on Terry O'Reilly, 151
Neely, Christine, 124
Neely, Jack, *127*
Neely, Marlene, 123
Neely, Michael, 123
Neely, Paulina, *127*
Neely, Scott, 123, 124, *125*
Neely, Shaun, 124
Neely Foundation for Cancer
    Research, 123, *125n*
Neely House, 123
NESN, 116, 120
netminders, 159–175
Neufeld, Ray, 219, 238
Nevin, Bob, *56*
New England Whalers, 9, 11, *11*
New Jersey Devils, *23n*
New York Golden Blades, 11

New York Rangers, 19, 20, 51, 57, 66, 69, 70–72, 83–85
NHL All-Star Game, 96, 102–103
NHL lockout, 166
NHL Winter Classic (2010), 241, 244–249
Nickulas, Eric, 238
Nicolson, Graeme, 192
Nielsen, Kirk, 238
Nienhuis, Kraig, 238
Nilan, Chris "Knuckles," *212, 220*, 221, 227
Nill, Jim, 238
Nokelainen, Petteri, 238
Nordstrom, Peter, 208
Norris, Jack, 52
Norris Trophy, 52, 54, *54n*, 57, 96, *186n*
Norton, Jeff, 192
Nota, Tony, *37*
Nowak, Hank, *55, 235*, 238
Nylander, Michael, 208
Nyrop, Bill, *30–31*
Nystrom, Bob, 81

O

Oates, Adam, *24*, 112, *124, 126, 194–195, 200, 204*, 208, *276*
O'Brien, Dennis, *132, 143*, 192
O'Brien, Frank, 55–56
O'Connell, Mike, *98*, 157, *188*, 192, *192*
Oddleifson, Chris, 208
Odgers, Jeff, 227, *227*
O'Donnell, Fred, *229n*, 238
O'Donnell, Sean, 192
O'Dwyer, Billy, *47*, 238
Ohlund, Mattias, *260*
Oliver, Murray, 1, 46, *185*
Oliwa, Krzysztof, 227
O'Neil, Paul, 208
"onetimer" shot, *9n*
Ontario Hockey Association, 51
Ontario Hockey League, 51
O'Reilly, Connor, *93*
O'Reilly, Evan, *93*
O'Reilly, Terry "Taz," *10, 30–31, 33–35, 47, 52, 76–77, 77, 77–93, 78, 79, 80, 81, 82, 84, 85, 86, 87, 88–89, 89, 90, 91, 92*, 97, 113, *135, 136, 138, 143*, 148, 151, 200, *212*, 222, *223*, 229, *249, 273, 274*, 280
    on Bobby Orr, 61–62
    captain, *89*
    coaching, 87, 89–91, *90*, 147, 149–152, 154, 157
    on Don Cherry, 141
    on fighting, 81–82, 83–85
    injuries, 92
    jersey retirement, 10, 77, 91, *92, 93*
    at Last Hurrah, 33
    Lunch Pail Gang, 130

mental makeup, 79
records and statistics, 91, 93, 157, *212*, 223
skating abilities, 78
on Stanley Cup finals, 1979, 136, 137
toughness, 79–83, 195, 217, 218, 223–224
Orr, Bobby, *1, 6, 6–7, 12, 14, 33–35, 50–51, 51, 51–63, 52, 53, 54, 55, 56, 57, 58, 59, 60, 61, 62*, 69, *70, 71, 93*, 98, *108*, 120, 177, 186, *222, 243, 244, 249, 271*
    awards, 52, 54, *54n*, 57, 63, 70
    final "full" season in NHL, 62–63
    Hockey Hall of Fame, induction
        into, *62*
    impact on hockey, 53
    injuries, *51n, 55n*, 58
    jersey retirement, *63*
    at Last Hurrah, 33
    and media demands, 59–61, *60*
    records and statistics, 59, 63, 68
    retirement, *62n*
    Stanley Cup winning goal, 54–58
Orr, Colton, 227
Oshawa Generals, 6, 51

P

Pachal, Clayton, 208
Pahlsson, Sammy, 108, 238
Paiement, Wilf, *42*
Paille, Daniel, 238, *246, 247*, 269
Palmer, Brad, 208
Panteleev, Grigori, 238
Parent, Bernie, 159
Parise, J.P., *162–163*
Park, Brad, *30–31, 55*, 66, *66, 67*, 91, 97–98, *135, 143, 176–177, 177–178, 178*, 192, 205, 248, *249*
Parker, Jack, 261
Pasin, Dave, 208
Payne, Davis, 239
Peat, Stephen, 220
Pedersen, Al "Beach," *31*, 149, 183–184, 185–186, *186, 189*, 192
Pederson, Barry, *8*, 111, *111n*, 112, 203, *205*, 209
Peeters, Pete, *161*, 161–163, 170, 175
Peirson, John, *33–35*
Pellerin, Scott, 239
Pelletier, Pascal, 209
penalty box, *29*, 219–220
penalty killers, 230, *230*
Penner, Jeff, 192
Perrin, Eric, 165
Pettie, Jim, *132, 143, 172*, 175
Peverley, Rich, 239, *255, 255*, 257, 260, 263, *268*
Philadelphia Flyers, 243–248, 251, 258
Phoenix Coyotes, 252

physical hockey, 81
Picard, Noel, 54
Pirus, Alex, *223*
Plante, Jacques, 159
Plett, Willie, 227
Podloski, Ray, 209
Pollock, Kevin, *253*
Pooh jersey, *163*
Popovi, Peter, 192
Potvin, Felix, 175
Potvin, Marc, 227
Poulin, Dave, *27, 31,* 112, *234,* 239
Prajsler, Petr, 192
press box, 27–29
Price, Carey, *256,* 257
Price, Noel, *12*
Primeau, Wayne, 239
Prince of Wales Trophy, *100, 125*
Pro Set, 14
Probert, Bob, 215
Professional Hockey Writers'
    Association, 118
Pronger, Chris, *247,* 248
Pronger, Sean, 239
Propp, Brian, *31,* 209
Prpic, Joel, 239
Puleio, Zibby Jr., 36
Puleio, Zibby Sr., 63

Q

Quintal, Stephane, 192

R

Ralby, Herb, 12
Ramage, Rob, *92*
Ramsay, Craig, 80, *201, 246*
Ranford, Bill, 106, *163, 165n,*
    170–171, 175
Raphael, Dick, 12
Rask, Tuukka, 175, 253, *261, 268*
Ratelle, Jean "Ratty," *8, 18, 33–35,* 66,
    97, *132, 143,* 178, *201,* 209, 231
Rathwell, Jake, 239
Ray, Rob, 100–101
Raycroft, Andrew, *127,* 165, *166,* 175
Raymond, Mason, *263*
Reasoner, Marty, 209
Recchi, Mark, 209, *241n,* 243, 246,
    246, 247, 250, 259, *262,* 265, 280
Redmond, Dick, *143, 189,* 192
Reece, Dave, *172,* 175
Reed, Tom, *185*
Reich, Jeremy, 227
Reid, Dave, 239
Richard, Rocket, 44
Richards, Mike, *247*
Richardson, Luke, *213*
Richer, Stephane, 193
Richter, Barry, 193
Riendeau, Vincent, *172,* 175

Riggin, Pat, 170, *172,* 175
Rindge Technical High School, 3
Rivers, Jamie, 193
Robbins, Tim, 248–249
Roberts, Doug, 239
Roberts, Gord, 193
Robertson, Torrie, 219–220
Robinson, Larry, 10, *69, 222*
Robinson, Nathan, 209
Robitaille, Randy, 209
Rochester Americans, *5n*
Rohloff, Jon, 193
Roloson, Dwayne, 259, *259, 260,* 261
Rolston, Brian, 108, *203,* 209
Romano, Roberto, 175
Rome, Aaron, 262, 263
Rookie of the Year. *See* Calder Trophy
Rosa, Fran, 29, 51, 52, 61, 134,
    138–139, 141
Ross, Art, 145
Roy, Andre, 227
Roy, Jean-Yves, 209
Roy, Patrick, *115*
Ruelle, Al, 12
Ruhnke, Kent, 239
Ruzicka, Vladimir, 209, *209*
Ryder, Michael, 209, 255, 257, 263,
    263, 265, *269*

S

Samsonov, Sergei "Sammy," 104, *108,*
    202, 209, *272*
Samuelson, Ulf, 116, *116*
Samuelsson, Martin, 209
Sanderson, Derek "Turk," 4, *4,* 6,
    33–35, 47, 54, *56,* 66, *108,* 222,
    229, 231, 239, *243,* 248
Sandford, Ed, 24–25, *33–35, 47*
Sanford, Ed, *37*
Sarner, Craig, 239
Satan, Miroslav, 209
Sator, Ted, 149, *189*
Sauve, Philippe, 175
Savage, Andre, 209
Savard, Andre, *78,* 231, *235,* 239
Savard, Marc, 206, 209, 243, 254–255,
    255
Sawchuk, Terry, 43, 159
Sawyer, Kevin, 227
Scapinello, Ray, *69*
Scatchard, Dave, 239
Schaefer, Peter, 239
Schlemko, Dave, *252*
Schmautz, Bobby, *128–129,* 130, 131,
    132, 138–139, 142, *143,* 178, 209
Schmidt, Milt, 20, 33, 44, 52, *93,* 145,
    243, 249, 266
Schneider, Cory, *263,* 265
Schoenfeld, Jim, 168, *188,* 193, *193*
Schultz, Dave, 10

Score, 14
scorers, 195–209
Secord, Al "Rocky," 130, *132, 143,*
    156, 218–219, *219,* 222, 224, *224,*
    225, 227
Sedin, Daniel, *263*
Seguin, Tyler, 209, 252, *252,* 259, *259,*
    265, 269
Seidenberg, Dennis, 193, 253–254,
    265, 269
Seiling, Rod, *46*
Serowik, Jeff, 193
Shaldybin, Yevgeny, 193
Shanahan, Sean, 239
Shand, Dave, *43*
Shaw, Dave, *24,* 101, *189,* 193
Sheehan, Bobby, 11, *11*
Sheehy, Tim, 11, *11*
Sheppard, Gregg, *56,* 209, *228–229,*
    231
Shields, Steve, 175
Shoebottom, Bruce, 227, *227*
Shore, Eddie, 20, *33–35,* 98, 177
Short, Steve, *41*
Sigalet, Jonathan, 193
Sigalet, Jordan, 175
Silk, Dave, 209
Simmer, Charlie, 209, *209, 270*
Simmons, Al, *188,* 193
Simmons, Gary "The Cobra," *233*
Simonetti, Frank, 54, 147, 181–182,
    183, *189,* 193
Simpson, Rob, 249, 277, 278
Sims, Al, *42, 69, 132, 138, 143, 188,*
    193
Sinden, Harry, 13, 24, *49,* 52, 65,
    66–67, 108, 111–112, 118, 131,
    144–145, 145, 145–147, 148–149,
    153, 155, 157, *163n*
Sittler, Darryl, *160*
Skriko, Petri, 209
Skudra, Peter, 175
Slegr, Jiri, 193
Sleigher, Louis, 227
Smith, Barry, 239
Smith, Brandon, 193
Smith, Dallas, *56, 57, 185,* 193
Smith, Mike, 259
Smith, Rick, *30–31, 143, 188,* 193
Smith, Zack, *255*
Smolinski, Bryan, 209
Smyl, Stan, 111
Sobotka, Vladimir, 239
Songin, Butch, *231n*
Songin, Tom, *143, 231, 231–233,* 239
Sports Action Images, *119n*
Sports Action Photography, 14, *15n*
St. Louis, Martin, 165, 209, 260
St. Louis Blues, 54, 69, 70
Staios, Steve, 193

Stamkos, Steven, *260*
Stanfield, Fred, *33–35*, 52
Stanley Cup finals
   1929, 19
   1939, 20
   1941, 20
   1943, 20
   1970, 53, 54–56, 69, 81
   1971, 57
   1972, 57, 69, 70, 81
   1978, *128–129*
   1979, 136–137
   1988, 105–106, 116, 151–152
   1990, *31*, 106–107, *107*, 121, 152
   2001, 108
   2011, 251, 261–267, *266, 267, 268, 269*
Stanton, Paul, 193
Stastny, Yan, 239
Stevens, Kevin, 152–153, 209
Stevens, Mike, 239
Stevens, Scott, *181*
Stevenson, Shayne, 209
Stewart, Al, 227
Stewart, Bob, *53*
Stewart, Cam, 239
Stewart, Jim, 164, 175
Stewart, Paul, 220
Stock, P.J., 215–216, *216*, 225, 227, *274*
Strelow, Warren, 163
strobes, 31
Stuart, Brad, 193
Stuart, Mark, 193, 257
Stumpel, Jozef, *204*, 209
Sturm, Marco, *205*, 209, *246*, 247, *248*, 253–254, 280
Subban, P.K., 257
Sullivan, Mike, *13*, 157, 239
Sutherland, Kiefer, 248, *249*
Sutter, Brian, *150–151*, 154, 157, *157n*
Sutter, Ron, 239
Sweeney, Bob "Swoop," *22–23, 31*, 90, *114, 205*, 223, *232–233*, 233, 239
Sweeney, Don, *31*, 95–96, 104, *104, 177, 179*, 179–181, 183, 184, *184*, 184–185, 193
Sweeney, Tim, 120–121, 152–153, 202–203, 209
Sylvestri, Don, 175
Syvret, Danny, 245

T

Tallas, Robbie, *172*, 175
Tampa Bay Lightning, 72–73, 258, 259–261
Tanabe, David, 193
Tatarinov, Mikhail, 193

Taylor, Chris, 239
Taylor, Tim, 239
TD Banknorth Garden, 33. *See* Fleet Center
Team Canada series (Summit 1972), 67
Team USA, *165n*
Tehabi Books, 275
Tenkrat, Petr, 209
Thelin, Mats, *190*, 193
Thelven, Michael, *190*, 193
Thomas, Tim, 165–167, *167*, 175, 245, 246, *247*, 248, *251*, 253, *254, 257, 257*, 258, 260, *260*, 261, *261, 262*, 263, *263, 265*, 267, *267*
Thomlinson, Dave, 239
Thompson, Cecil "Tiny," 19, 159
Thompson, Nate, 239
Thornton, Joe "Jumbo Joe," *14*, 104, *127, 195, 195, 202*, 209, *272, 278n*
Thornton, Shawn, *214*, 227, 245, *245, 257*, 262, *268*
Thunder and Lightning: A No B.S. Hockey Memoir (Esposito), 65
Timander, Mattias, *190*, 193
Timonen, Kimmo, 246
Tocchet, Rick, 221, 239
Toivonen, 175
Toppazzini, Jerry, 1, *33–35*
Topps, 14, 271
Torres, Raffi, 262
Townshend, Graeme, 239
"The Trade," 52, 66
Traverse, Patrick, 193
Tremblay, Mario, 137, *212*
Tugnutt, Ron, 202
Turgeon, Pierre, *25*
Turnball, Ian, *142*
Tuzzolino, Tony, 239

U

Upper Deck, 14

V

Vachon, Rogie, *84*, 102, *139*, 175, *175*
Vadnais, Carol, *58*, 66, *189*, 193
Vancouver Canucks, 261–267
Vancouver Giants, *269n*
Van Dorp, Wayne, 220
Van Impe, Darren, 193
Varitek, Jason, *249*
Vaske, Dennis, 193
Vasko, Elmer "Moose," 272
Velischek, Randy, *117*
Vernarsky, Kris, 239
Vesey, Jim, 239
Vezina Trophy, 161, *161n, 165n*

Vial, Denis, *219*
Vigneault, Alain, 263, 264
Virtue, Terry, 193
Von Stefenelli, Philip, 193

W

Walter, Ben, 239
Walton, Mike, 209
Walz, Wes, 239
Ward, Aaron, 193
Ward, Dixon, 239
Ward, Geoff, *246*
Weiland, Cooney, 19, 20
Weinrich, Eric, 193
Wensink, John "Wire," 77, 92, 130, 132, *132*, 135, *136, 138*, 139–140, 143, *143*, 216–218, 222, *222, 223*, 224, 227
Wesley, Glen, *31*, 106, 111, *111n*, 168, *180–181, 189*, 193
Westfall, Ed, *33–35, 40*, 231
Wheeler, Blake, 239, *246*, 255
Whitfield, Trent, 239
Whitmore, Kay, 175
Wideman, Dennis, 193
Wiemer, Jim, *31, 189*, 193
Williams, Dave "Tiger," *215*
Williams, Tommy, 46
Wilson, Bob, *36*, 39
Wilson, Landon, *234*, 239
Winnes, Chris, 239
Wisniewski, James, *256*
Wolanin, Craig, *124*
Woods, Tiger, 52
World Hockey Association (WHA), 9, 65, 66
Wozniewski, Andy, 193

Y

Yelle, Stephane, 239
York, Jason, 193
Young, C.J., 209
Young, Neil, *276*, 276–278, *277*
Young, Peggi, 247
Young, Scott, 276, *277*
Yushkevich, Dmitri, *27*
Yzerman, Steve, 258

Z

Zamboni, 23
Zamuner, Rob, 239
Zanussi, Joe, 66, 193
Zehr, Jeff, 239
Zhamnov, Alexei, 209
Zholtok, Sergei, 209
Zinovjev, Sergei, 209
Zombo, Rick, 193, *198*